Windows® 8.1

ABSOLUTE
BEGINNER'S
GUIDE

Paul Sanna
Alan Wright

800 East 96th Street,
Indianapolis, Indiana 46240

Windows® 8.1 Absolute Beginner's Guide

ISBN-13: 978-0-7897-5224-6
ISBN-10: 0-7897-5224-7

Library of Congress Control Number: 2013947525

Printed in the United States of America

Second Printing: January 2014

Trademarks

Warning and Disclaimer

Bulk Sales

Que Publishing offers excellent discounts on this book when ordered in quantity for bulk purchases or special sales. For more information, please contact

> U.S. Corporate and Government Sales
> 1-800-382-3419
> corpsales@pearsontechgroup.com

For sales outside the United States, please contact

> International Sales
> international@pearsoned.com

Editor-in-Chief
Greg Wiegand

Executive Editor
Loretta Yates

Development Editor
Todd Brakke

Managing Editor
Kristy Hart

Project Editor
Andy Beaster

Indexer
Lisa Stumpf

Proofreader
Dan Knott

Technical Editor
Laura Acklen

Editorial Assistant
Cindy Teeters

Interior Designer
Anne Jones

Cover Designer
Matt Coleman

Compositor
Gloria Schurick

Contents at a Glance

Table of Contents

About the Authors

Paul Sanna is a software professional and the author or co-author of two dozen computer books on topics such as Windows 2000, Internet Explorer, VBA, Windows security, and more. He has been writing about computers since his first literary agent said to him many years ago, "I didn't know Boston University had an English program," and "Have you heard of this Windows 95 thing?" Mr. Sanna has worked in the IT field his entire career, building software, selling high tech, helping customers understand how to be successful with technology, and helping to market breakthrough analytics technology. His home with his family is in Charlotte, NC. Go Gamecocks!

Alan Wright has worked professionally in and around IT for more than 10 years. He has provided enterprise-level support in the Detroit, Michigan, area and continues to provide software and hardware support for small businesses and residential users. He holds several certifications from CompTIA and Microsoft and enjoys working with technology and teaching others how they can make technology work for them. Alan has been the technical editor on other books from Que Publishing, including *Using Windows 8* and *Microsoft Project 2013 In Depth*, and he co-authored *Visio 2013 Absolute Beginner's Guide*. When not working with computers, he enjoys working on projects in his cabinet shop. Alan lives in northern Michigan with his wife, Pam, and their two children, Joshua and Jonathan.

Dedication

To Andrea—my beautiful bride of almost 25 years.

—Paul Sanna

To my wife Pam, no one knows how patient you are. Thank you!

—Alan Wright

Acknowledgments

No one deserves more credit for helping this project cross the finish line than Loretta Yates, my editor. Thanks for having faith in me, for working with my strengths and interest to come up with a project, for the support and great ideas, and for gently whacking me every time I looked for more time. Todd Brakke, the development editor, hereby known as "The Architect," is the man for keeping the book cohesive, smart, focused, and organized. Laura Acklen, the technical editor, kept me honest and accurate, and thanks to Barbara Hacha, who deserves a big raise after editing my work!

The unnamed co-captain of this project is my wife, who kept me happy, well fed, focused, and in clean clothes throughout. This could not have been done without her. Thanks also to the three absolute beginners whom I channeled, namely Andrea, Mom, and Bob—thanks for the ideas and perspectives. Please stay novices forever (or as long as I write beginner books).

I have to acknowledge my precious daughters, Rachel, Allison, and Tori, for checking on me and bringing me smoothies, snacks, candy, and sandwiches (and imploring me to get sleep!). Thanks to Karsyn and Camryn for their regular visits to Mr. Paul. Finally, no list of acknowledgments would be complete without mentioning Abby, my 15-pound cocker spaniel/golden retriever mix, who never left my side from proposal to last chapter.

—Paul Sanna

Loretta Yates, Andy Beaster, Todd Brakke, and Barbara Hacha have all done an outstanding job of ensuring this book was pulled together and done well. Laura Acklen has been a great Technical Editor on this book, and I enjoy her sense of humor. Paul Sanna, my co-author, deserves a lot of credit, and I appreciate the opportunity to be able to assist him with this book.

I have to thank my family and friends for their patience while I worked on this project; I often wanted to be in three places at once, which everyone seemed to understand. I'll also take the opportunity to thank my parents, Paul and Verna, for always being there to encourage me.

—Alan Wright

We Want to Hear from You!

As the reader of this book, *you* are our most important critic and commentator. We value your opinion and want to know what we're doing right, what we could do better, what areas you'd like to see us publish in, and any other words of wisdom you're willing to pass our way.

We welcome your comments. You can email or write to let us know what you did or didn't like about this book—as well as what we can do to make our books better.

Please note that we cannot help you with technical problems related to the topic of this book.

When you write, please be sure to include this book's title and author as well as your name and email address. We will carefully review your comments and share them with the author and editors who worked on the book.

Email: feedback@quepublishing.com

Mail: Que Publishing
ATTN: Reader Feedback
800 East 96th Street
Indianapolis, IN 46240 USA

Reader Services

Visit our website and register this book at quepublishing.com/register for convenient access to any updates, downloads, or errata that might be available for this book.

IN THIS INTRODUCTION

- What this book covers
- How this book is organized
- Conventions for menu commands, keyboard short-cuts, and mouse and touch screen actions used in this book
- Special elements used to call your attention to notes, tips, and cautions
- How to send the author your feedback

INTRODUCTION

We are delighted you are reading this introduction, whether you're considering buying this book or because you already own it. We know you'll find value reading it and using it while you wrestle with this beast called Windows 8.1.

Windows 8 is just a few years removed from Windows 7, but it's incredibly different from its predecessors. Windows 8.1 has added even more new features and enhancements to existing apps and tools within Windows 8. Microsoft easily could have called it "Windows 2020" or "Not Your Parents' Windows." The user interface (UI), which Microsoft dubs Modern, is the near-technical term that describes the part of the software you see and touch and control, and it is quite different. Gone is our old friend the Start menu, and in its place is an exciting layout of tiles, each representing a piece of software installed on your system.

 NOTE You might find yourself asking, "I have Windows 8, but how do I know if I have Windows 8.1?" Microsoft hasn't exactly gone out of its way to differentiate 8 from 8.1. Mostly that's because 8 remains the brand and 8.1 is just their way of updating and refreshing it a bit, which is why 8.1 is a free upgrade for all Windows 8 users. For that reason, this book sticks to referring to Windows 8 for anything that isn't specifically unique to Windows 8.1.

The new style of applications, using the Modern UI, that you use in Windows 8 are attractive, engaging, and fast. They run full screen, sit flat on your monitor with no raised buttons or widgets, take advantage of video and animation better than any prior Windows release, and behave quite nicely in the sandbox with other apps. Crashes and lockups because of applications are a thing of the past!

The Windows 8 start-up process is so quick, you'll wonder whether you really clicked Restart or you just imagined doing so. And if you're pining for the old Windows Desktop, which is still there and runs all your existing applications, it's just a touch, click, or swipe away.

Yep, for you beginners, that means there's basically two wholly different Windows environments to learn. Good thing there's a book out there for the absolute beginner—are we right?

This book is intended to help you, whether you're new to Windows or just new to Windows 8.1, accomplish whatever it is you need or want to do during your personal or professional day. If you walk into the office and find your computer has been upgraded to Windows 8.1, you can read how to run (and where to find) your old programs. You can learn how to move around the system and how to work with your old files. You can also learn how to do those seemingly difficult administrative functions, such as setting up a printer or a second monitor.

If Windows 8.1 is loaded on a new computer you acquire for use at home, you can learn how to connect to all those social media networks, like Facebook and Twitter. You can see how to have fun with the photos you take and those that are shared with you. You can read how to buy and enjoy movies, music, and games.

And for those times when work follows you home or your personal time is overrun by home business tasks, such as homework or creating a budget, you can learn how to be productive and efficient.

For the hardware you use to run Windows 8.1, Microsoft has made a big deal about how Windows 8.1 can run on laptops, workstations, servers, and tablets. Allowing for form-factor differences, the user interface is identical on all devices with the exception of how you interact with it: mouse, keyboard, stylus, speech, or touch. This book works for you regardless of the hardware you use. Although this book doesn't cover the unique capabilities of certain models, such as the Acer Iconia W3, you can follow along with the lessons, how-tos, and explanations using whatever hardware you have. The screenshots shown in this book come from a wide range of devices—some from small laptops, others from gigantic servers, and a few from tablets. Odds are you won't see a difference between them.

What Is an Absolute Beginner?

The book is respectful of your level of expertise. You are probably either new to Windows or, especially, new to Windows 8.1. You probably can handle a mouse and a keyboard, but the book guides you from the moment your computer or tablet starts through all the most common functions you're likely to demand from it.

How This Book Is Organized

The book follows a logical path, starting with the most basic chapters and getting into more specific topics later in the book. Chapter names describe the type of information you will find, which will help you if you need to jump around in the book. For example, Chapter 11, "Connecting to the Internet," may be a chapter you need right away if you have a new device and cannot figure out why things are not connecting to the Internet. You can read chapters and parts in any order you like, with one exception:

- Chapter 1, "Your First Hour with Windows," covers the new Windows 8-style bells, buttons, windows, and whistles in some detail. Chapter 2, "Interacting with Windows," picks up from there to help you interact with Windows 8, and Chapter 3, "Organizing the Start Screen," focuses on setting up your Start screen. If you are new to Windows 8.1, you should give these chapters a close read.

- If you are brand new to Windows, you'll also want to spend some time with Chapter 8, "Learning About the Windows Desktop," which is still the place that a host of important applications call home.

Each chapter in this book follows a standard format, but diversions from the format occur here and there. The first section in each chapter is a short list describing the things you can learn and do in the chapter, along with a brief description and why it's important to you. This short section also alerts you to any techniques or gestures you need to know to complete the tasks described in the chapter, as well as where in the book to find that guidance.

Conventions Used in This Book

This book is easy to understand. Even though Windows 8.1 might seem hard to learn, to help make your task of learning Windows simpler, certain types of instructions are formatted or written in a specific way to keep them consistent. Some decisions were made as to how to handle all the interfaces to Windows 8.1: keyboard, mouse, and touch. You can read about how to handle the keyboard instructions, as well as all these conventions, in the next few short sections.

Selects and Selecting

Windows asks you to do lots of things. You're asked to click here, choose that, press this, and enter these. Given that you might use a touch-driven tablet or a mouse and keyboard, some of the instructions in the book are streamlined to reduce confusion by settling, as often as possible, on using the word "select." When you see "select," you complete the most natural action for the thing you are asked to select, whether that's a click of the mouse or a finger tap of the screen.

That established, this book loves and features the mouse. Every how-to, detailed explanation, or quick tip or timesaver leads with use of the mouse. You'll have no trouble following instructions such as, "With your mouse, click here," or "Double-click the smiley face picture."

Touchscreen users can find countless sets of specific instructions to interact with Windows via touch whenever the gesture for doing so with a touchscreen device is not obvious or is notably different from doing so with a mouse.

Finally, although you can accomplish most tasks in Windows with a mouse or via touch, you can still do a lot with a keyboard that enables you to work faster than with a mouse or touch. With that in mind, you'll find plenty of keyboard shortcuts throughout the book.

Special Elements

A few special tools emphasize certain points and concepts that might not be directly related to the topic discussed but are important enough to mention. These elements come in the form of Tips, Cautions, Notes, and Sidebars.

NOTE A note is a useful piece of information that is not quite part of the core topic of the chapter or the section of the chapter where the note appears.

TIP A tip is a useful piece of information that should help you get your work done a bit faster or a bit better in Windows 8.1.

CAUTION A caution appears if there is a particular pitfall you must avoid or if there's a chance of losing your data executing one of the procedures in the book.

SIDEBAR

Sidebars will point out additional information that may be slightly off-topic. It may be additional background information or other details that are good to know.

1

YOUR FIRST HOUR WITH WINDOWS

If you just brought home a new computer with Windows 8 preinstalled, or if your computer has been upgraded to Windows 8, maybe you're thinking, "Now what?" The obvious answer is to power up your computer and sign in. If you're making the jump to Windows 8 from Windows 7 or an even older version, you'll notice this process is all quite a bit different from what you're used to. And if you haven't used Windows before, the start-up process appears unique. For these reasons, this chapter walks you through the steps necessary to start your computer and then sign in to Windows.

The most obvious change from older Windows versions is the Start screen, which you will become familiar with as soon as you log in to your computer. Next, you get a quick tour of the capabilities of the Charms bar, which is a new and exciting concept if you've not had exposure to Windows 8. You also learn how to put your computer to sleep if you won't be using it for a while, and you learn how to exit Windows 8.

First, though, is powering up your Windows 8 hardware and signing in to Windows 8.

Starting Up Windows

Before you can start up Windows 8 for the first time, there are a few things you should have in mind:

- If someone other than you installed Windows 8, check with that person for the user ID and password you should use. Be sure to ask whether a *local account* or a *Microsoft account* was used. You'll learn more about these two account types in Chapter 17, "Sharing Your Windows Computer with Others."

- If you sign in to Windows 8 for the first time at your place of business, check with a person from your IT or support organization for your user ID and password and, if required, your domain. The domain identifies what part of the corporate network you log in to. If your computer has been upgraded to Windows 8, your user ID, password, and domain are probably the same as you used previously.

- If you are upgrading or starting up the Windows 8 device for the first time, you will be asked to sign in with a Microsoft account as the recommended sign-in option. You may choose to create a Microsoft account or a local account. Chapter 17 can guide you through the use of these two account types if you are unsure, but the intention is for you to have a Microsoft account (it's free). You need an active internet connection to login with a Microsoft account for the first time.

With these log in options in mind, go ahead and boot up your Windows 8 computer. It should take no more than a minute or so before the sign-in screen appears.

NOTE If another version of Windows was installed and running properly on your computer when Windows 8.1 was installed, the person who installed it may have chosen to create a *dual-boot* setup. Instead of replacing the old operating system with the newer one, this kind of setup enables you to choose the operating system to use when the computer is turned on—yes, this is possible. If, when turning on your computer, a screen appears asking you to select an operating system, select Windows 8.

Signing In

With your computer running and Windows 8.1 booted up, the next step is to sign in to Windows. If you've signed in with a Microsoft account, you should already have a standard password in place and be able to log right in. However, if you're working with an existing local account or one that someone else has set up for you, you should know about some alternative password types.

TIP   If you wonder if "signing in" is the same as "logging in," you are correct. Microsoft has adopted the term "signing in" to describe that process to identify one's self to Windows.

Windows 8 provides an alternative to the conventional password for use when signing in. When you create your first user account in Windows, you need to supply a password, but you can also specify one of two alternative sign-in options: **PIN** and **Picture Password**. Besides saving you the repetitive stress of entering your password, these two new options offer a lot of flexibility to determine how to access your user account.

- **PIN**—A PIN is a 4-digit number you use to identify yourself when you sign in to Windows. A PIN is particularly useful to tablet users who normally don't have a physical keyboard.

- **Picture Password**—A picture password is a combination of a picture and touch gestures. To define a picture password, choose a picture from your Pictures folder and then make three gestures: you can choose to tap or draw lines or circles. Windows records the position of the gestures, their length, and the order in which you make them.

If you did not set up Windows, be sure to ask the person who did set up Windows what kind of password your account uses. For information on setting up one of these two options, refer to Chapter 17.

Now that you're finished with the preparation and explanations, follow these steps to sign in to Windows:

1. You can sign in to Windows if the Welcome screen—also known as the Lock screen—appears, as shown in Figure 1.1. The picture in your Welcome/Lock screen might be different from the one shown here, but you can tell you're in the right place if you see the time and date superimposed on your picture.

FIGURE 1.1

The Windows Welcome screen appears when Windows is locked, which occurs if you do not enter your user ID and password promptly or if you enter the command to lock Windows.

2. From the Welcome screen, swipe up, tap the spacebar, or click once on the screen. Any of these three gestures reveals the sign-in screen.

3. Select your portrait if more than one portrait appears (see Figure 1.2). If your portrait is the only portrait on the screen, skip this step and continue with step 4.

FIGURE 1.2

Select your portrait to sign in.

4. Your portrait should appear alone on the screen. From there, how you sign in depends on the type of password protection you have:

   • To sign in with a conventional password, enter it into the Password box and press Enter. If you want to verify you entered your password correctly, tap and hold or click and hold the eye-shaped icon near the end of the Password box, as shown in Figure 1.3.

FIGURE 1.3

You can check that you entered your password accurately.

- To sign in with your PIN, enter its four digits. Note that you will be signed in immediately after correctly entering the last digit of your PIN.

- If you used your picture password the last time you signed in, a screen like the one shown in Figure 1.4 appears. (Your picture will be different from the one shown here.) Make your three gestures on the picture. If you successfully make the three gestures, you are signed in and the Start screen appears.

FIGURE 1.4

The Picture Password screen appears if you last signed in using your picture password.

 NOTE If you made a mistake signing in with a picture password, Windows 8 prompts you to try again. Select **OK** and (more accurately) make your three touch gestures on the picture. To redo the gestures before Windows prompts you, select **Start Over**.

Introducing the Start Screen

Fitting to its name, the Start screen is where you begin your work and play. After signing in to Windows, you are dropped off at the Start screen. In Windows 8, the Start screen has been designed to replace the Start button from previous versions of Windows so that you see your most important or highly used apps. In this new Windows, the Start screen shown in Figure 1.5 is highly customizable; you don't see the tools unless you need them.

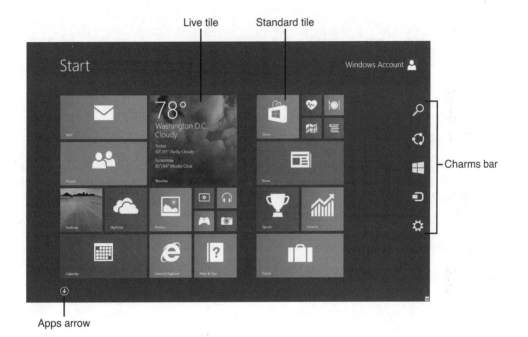

FIGURE 1.5

The Start screen is your gateway to everything Windows has to offer.

To start, here's a short review of the items you can see on the Start screen:

- **Tiles**—A tile is the representation of an app or program. Tiles can be live, displaying updated information from the app, such as a new email alert, weather details, or recent social network status updates. This chapter and Chapter 4, "Making Windows Your Own," provide plenty of information about using, organizing, and manipulating tiles. To activate a tile, click it or tap it.

- **Charms bar**—The Charms bar is a special toolbar that contains a set of five buttons, known as *charms*. Each charm represents an important, very useful feature or tool in Windows, such as search, work with devices such as printers, change Windows or app settings, and a few more. These charms are available everywhere in Windows. There are a few methods you can use to display the Charms bar. You can find details about charms later in this chapter in the "Using the Charms Bar" section.

- **Apps arrow**—Touching or clicking this down arrow reveals a list of all apps, accessories, and Windows system utilities installed on your computer.

 TIP With Windows 8.1 you can boot to the Desktop environment instead of the Start screen if you prefer. To learn about setting this as your default boot up preference, see Chapter 9, "Working with Windows Desktop Programs."

Returning to the Start Screen

Although most of your work in Windows initiates from the Start screen, when you're in an app, all of which run in full screen mode, you need to know how to return to the Start screen. The first time you open an app in Windows 8.1 you will see a tip that shows how to return to the Start screen using your mouse as shown in Figure 1.6. Based on the device you use, follow one of these methods to return to the Start screen.

Swipe in from the middle of the right border and then tap the Start button that appears on the Charms bar.

Press the Windows key.

Point to the bottom-left corner of the screen and click the Start button icon when it appears. (This icon appears as a permanent button on the Windows Desktop, so when working from the Desktop, you do not need to mouse over it to make it appear.)

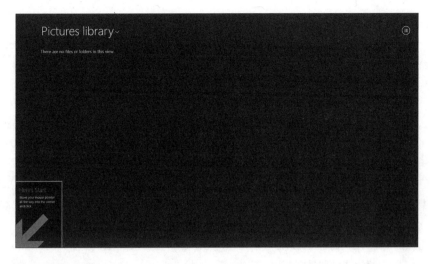

FIGURE 1.6

Windows 8.1 will show you a helpful tip to reveal the Start portrait by pointing to the bottom left corner of the screen.

Seeing Tiles off the Screen

It doesn't take long for new tiles to start to appear on the Start screen. When you install new software and when you pin apps, pictures, and documents to the Start screen, your display of tiles starts to grow. The collection of tiles won't fit on a single screen, so you need to scroll to the right to see the rest of them; then you scroll back to the left to see the tiles you passed.

To see tiles off the screen, follow these steps based on the device you use:

- Pan to the right by placing your finger or stylus on the screen and then swiping it to the left. You can reverse the direction by swiping to the right. Try to swipe on an empty spot on the Start screen, avoiding tiles.

- Use your left- and right-arrow keys to move across the Start screen. If pressing the left- or right-arrow key has no effect, either you are already at the edge of the Start screen or the pointer is not on the Start screen. Press Tab once or twice to move the pointer to the Start screen.

- Use the horizontal scrollbars at the bottom of the screen to move left and right. Click the dark colored areas of the scrollbar to scroll in that direction. You can also use your scroll wheel if your mouse is so equipped.

Displaying All Apps

Certain types of apps do not appear on the Start screen automatically. These apps include Windows accessories, such as the Calculator and Notepad; Windows Ease of Access tools, such as the Magnifying Glass tool; Windows System tools, such as the Control Panel and the virus protection tool, and many more.

Windows 8.1 makes accessing these apps a bit easier than it was in Windows 8, and you can still add (pin) their tiles to the Start screen, making it easy to select the app the next time. When you pin an app to the Start screen, the tile always appears on the Start screen. Pinning an app is covered later in this chapter.

To show all the apps in Windows 8.1, as shown in Figure 1.7, do one of the following based on the device you use:

- Swipe up from an empty spot on the Start screen, which reveals all the apps installed on your computer.
- Touch or click the downward pointing arrow in the lower right of the Start screen, as shown in Figure 1.5.

FIGURE 1.7

You can easily see all the apps installed in Windows in the Apps view.

NOTE There is a group of applications known as administrative tools that Windows hides from view. If you want to display these specialized tools, open the Settings charm from the Start screen and, under Tiles, move the Show Administrative Tools slider to the Yes position. These tools are not discussed in this book, and you shouldn't use them unless you know what you're doing; refer to an advanced-level book for help with these programs.

Using the Charms Bar

Charms are one of the cooler features first introduced in Windows 8. Each charm (there are five) represents a tool, a capability, or a way to do things in Windows.

Now you might think that search and sharing functions aren't new to Windows. You are correct, but here's the difference: Before Windows 8, changing a program's settings, including how the program prints or how you can share your information from the program with other users, differed with each program you used. For example, the printer that worked perfectly with your word processing program, a moment later might not work with your greeting card software. These scenarios change with Windows 8 charms.

Charms are the responsibility of Windows, so no matter which app is open when you open the charm, and no matter what you do with that app, the feature that the charm represents still works the same way.

Here's how it works inside of Windows. When smart developers create a program to run in Windows 8, they decide to *contract* with Windows for certain functionality, such as printing, sharing, or using a device such as a second monitor. By entering into that contract, your program says, "Windows, I grant you responsibility for printing/sharing/devices. Thanks for letting me pay attention to the important stuff that I want to do!"

The five charms in Windows are the following:

- **Search charm**—Search for files, apps, programs, and settings, as well as content from the Internet.

- **Share charm**—Share what you are looking at with another app.

- **Start charm**—Go to the Start screen.

- **Devices charm**—Access the devices and hardware attached to your computer, such as a printer or a second monitor.

- **Settings charm**—Change settings for whichever Windows 8 app you're working with. Opening the Settings charm from the Start screen gives you access to most Windows settings.

These capabilities are available from a handy pop-up menu available at all times. That menu is known as the *Charms bar*. You can display the Charms bar, which gives you access to the capabilities previously described, or you can use some handy shortcuts that bring you directly to those capabilities.

To open the Charms bar, do one of the following based on the device you use. The Charms bar appears, as shown in Figure 1.8.

Swipe in from the right edge of the screen.

Press Windows+C.

Point to the top- or bottom-right corner of the screen.

FIGURE 1.8

The Charms bar gives you access to important tools across Windows 8.1.

There are also a series of keyboard shortcuts that each open an individual charm directly (see Table 1.1).

TABLE 1.1 Charms and Charms Bar Quick Key Combinations

Press This	To Do This
Windows+C	Display the Charms bar. Also displays the time/date tile.
Windows+F	Open the Search Files charm.
Windows+H	Open the Share charm.
Windows+I	Open the Settings charm.
Windows+K	Open the Devices charm.
Windows+Q	Open the Search charm.
Windows+W	Open the Search Settings charm.

Using the Search Charm

Use the Search charm, which has been significantly updated in Windows 8.1, to search for anything in Windows (such as a file or folder), a setting, an app, or the Web.

 NOTE You can use any search tool you can find on the Web, such as Google. To search with a web-based search tool, you must open Internet Explorer and navigate to a page where you can launch the search. However, a search tool that you open in your web browser cannot find apps or files in Windows 8.1.

Like the other charms, the Search charm provides a capability regardless of what you are doing, what apps are running, and what device you're using. You can search for files, apps, or programs, and even for specific settings, such as "volume" or "email address." Figure 1.9 shows the screen after the Search charm is opened.

FIGURE 1.9

Use the Search charm to search for apps, settings, or files, as well as to search the Web.

Here's what you need to know about the Search charm:

- When the Search charm appears, you can select Everywhere, Settings, Files, Web Images, or Web Videos to narrow the focus for what you want to search for.

 NOTE Windows sorts the results of your search by popularity.

- From the Start screen, you can type any search terms without opening the Search charm first.

- How many times have you hunted through menus, looking for some option or feature you know exists? With the Search charm, you can search for the setting. When it's found, you can open the area of the software where the setting is located. For example, if you receive so much email that you would like to mute the sound that plays when an email arrives, you can enter the word **sound** to search for a setting where you change the mail notification setting. Figure 1.10 shows how to search for settings whose name matches "sound." You'll notice that Settings is selected for the search filter.

Filtering a search makes it easier to get the results you want.

FIGURE 1.10

This image shows the results of a search for settings that contain the word sounds.

Using the Share Charm

The Share charm provides a simple way to pass information from one app to another. The app you're working with is the one doing the sharing. Not every app is capable of receiving shared information, so Windows filters the list of apps shown when you open the Share charm. Two examples of apps you can share with are Mail and People, but apps can be configured by the teams that build them to share with just about any other program.

When you summon Share, Windows prepares a link or some other capsule of the page you're looking at. Windows then creates a message containing the link or capsule for the app doing the sharing.

The most obvious example of using the Share charm is with Internet Explorer. When you open the Share charm from Internet Explorer, you'll see Mail as an option (see Figure 1.11). If you select Mail, Windows creates a message containing an image plus a summary of the page you had open. It can do so for any page on any website.

FIGURE 1.11

You can use the Share charm to pass along information from the page you are looking at via email.

To open the Share charm, do one of the following based on the device you use:

- Swipe in from the right and then tap the Share charm.
- Press Windows+H.
- Point to the top- or bottom-right corner of the screen. When the Charms bar appears, click the Share charm.

Using the Devices Charm

When you think about the stuff that makes computer users a bit nervous, especially beginning users, working with hardware—such as printers, scanners, projectors, and other gear—is near the top of the list. Now if you don't routinely think about these things, it's okay—this book has done the work for you.

It's not a surprise that hardware causes confusion. Think about it: When you print, you usually select File and then Print from a menu. But when you scan a document, you need to figure out if you should use the software on your computer or the controls on the scanner. Who knows? But if you need to project from your computer, do you work with the display settings in the software you're using or maybe turn the projector on and off? There was no such thing as consistency—until the Devices charm.

When you connect hardware to your computer or when Windows notices the hardware attached to your system when you upgraded to Windows 8, it figures out what these devices do. Windows also notes what kind of hardware typically is used with each of your apps and programs. When you open the Devices charm, Windows shows you just the devices that would work (and should work) with your app. From the Devices charm, you can carry out your job, such as print or project or scan.

To open the Devices charm, do one of the following based on the device you use:

- Swipe in from the right and then tap the Devices charm.
- Press Windows+K.
- Point to the top- or bottom-right corner of the screen. When the Charms bar appears, click the Devices charm.

When the Devices charm appears, select the task you want to perform and follow the onscreen instructions to specify your device. Yes, it's as easy as that.

Using the Settings Charm

Most apps you run have various options that you tweak to control how the app works. However, Windows also has some control over how apps run. There are a few settings for each app that control how the app works with Windows. The Settings charm also enables you to reach some common Windows settings that have nothing to do with an app, such as volume, network connection, screen brightness, and more. Figure 1.12 shows the settings for a web page.

To open the Settings charm, do one of the following based on the device you use:

- Swipe in from the right and then tap the Settings charm.
- Press Windows+I.
- Point to the top- or bottom-right corner of the screen. When the Charms bar appears, click the Settings charm.

FIGURE 1.12

The Internet Explorer settings (with a menu of commands under the heading Options) enable you to alter settings for browsing the Web.

The Help and Tips App

Windows 8.1 has introduced a new app named Help+Tips which you should be aware of as you get to know your new Windows 8 device. This app appears by default on your Start screen as a tile with a large question mark. Select the app to open the Help+Tips screen shown in Figure 1.13.

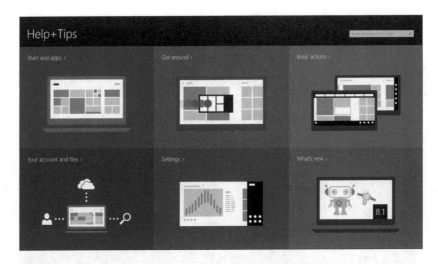

FIGURE 1.13

The Help+Tips app has been designed to help you quickly get familiar with Windows 8.1.

This app provides six fields of information that can be very useful references, especially if you are having trouble with revealing hidden tools or using new navigation gestures. You will find helpful animated video clips that show how to perform basic navigation and tasks. In addition, it provides basic how-to information. Finally, you can search for additional information on Microsoft.com from the Search field in this app.

Handling Special Startup Situations

As pointed out earlier in this chapter, starting up Windows is easy. Every once in a while, though, the unpredictable happens, and sometimes you do things that are out of the norm. The next three sections look at some special situations that could occur during startup.

Restarting Windows After a Problem

The Microsoft engineers built Windows to handle many problems, but there is always a chance that something can go wrong. Some software programs might interfere with others; hardware you add to your computer might interfere with Windows; and programs you download from the Internet can cause issues. As a result, Windows can freeze, become sluggish, or shut down unexpectedly, and sometimes you may need to force your computer to power down. If Windows shuts down while experiencing problems, you might see the screen shown in Figure 1.14 when your computer restarts.

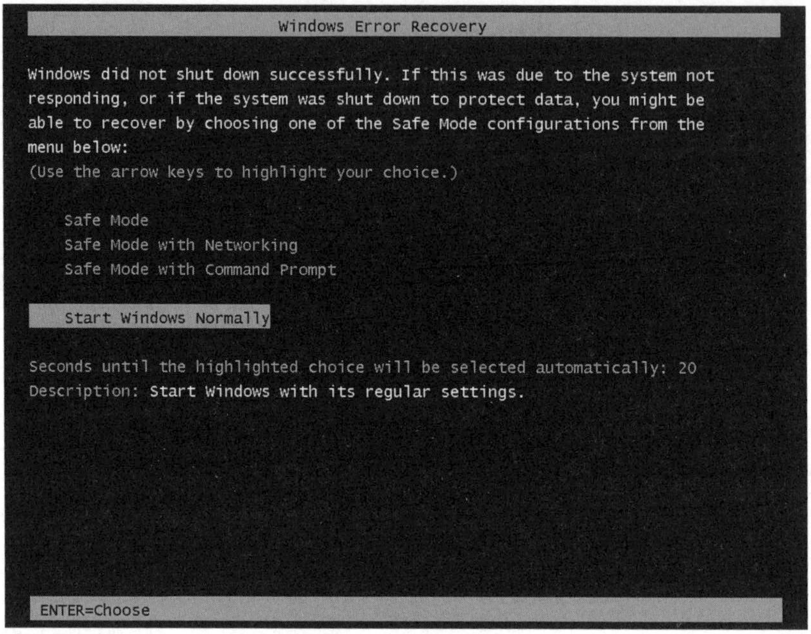

```
┌─────────────────────────────────────────────────────────────────┐
│                    Windows Error Recovery                         │
│                                                                   │
│  Windows did not shut down successfully. If this was due to the system not │
│  responding, or if the system was shut down to protect data, you might be │
│  able to recover by choosing one of the Safe Mode configurations from the │
│  menu below:                                                      │
│  (Use the arrow keys to highlight your choice.)                   │
│                                                                   │
│     Safe Mode                                                     │
│     Safe Mode with Networking                                     │
│     Safe Mode with Command Prompt                                 │
│                                                                   │
│     Start Windows Normally                                        │
│                                                                   │
│  Seconds until the highlighted choice will be selected automatically: 20 │
│  Description: Start Windows with its regular settings.            │
│                                                                   │
│                                                                   │
│                                                                   │
│                                                                   │
│  ENTER=Choose                                                     │
└─────────────────────────────────────────────────────────────────┘
```

FIGURE 1.14

If it crashes or shuts down unexpectedly, Windows guides you when it restarts.

If you have experience running Windows in one of the diagnostic modes listed, such as Safe Mode or Safe Mode with Networking, you can use one of those options. If you are like most users, select **Start Windows Normally** and press **Enter**. Ideally, everything should run like normal at this point. If it doesn't, refer to Chapter 25, "Troubleshooting and Solving Common Problems," for assistance troubleshooting Windows problems.

Waking Up Windows

If, instead of powering off your system, you place Windows in sleep mode, eventually you need to wake up Windows to resume using your computer. Although some computers might use a different button for waking from sleep, it's most likely that you use the Power button on your computer. (Usually just moving or clicking your mouse works, too.) This doesn't mean you should press and hold the Power button until you see something happen. Rather, press the Power button once and then release it to wake up Windows. It's best to check the documentation that came with your computer or to check the computer manufacturer's website to confirm how to wake your computer.

TIP   Be sure you do not hold the Power button too long. Doing so typically restarts the computer, which might cause you to lose any unsaved work.

Password Notifications

Passwords are the one area of your account that, depending on your settings, may require regular maintenance. In these cases, Windows sends messages to you, reminding you what needs to be done with your password.

Expiring and Expired Passwords

You might see a message when you sign in informing you that your password will soon expire (see Figure 1.15). Unless you have extremely tight controls over computer use at home, you will see this message only at work. If you do, it means your company has established a policy requiring you to change your password on a regular, scheduled basis, and you need to create a new one before you can use Windows.

FIGURE 1.15

This message appears if your password has expired.

Password Not Complex

If you see the message shown in Figure 1.16, your company has established a policy that passwords must be complex, and your password is too simple and easy to figure out. This message appears when you try to change your password, such as when it expires or when you change it on your own.

FIGURE 1.16

The password entered did not meet the minimum complexity requirements.

The actual password requirements can vary based on the policies put in place, but in general, a good password should meet the following guidelines:

- The password should not contain the user's account name or any more than two consecutive characters from the user's full name.

- The password should be at least six characters long.

- Of the four categories that follow, the password should have at least three of these characteristics:

  - Contains at least one English uppercase character (A through Z)

  - Contains at least one English lowercase character (a through z)

  - Contains at least one digit (0–9)

  - Contains at least one nonalphabetic character (for example, !, $, #, %)

Exiting Windows

When you need to take a break from your computer, perhaps to shop for computer books, you should consider how long you will be away and in what state you should leave your computer. For example, if you are going to be away from your computer for a short period of time but you are working on sensitive information, you should lock your computer. Locking your computer immediately displays the Lock screen without affecting the programs running or the files that are open. This enables you to get back to work quickly as soon as you sign back in. With the sleep option, there are four choices available to manage your computer while you take a break. You can also completely power down your computer if you think you're going to be away for a longer period of time.

Signing Out of Windows 8.1

You leave no trail behind when you sign out of Windows. Any programs running when you signed out are shut down, and any connections you had open are closed. If you attempted to sign out with unsaved work in either a Desktop or Windows app, Windows prompts you to save the work, as shown in Figure 1.17.

Closing 1 app and signing out

Letter to Maria and Jeff - WordPad
This app is preventing you from signing out.

FIGURE 1.17

You see a warning on the Start screen if you try to sign out with unsaved work.

To log out of Windows, go to the Start screen, select your portrait, and then select **Sign Out**. This leaves your computer powered on, but available for other users to sign in with their own accounts.

Locking Windows 8.1

Locking Windows 8.1 is useful if you are going to be away from your computer, but you want to resume your work or play when you return. Locking also prevents others from accessing the information on your computer.

To lock Windows, follow these steps:

1. On the Start Screen, select your portrait on the Start screen and then select **Lock**.

2. Press **Windows+L**.

Putting Windows 8.1 to Sleep

If you don't intend to use your computer for a longer period of time (for example, a few hours or even a full day), it makes sense to put the computer to sleep. When a computer is asleep, it is still running, although in a low-power mode. Because you can leave your applications and documents open when you put your computer to sleep, it usually takes far less time to start work again by awakening a computer than to power it up from scratch and reopen whatever program you were working on.

To put Windows to sleep, follow these steps:

1. From the **Settings** charm, choose **Power**, and then select **Sleep**.

2. Press **Ctrl+Alt+Delete**. Then, click or press the power button in the lower right and select **Sleep**.

To wake your computer from sleep mode, moving the mouse, typing, or pressing and releasing the power button typically wakes it. Do not press and hold the power button; doing so will typically shut down your computer.

Shutting Down Your Windows 8.1 Computer

If you're going to be away from your computer for an extended period of time and don't want it sucking away even the minimal amount of power sleep mode uses, you can shut it all the way down. You don't need to close any running programs or apps, but you must save any unsaved work or you will lose your changes since the last time you saved.

To shut down Windows at the Start screen, do the following:

1. From the Settings charm, choose **Power**, and then select **Shut Down**.

2. Press **Ctrl+Alt+Delete**. Then, click or press the power button in the lower right and select **Shut Down**.

THE ABSOLUTE MINIMUM

Here are the key points to remember from this chapter:

- You can use a PIN or a picture password instead of a password to sign in to Windows 8.1. These password types are particularly useful if you use a Windows 8 tablet.

- Get comfortable with using the Start screen; you will be using it frequently.

- The Charms bar is easily accessible from anywhere in Windows. The charms behavior is very predictable and can make activities like sharing and printing much easier and faster.

- You have a wide choice of options when you want to pause your work and protect your files. Be sure to make the right choice—sleep, sign out, lock, or shut down—based on how long you will be away from your computer and where your computer is located.

2

INTERACTING WITH WINDOWS

Although this chapter's title suggests a broad presentation about working with Windows and does not identify a specific version, the focus of this chapter is relatively narrow. Windows 8 enables new ways to control what happens on the screen while continuing to support more traditional methods. The methods you employ will make your experience more satisfying which is why this book devotes an entire chapter—this one—to helping you learn how to interact with the various switches, dials, knobs, buttons, and pulleys that enable you to control what Windows does. The newness of Windows 8, though, is not the only challenge in learning to work with it.

One of the more notable new features in Windows 8 is the support for mobile devices, such as tablets. Microsoft planned to simultaneously release versions of Windows 8 that run on laptops, desktop, servers, and tablets. Allowing for form factor differences, the user interface (the part of the software that you touch, look at, and respond to) is identical on all devices, but how you interact with each is different. There are some things the mouse can't do that the finger or stylus can, and the keyboard can bring 100 keys to the party, whereas the mouse brings just 2.

Getting to Know the Windows 8 Interfaces

Because Windows 8 has to work across a range of hundreds of different models of desktops, servers, laptops, and tablets, Microsoft dictated specific guidelines as to how all these hardware devices should work with it. These guidelines apply to traditional personal computers as well as tablets. So the product of all this consistency is a batch of techniques (for example, "Click like this," "Swipe like that") that work across all kinds of different devices. In this section of the chapter, you can review how to interact with Windows 8 computers using the four main interfaces: touch, the mouse, the keyboard, and the virtual keyboard. Some of the combinations are natural, such as touch and a tablet, and some combos aren't as obvious. You can read about both and everything in between in this section.

Using the Mouse in Windows 8

The mouse is a great choice for any device, although touch is probably more efficient and easier to use with a tablet. Following are the commands you see associated with use of the mouse:

- **Point**—Unless you have a special version of Windows that can read your mind, you use a mouse to point to the item on the screen that you want to work with. The mouse pointer is usually in the shape of an arrow, but you can always change it to another shape, as explained in Chapter 10, "Performing Easy Windows Configuration." You can also download Windows *themes* that bring together a new color scheme and fun graphics, including cool, new mouse pointers, to give Windows a different look and feel.

- **Click**—Besides picking up dust, the most common action you take with the mouse is *click*. You click to select items, to start and stop actions in Windows, to indicate where text you write should be inserted, and more. To click with your mouse, just tap the primary mouse button.

- **Double-click**—The double-click mouse action traditionally has been used in Windows to start a program or launch a task. In Windows 8, most of those double-clicks have been changed over to single-clicks, mainly to make things more consistent for all users. Any of the programs you ran in previous versions of Windows that required a double-click have the same requirements if you run the same programs on the Desktop.

- **Right-click**—The right-click traditionally is used to display a menu of commands related to the item you right-click on. For example, right-clicking on a photo might present commands to open your photo editing application and to add the picture to a slide show. This convention still works on the Desktop, but not on the Start screen. On the Start screen, right-clicking displays the Apps bar, and in Windows 8 apps, right-clicking displays the Command bar. The App bar and Command bar are described in Chapter 5, "Using Windows Store Apps."

   NOTE When you see the command to select or click, this always refers to use of the primary mouse button, as described in this section. Any task that requires you to click the secondary mouse button clearly says to use the *secondary* or *right* mouse button. You can also specify which button on your mouse is the primary button. Refer to Chapter 17, "Sharing Your Windows Computer with Others," for help with configuring the mouse.

- **Click and drag**—The click-and-drag action is used to move files, folders, or any other item from one place to another in Windows 8. You can always use the cut-and-paste menu convention (when available) to move things, but you can save time and look smarter by using click and drag. Click and drag is also known as drag and drop. One of the most prominent areas in which you can employ click and drag on the Windows 8 Start screen is where you can drag a tile to a new location on the Start screen.

   TIP Windows always treats click and drag as a move action. This means the item you were dragging will no longer be in the location from which you dragged it. To use click and drag as a copy action, press and hold down the Ctrl key before you release the mouse key to drop the file in its new location. Windows will copy the file rather than move it.

- **Right-click and drag**—A cousin to the click and drag is the right-click and drag. Just as the right-click displays a menu with commands specific to the item you click, so does the right-click and drag. Windows recognizes the item you are dragging and pops up a menu relevant to the item and the destination of your drag.

Using the Keyboard in Windows 8

Windows 8 includes an onscreen keyboard that appears when you need it. This section is dedicated to the physical keyboard. You can read about the virtual keyboard in a bit, in the section, "Using the Virtual Keyboard."

The keyboard is an important tool for interacting with Windows 8, but its role is for more than entering text and punctuation. You can use a large number of quick-key combinations to issue commands to Windows 8. A quick-key combination refers to two keys pressed simultaneously to issue a specific command, such as Windows Key+F to use the Search charm. The quick-key combinations in Windows 8 use the Windows key as the first key in the combination. Keep in mind when using quick-key combinations that you should always press the Windows key slightly before pressing the second key.

Table 2.1 lists some useful quick-key combinations you can use with Windows 8.

TABLE 2.1   Quick Key Combinations

Press This	To Do This
Windows (alone)	Switch to the Start screen
Windows+B	Opens the Desktop app
Windows+C	Displays the Charms bar; also displays time/date tile
Windows+D	Opens the Desktop app, minimizes open applications, and shows desktop
Windows+E	Starts Windows Explorer
Windows+F	Opens the Search Files charm
Windows+Ctrl+F	Searches for computers on the network
Windows+G	Cycles through Desktop gadgets (you must be on the Desktop for this to work)
Windows+H	Opens the Share charm
Windows+I	Opens the Settings charm
Windows+J	Switches between two snapped apps
Windows+K	Opens the Devices charm
Windows+M	Minimizes all windows on the Desktop
Windows+O	Locks screen orientation
Windows+P	Configures a projector or second display device
Windows+Q	Opens the Search charm

Windows+T	Goes to taskbar on the Desktop and cycles through running apps
Windows+U	Opens Ease of Access Center
Windows+V	Cycles through notifications
Windows+W	Opens the Search Settings charm
Windows+Z	Opens the App bar (you must be at the Start screen for this to work)
Windows+Comma	Peeks at the Desktop
Windows+Period	Cycles through the three docked app positions: snapped left, docked right, and snapped right.
Windows+Shift+Period	Cycles backward through the three docked app positions: snapped right, docked left, and snapped left
Windows+Tab	Cycles through the list of apps you most recently used; doesn't include programs you run on the Desktop
Windows+PrtScn	Takes a picture of a screen and places the picture in the Photos folder in Screenshots
Windows+PgUp	Using multiple monitors, moves the Start screen to the left monitor
Windows+PgDn	Using multiple monitors, moves the Start screen to the right monitor

Using Touch in Windows 8

The touch interface is new to Windows 8. In previous versions of Windows, you could use a stylus, a mouse, and the keyboard to work with Windows, such as to sketch and trace. With Windows 8, you can now use your finger or another touch device to completely interact with Windows and issue commands. A number of hardware manufacturers have brought mobile devices to market to take advantage of the new Windows touch interfaces, including Microsoft with its Surface brand of tablets. Here are some of the devices that leverage the new touch capabilities:

- Tablets
- Touch-sensitive displays
- Phones

Where you use the word click to specify the action you take with a mouse to interact with Windows, touch-specific commands generally use the word *gesture* because it's a word that describes just about any action you take with your touch device. Here is a list of the gestures used with Windows 8, including some tidbits on how the gesture works:

- **Swipe**—The swipe is a short movement with your finger or fingers across the screen of the device. The fingers are on the screen only for a short period of time. A direction is usually given when you are instructed to swipe, such as Swipe Down from the top of the screen.

- **Tap**—It doesn't get any easier than this gesture. To tap, just touch your finger to the screen.

- **Press and hold**—The press-and-hold action is the touch equivalent of the mouse right-click. You usually press and hold a specific item, such as a file or folder. This action is used predominantly to display a special menu that contains commands relevant to the item that you pressed and held. You can tell you pressed long enough by the appearance of a small circular symbol at the point on the screen where you held.

- **Rotate**—Windows 8 supports a *rotate* gesture, which enables you to turn an image or document clockwise or counterclockwise. You might not see regular use for this gesture on a computer or laptop, but a tablet user should take advantage of the capability to pivot an image to better see it on a device with limited screen real estate.

  To pivot a document or an image with the rotate gesture, place two or more fingers on the display. Turn your fingers and wrist in a circular motion while keeping the display stationary.

- **Pinch and stretch**—Use the pinch gesture and the stretch gesture to expand an image (stretch) or to shrink an image (pinch). To pinch, place two fingers on the display separated a bit over the image you want to change. While keeping contact with the screen, slowly draw both fingers together as if you were softly pinching a baby's cheek. You can stop drawing your fingers together when you are happy with the results of the pinch, such as reducing the size of an image.

  To stretch, place two fingers on the display slightly touching one another over the image you want to affect. While keeping contact with the screen, slowly draw both fingers apart. You can stop drawing your fingers apart when you are happy with the new size of the image.

Using the Virtual Keyboard

Windows 8 displays an onscreen keyboard when it detects one is necessary, as shown in Figure 2.1. Here are the two conditions that, together, let Windows 8 know that a virtual keyboard is needed.

- You use a touch device, such as a tablet or a touch screen. (Windows 8 can detect it.)
- You are on a screen requiring text input and no physical keyboard is detected.

FIGURE 2.1

Windows displays a keyboard automatically when it believes you need one.

You can choose between three keyboard modes. To choose the keyboard mode, tap the main keyboard key at the bottom-right corner of the virtual keyboard, and then tap the tile for the keyboard mode you need:

- Split Keyboard
- Regular Keyboard
- Handwriting Recognition

Although the keyboard automatically appears when you use a Windows 8 app, you must make a few clicks for the keyboard to display on the Desktop. To display the virtual keyboard on the Desktop, follow these steps:

1. Press and hold on the taskbar.

2. Tap **Toolbars** and then **Touch Keyboard**. A keyboard icon appears on the taskbar.

3. Tap the keyboard icon on the taskbar.

 NOTE If you have a physical keyboard attached, the virtual keyboard may not automatically appear. Select the Settings charm to call up the virtual keyboard by selecting Keyboard when using a touchscreen device.

Using Windows Controls You Find on the Desktop

If you have experience with Windows 7 or an earlier version of Windows, you can skip this section unless you would like a refresher. If you are a beginner to Windows or are new to computers in general, this section of the chapter helps you get comfortable with the tools and objects you use on the Desktop. Remember, the Desktop app is an environment for working with traditional desktop applications and programs.

Window

The window is the big cheese of controls. A window is the control that organizes and stores other controls. It is the main organization unit in all Windows software—that's right, all Windows Desktop software. The window is so important Microsoft named its operating system after it. Software programs present their options and settings in a window, you supply information to those programs in a window, and the messages the program reports back to you are organized in a window.

Figure 2.2 shows a window and points out a few key parts. You can find a lot of information about windows in Chapter 8, "Learning About the Windows Desktop."

Button

A button's use is fairly obvious. You click a button to execute the command indicated by the text on the button. In many cases, a button that is labeled OK means *proceed as planned* or *I am through making choices—go ahead and finish the job.* A button with the label Cancel usually indicates *forget it, I changed my mind* or *don't finish what you started.* Sometimes a picture or an image is used as a button. You click the picture to execute the command portrayed by the picture. Figure 2.3 shows examples of different buttons, including both traditional buttons and new tile buttons used in Windows 8.

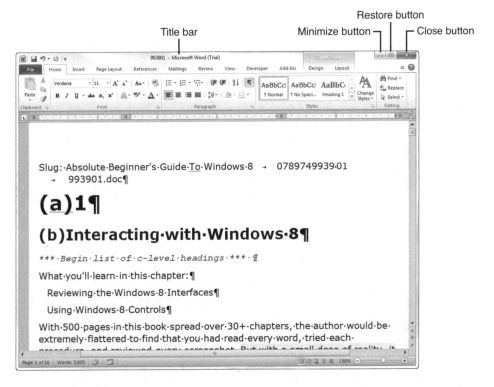

FIGURE 2.2

A typical window found on the Desktop.

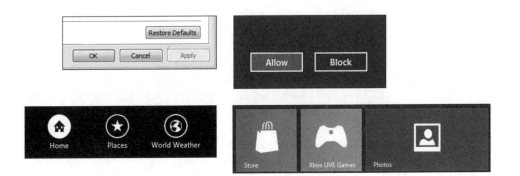

FIGURE 2.3

Most buttons in Windows look the same; however, buttons can appear as pictures on your screen.

Option Button or Group

Software designers use something known as an option button inside of a group of these buttons to enable you to make a single choice from a group of possible options. A border with a label usually is used to organize the group of option buttons on the screen, as shown in Figure 2.4. Option buttons are also known as *radio buttons*.

Camera roll folder

If you automatically upload photos and videos from your camera Roll folder to SkyDrive, you can get to them from any device. Higher quality photos will take up more space on your SkyDrive.

○ Don't upload photos

◉ Upload photos at good quality

○ Upload photos at best quality

FIGURE 2.4

Option, or radio, buttons are organized for you to choose only one from the group.

Text Box

If you have ever entered your name or address to register a new program or to identify yourself to a website, you have used a text box. If the program you use requires more information from you than just a single line of information, you will see a much larger text box.

TIP Most text boxes work properly with the Windows cut/copy/paste mechanism. This means you can copy information from a document or email and then paste it into a text box (Ctrl+C is the keyboard shortcut to copy selected text). Sometimes you can't access a menu when entering information into a text box, and sometimes you can't choose Paste. In these cases you can usually use the keyboard command to Paste by pressing Ctrl+V while the cursor is inside the text box.

Check Box

You will see a check box when you must select whether some state or condition is ON or OFF. The label determines whether checking the box indicates on or off. In most uses, a check box actually isn't checked. Rather, an "x" symbol fills the box part of the control. Figure 2.5 shows examples of check boxes.

To check or uncheck a check box

🖰 Click in the check box or on the text to change it.

👆 Tap in the check box or on the text to change it.

Turn messages on or off

For each selected item, Windows will check for problems and send you a message if problems are found.
How does Action Center check for problems?

Security messages

☑ Windows Update   ☑ Spyware and related protection
☑ Internet security settings   ☑ User Account Control
☑ Network firewall   ☑ Virus protection
☑ Microsoft account   ☑ SmartScreen

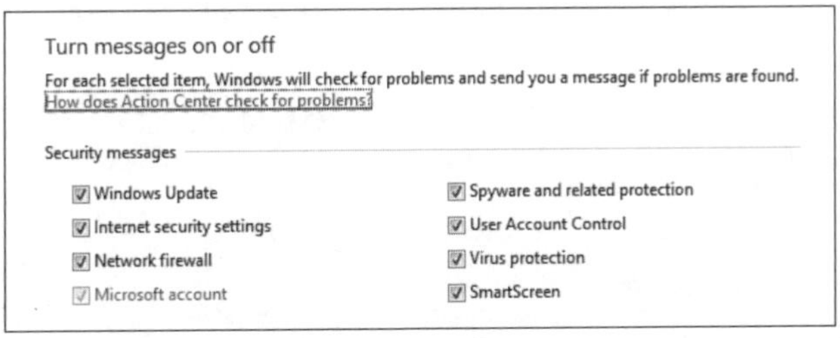

FIGURE 2.5

A check box indicates an ON or OFF condition.

Windows 8 Toggle

Like the check box control, the toggle presents an on or off condition. The label next to toggle tells you what setting is controlled. It's easy to slide the toggle to on or off with the mouse or touch, as shown in Figure 2.6.

To switch a Windows 8 toggle

🖰 Click and drag the bar to the other end of the toggle.

👆 Press and hold on the bar, and then drag it to the far end of the toggle.

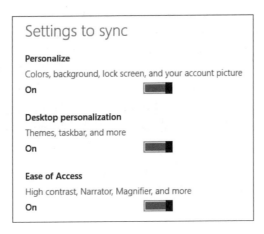

FIGURE 2.6

The toggle is used to turn some settings on or off.

List Box

The list box appears when you must select an item from a list of options. Sometimes you need to select one item from the list; other times you may be asked to select multiple items. Figure 2.7 shows an example of a list box.

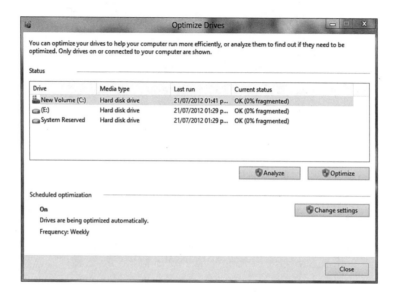

FIGURE 2.7

A list box is used for you to review and select items from a list.

To select one item in a list:

- With your mouse or touch, scroll through the list to locate the item you're looking for. Tap or click once on the item.

To select multiple contiguous (next to one another) items in the list:

- With a mouse, click and drag the mouse pointer over all the items. Windows 8 highlights the area of the screen selected, making it easy to see the files and folders selected.

- Also with a mouse, click once on the first item. Next, press and hold Shift while you click once on the last item.

- With your finger or a stylus, tap once on the first item. Next, press and hold Shift while you tap on the last item.

To select multiple noncontiguous (not next to one another) items in the list:

- With a mouse, click once on the first item. Next, press and hold Ctrl while you click each remaining item. Do not release Ctrl until you have clicked each of the items you intend to select.
- With your finger or a stylus, tap once on the first item. Next, press and hold Ctrl while you tap each remaining item. Do not release Ctrl until you have tapped each of the items you intend to select.

Drop-Down List

A drop-down list, like the list box described previously, presents a list of items you can choose from. The items in the list appear to drop down beneath the control when you select the arrow button on the right side of the control, as shown in Figure 2.8. The selected item in the list is always shown in the visible portion of the drop-down list, even after you close the dialog box or the window where the drop-down list is located.

To select an item from a list in a drop-down control

- Click the arrow at the end of the control. Then scroll through the list to find your item. Click your item when you find it.
- Tap the arrow beside the control to drop down the list of choices. Scroll through the list until you find your item. When you do, tap it.

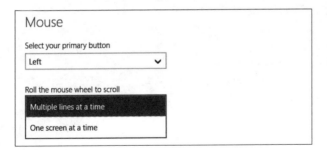

FIGURE 2.8

A drop-down list takes up less room than the list box, but it's harder to find the item you are looking for.

Combo Drop-Down List

A combo drop-down list is similar to the drop-down list control described earlier. The only difference is you can enter the name of the item you want to select in the part of the control that displays the selected item with the combo drop-down list.

The list automatically selects the first item in the list whose name matches the text you type. This control is used when it is believed you might not know if the item you're interested in is actually in the list. It's quicker to verify that the item you want is listed by entering its name rather than scrolling through the list.

THE ABSOLUTE MINIMUM

- There are four interfaces you can use to interact with Windows 8: mouse, keyboard, virtual keyboard, and touch.

- Windows 8 appears and operates almost identically on the different devices that it runs on.

- Make sure you recognize and know how to use the tools to interact with Windows 8 such as the On/Off toggle and drop-down menus.

- Although the keyboard alone does not have the capability to access all the buttons, lists, and switches that a mouse or your finger does, approximately 30 quick-key combinations are available that automate many of the important tasks in Windows.

3

ORGANIZING THE START SCREEN

Because the Start screen serves as your dashboard to access the many features and applications contained with Windows 8, you will likely want to spend some time organizing and customizing how it looks. There are endless possibilities of tile arrangements now that Microsoft allows four tile sizes. You can also name organized groups of tiles, or applications, utilizing logical labels.

Organizing All Those Tiles

In Chapter 1, "Your First Hour with Windows," you had a quick introduction to the Start screen and became familiar with the basics. Here you will find out how to change the look and feel of the Start screen. This coverage will help you understand how to truly make Windows fit your needs.

Selecting a Tile

Before you change any tile's appearance or function, you need to indicate to Windows which tile you want to work with. This is known as *selecting*, and in this case, you are selecting a tile.

When a tile is selected, a check mark appears in the top-right corner of the tile, as shown in Figure 3.1. To select a tile, do one of the following based on the device you use:

🖐 Touch and hold the tile you want to select until the check mark appears.

⌨ Use your left and right or up and down arrow keys to move across the Start screen. As you do so, a colored border appears around tiles as you pass over them. Press the spacebar when you have moved to the tile you want to select.

🖱 Right-click the tile.

 TIP To deselect a tile, just repeat what you did to select the tile.

FIGURE 3.1

A check mark appears in the top-right corner of a selected tile.

Moving a Tile

You can reorganize the tiles on the Start screen as you like. No rules dictate where certain tiles should appear, so you can move a tile to whatever position you like.

To move a tile, do one of the following based on the device you use:

- Touch and hold on the tile to be moved and immediately drag it to its new location.

- Click and drag the tile to its new location. Notice when you click and hold the tile, it seems to tip backward slightly. Also notice how the other tiles on the Start screen seem to move out of the way and open an empty spot as you drag a tile across the screen (see Figure 3.2).

FIGURE 3.2

Moving a tile.

Making a Tile Bigger or Smaller

You can select the size for any tile. There are four sizes: large, wide, medium, and small (see Figure 3.3). You might prefer smaller tiles to fit more tiles on the screen. You might also use the size of a tile to distinguish certain types of tiles from another. For example, apps you use online, such as News and Mail, might be represented by large tiles, and apps you use on your computer or tablet, such as the Photo app, might be represented with small tiles. The size of the tiles can be changed to suit your individual preference—there is no right or wrong tile size.

To change a tile's size, do one of the following based on the device you use:

Select the tile (see the earlier section "Selecting a Tile"). Tap **Resize** on the bar at the bottom of the screen and then choose your desired size.

Select the tile. Then press the left or right arrow to highlight the Resize icon and then press the spacebar. Use the up or down arrow keys again to highlight your desired size. Press the spacebar one more time.

Select the tile and then click **Resize** on the bar at the bottom of the screen. Select from the displayed sizes to make your change.

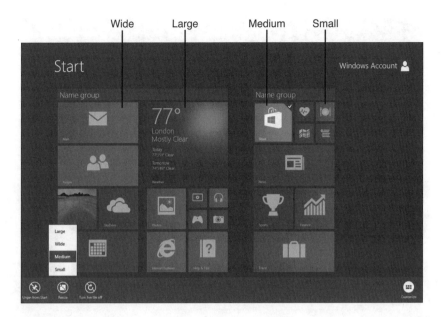

FIGURE 3.3

Resizing a tile.

Adding a Tile to the Start Screen

Adding a tile to the Start screen is less challenging than you might expect. You can add a tile for an installed application only, so you first must install any program you'd like to show on the Start screen. Most of the Windows programs (those components of Windows not delivered as Windows 8.1 apps) do not appear on the Start screen. You can access them in one click by adding a tile for the ones you expect to use often (see Figure 3.4).

To add a tile to the Start screen, do one of the following based on the device you use:

Show the Apps page (click the down arrow on the Start screen) and then select the tile to be added. Tap **Pin to Start** from the App bar.

Show the Apps page and then select the tile to be added. Press the left or right arrow key, which moves the selector down to the bar at bottom of the screen. Press the right-arrow key to select **Pin to Start**. Press the spacebar.

Show the Apps page and then select the tile to be added. Click **Pin to Start.**

FIGURE 3.4

Adding a tile to the Start screen.

Show More Tiles

One result of pinning more tiles to your Start screen is that your screen can only display so many tiles at a time before you need to scroll over to see additional tiles you have pinned. This is especially noticeable on devices with smaller screens. One way to tweak how your tiles display is to add more tiles to your display using a new setting in Windows 8.1. Instead of the default three rows of tiles, your screen can be scaled to show additional rows of tiles as shown in Figure 3.5. For some devices with larger screens, this may not appear as an option.

To Show more tiles follow these steps:

1. From the Start screen, select the Settings charm.

2. Select **Tiles**. The Tiles pane will be displayed.

3. Under Show more tiles, Slide the slider to Yes as shown in Figure 3.5. Your screen may take a few seconds to re-scale the tiles.

FIGURE 3.5

Show more Tiles to increase the number of tiles visible on your display.

Personalizing Tile Groups

Your collection of tiles is bound to grow as you install new programs and apps. You can also pin documents and web pages to the Start screen, so it's likely you will add many, many tiles to the Start screen in a short period of time. To help keep track of tiles and to easily locate them, you can organize tiles into groups of your own design. For example, you might create a group of tiles of all your photo-related applications. The groups are organized into columns on the Start screen. A wider margin separates one group from another. You can move your tile groups when you like, and you also can place a name above each group. An example of a number of tile groups appears in Figure 3.6.

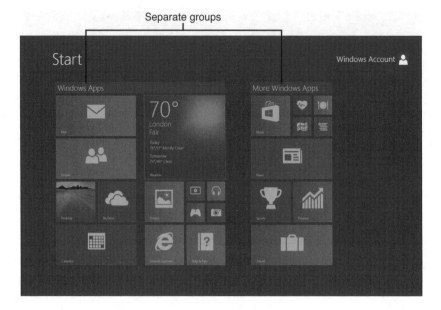

FIGURE 3.6

You can organize the tiles on the Start screen into groups.

Creating a Tile Group

Tile groups, as the name would imply, are groupings of tiles into a collection where there isn't any separation by margins or blank space. Within these groups you may adjust tile size and where they appear within the group. Sometimes it is easier to break out particular tiles into a separate group so they are easier to find or to where they make more sense from an organizational standpoint. Windows puts its default tiles into somewhat logical groups, but they may not appeal to you.

To create a tile group, do one of the following based on the device you use:

Touch and then drag the first tile in the group to the right beyond the last tile of a group until a vertical bar appears on the screen. Be sure the first tile is to the right of the bar. Release your finger or the stylus from the tile. Drag other tiles in the group the same way, either to the right or below any other tile in the group.

Click and drag the first tile in the group to the right beyond the last tile until a vertical bar appears on the screen. Be sure the first tile is to the right of the bar. Release the mouse. Drag other tiles in the group either to the right or below any other tile in the group (see Figure 3.7)

FIGURE 3.7

Dragging a tile to create a new group.

Figure 3.8 shows that you have created a new group illustrated by the fact that the Adera game tile is separated by margins on either side.

FIGURE 3.8

A newly created group.

Moving Tile Groups

You may want to change the order of your groups so that frequently accessed tiles require less scrolling or if you have changed your organizational structure.

To move a tile group, follow these directions based on the device you use:

- From the Start screen, press **Ctrl+Mouse-Wheel-Scroll-Forward**. This creates an effect of zooming out from the Start screen, as shown in Figure 3.9. With your mouse, click the group to move, and then drag the group to the new location.

- Use a pinching motion on the Start Screen. This creates an effect of zooming out from the Start screen (see Figure 3.9). Touch the group you want to move, and then drag it to a new location.

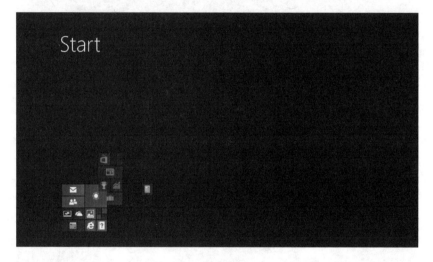

FIGURE 3.9

By zooming out from the Start screen, you can easily rearrange tile groups.

Naming a Tile Group

It may make sense for you to name your groups so you can more easily locate your tiles, rather than trying to remember into which group you put a tile.

To label a tile group, follow these directions based on the device you use:

- Right-click a tile in the group that you want to name. You'll then notice a shaded area at the top of the group that reads Name Group.

- Tap-and-hold on a tile in the group you want to name. You'll then notice a shaded area at the top of the group that reads Name Group.

Now whether you use touch or a mouse, select or click the **Name Group** box, and then enter the name of the group in the box that appears as shown in Figure 3.10. You can repeat these steps for another group, or click or tap anywhere on the screen to return to the normal Start screen.

FIGURE 3.10

You enter the name of the tile group in the small box that appears when you select the Name Group button.

THE ABSOLUTE MINIMUM

- You can customize the appearance of the tiles on the Start screen. You can change their size and move them around. You can also add new tiles to the Start screen.

- Leverage the ability to pin apps so that both Desktop and Windows 8 apps are easy to locate on your Start screen.

- Use the Show more tiles feature to instantly provide additional space on your smaller device screen.

- You can create new groups for tiles, add names to groups, or re-arrange groups of tiles.

4

MAKING WINDOWS YOUR OWN

Short of playing games and keeping up with Twitter and Facebook, there probably is no greater distraction from real work than tweaking and adjusting all those preferences that make Windows your own. You wouldn't be the first person to spend more time picking colors and pictures for your Windows background than actually working. Although this version of Windows may seem like it has fewer options you can use to personalize Windows than previous versions had, there certainly are enough new options in Windows 8.1 to help you make it your own. This chapter takes you through the various personalization settings, including providing some before and after examples.

Personalizing Windows to your liking requires you to work with a number of areas of Windows. Many of the procedures and skills necessary to set these personal options are described in Chapter 2, "Interacting with Windows." If you run into difficulty with this chapter, refer to the two previous chapters. In addition, review the sections "Returning to the Start Screen" and "Using the Charms Bar" in Chapter 1, "Your First Hour with Windows 8."

Personalize the Start Screen

When you first install Windows, you are asked to personalize it with your own color selections. In this color section, you see how you can modify those choices and use colors and photos to personalize Windows at any time. You can further personalize Windows using one of your own photos as the background of the Lock screen, and you can use any photo you like for your account picture. You also can select from a palette of color themes and choose from a selection of background patterns to personalize Windows. The color and photo selections appear in several places in Windows, including the Start screen, as shown in Figure 4.1, which is where this section begins.

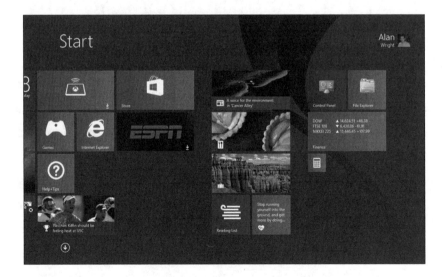

FIGURE 4.1

The Start screen is all about personalizing.

NOTE If you are using a Microsoft account, your personalization settings can be synchronized to any Windows 8 devices that you log into using your Microsoft account. By default, synchronization is enabled so that you have the same appearance on any device without the need to repeat these steps. To learn more about this feature and how to enable or disable it on a device see Chapter 20, "Working with SkyDrive."

The color you choose for the Start screen applies not only to Start, but to any Windows app you have installed. The color selection finds its way to the banner where certain apps display their name, as well as a few other places.

To change the color of your Start screen, follow these steps:

1. Open the Charms bar and select **Settings**.

2. Select **Change PC settings**.

3. Select **Personalize** from the list on the left side of the screen. A fly-out pane titled Personalize appears with three groups of choices (see Figure 4.2).

FIGURE 4.2

You can personalize the color used throughout Windows 8.1, as well as the background of the Start screen.

4. The topmost group of tiles shows thumbnails of Start screen backgrounds; some of these even have animation. Select a tile to see a preview on the Start screen; animations will not be visible until you leave the Personalize pane and lock your choice in. The last tile in this group is special and new with Windows 8.1; it is a match to your current Desktop wallpaper, and selecting this tile keeps the Desktop background and the Start screen synced. Select the Start screen wallpaper you like.

5. The second group of colors is titled Background Color. Select from the colors here to set the color that will appear throughout Windows. The Accent Color you select is used in menus and text and is the color that pulses on the Start button. In both groups, you can use the color bar across the bottom to get an approximate color, and then use the larger color swatches to fine-tune your preference. Click or select a spot on the Start screen to exit the Personalize pane and keep your choices.

Compare Figures 4.1 and 4.3 after changes to just three settings. Windows has a lot to offer if you like to make Windows your own. In the following sections, you learn additional ways to personalize Windows.

FIGURE 4.3

You can preview the effects of your color choices and Start screen backgrounds as you make choices.

Personalize Your Account Picture

You can select one of your personal photos to use as your account picture. Your account picture appears not only on the screen where you sign in, but also on the upper-right corner of the Start screen.

To change your account picture, follow these steps:

1. From the Start screen, select your name and current picture (if any) that appear in the upper-right corner of the screen.

2. Select **Change Account Picture** from the list that appears (see Figure 4.4). The Settings pane opens to Accounts, and Your Account is selected on the left.

3. Select **Account Picture**. The Account Picture screen appears, as shown in Figure 4.5.

FIGURE 4.4

Update your account picture from the current account information displayed on the Start screen.

FIGURE 4.5

You can select a photo to use as your account picture or shoot a new photo to use.

4. To shoot a picture using a camera connected to your computer, select **Camera**. When the Camera app starts, snap the photo, set the crop marks, and select **OK**.

   To choose a photo stored on your computer, select **Browse**. The File Picker window appears as shown in Figure 4.6. Select the photo to use as your account picture, and select **Choose image**. (For information on navigating your folder system, refer to Chapter 2.)

5. The image you chose appears in the portrait back on the Account Picture screen.

6. You are returned to the Account Picture screen. Your account picture now reflects the photo you selected, as shown in Figure 4.7. There is no Close or Exit button on the Account Picture screen, so to return to the Start screen, press the Windows key, or slowly move to the bottom-left corner with your finger or mouse to display the Start portrait. Select the portrait.

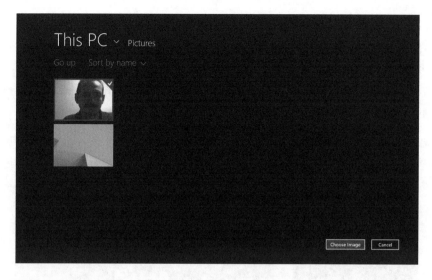

FIGURE 4.6

Choose your account picture from any photo on your computer, or shoot a new photo to use easily to update your account picture.

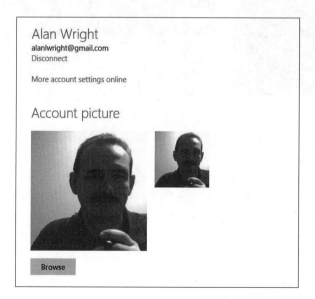

FIGURE 4.7

Your Account picture will update to show the picture you have selected.

Personalize the Lock Screen

The Lock screen appears when you have signed out of Windows or you haven't used Windows for a period of time and it kicks you out.

To change the picture that appears on your Lock screen, follow these steps:

1. Open the Settings charm, and select **Change PC Settings**.

2. Select **PC and Devices** and then **Lock Screen**. Your current Lock screen picture appears as the large image in the right pane, as shown in Figure 4.8.

FIGURE 4.8

Choose from the available Lock screen images, or use your own.

3. Under your current Lock screen image you can see additional Lock screen images that come with Windows 8.1. Do one of the following:

   • To use one of the pictures that ships with Windows, select the picture you like. The picture you choose replaces the current Lock screen picture on the screen.

   • If you want to use one of your pictures as the Lock screen background, select **Browse**.

4. Your screen displays the photos in your Picture folders. Look through the photos to find one to use as your Lock screen. Select the photo to use and then select **Choose Image**.

Setting a Lock Screen Slideshow

A very nice feature in Windows 8.1 is the capability to turn your Windows device into a digital picture frame. By default, Windows pulls pictures from your Pictures library on the device. You can add additional folder locations as well.

To set up a slideshow on your Lock screen, follow these steps:

1. Open the Settings charm, and select **Change PC Settings**.

2. Select **PC and Devices** and then **Lock Screen**. Below the wallpaper choices for your Lock screen you will see the option to Play a Slide Show on the Lock Screen. Turn this slider switch to On, as shown in Figure 4.9.

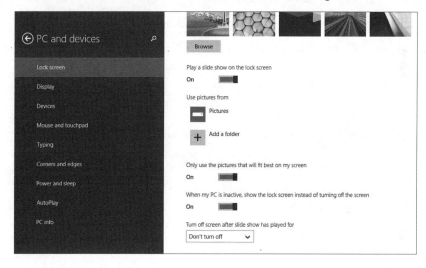

FIGURE 4.9

The Lock screen can play a slideshow from your Pictures folder.

3. Select **Add a Folder** to use the File Picker to point to additional folder locations. If you need to remove a folder that you've included, select the folder name and then select the **Remove** button that appears.

4. It is best to leave the switch to On for showing pictures that fit best on the screen.

5. Leave the switch to On to show the Lock screen when the computer is inactive if you want to see your slideshow.

6. The last setting for your slideshow is related to how long the show can continue before the screen goes dark. By default this is set to Don't Turn Off, which means your slideshow will play until you unlock the screen. You can shorten this to 3 hours, 1 hour, or 30 minutes.

The slideshow that plays shows individual pictures as well as mosaics with panning effects. Your slideshow displays the time as well as any notifications that are allowed to display on the Lock screen.

Lock Screen Apps

When you are not using your computer, you can still receive notifications from apps on the Lock screen. This allows you to know that emails have arrived, calendar appointments need attention, or chat messages or Skype calls perhaps need a reply.

To allow an app to send notifications to your Lock screen, follow these steps:

1. Open the Settings charm, and select **Change PC Settings**.

2. Select **PC and Devices** and then **Lock Screen**. Scroll down to the section titled Lock Screen Apps, as shown in Figure 4.10.

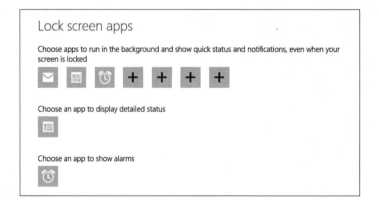

FIGURE 4.10

You can determine which apps can send notifications via the Lock screen.

3. Select an empty space, indicated by a + sign, to add an app.

4. In Figure 4.11, Skype is listed as an app that could be added. Select an app from the list to add it to your Lock screen apps.

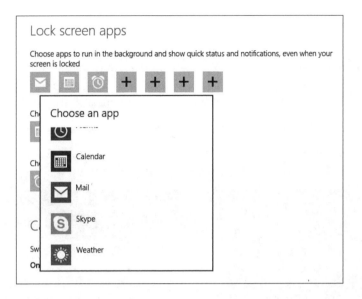

FIGURE 4.11

Select an app from the list of installed apps to allow notifications to appear on the Lock screen.

5. Select any additional apps that appear on the list to allow notifications to appear from the Lock screen.

6. To prevent an app from giving notifications, select it from the list and in the Choose an App pane select **Don't Show Quick Status Here**.

 TIP If you are bothered by chimes and other sounds that notifications might make, you should know that they can be silenced. To learn more about additional settings that control notifications, look over information in Chapter 7, "Setting Up Search, Share, and Notifications."

Personalizing the Desktop

One of the most enjoyable tasks in the computer world is to make Windows feel like home. This applies to the Desktop, too. You can tweak the color of everything from the window border to the text on the screen; use your favorite photo as a background on the Desktop; change the icon representing the Recycle Bin to one of 400+ icons provided in Windows; and change many other settings to make the Desktop reflect your mood and personality. In this section, you learn how to personalize the Desktop environment.

Changing the Desktop Background

The Desktop background is the best place to show your own personality and preferences in Windows. You can choose a stock image that comes with Windows, or you can choose a picture that you have imported from a camera or received in email. To change the Desktop background, follow these steps:

1. Right-click or tap and hold a clear spot on the Desktop; then click **Personalize**.

2. Select **Desktop Background** at the bottom of the window. The Desktop Background window appears, as shown in Figure 4.12.

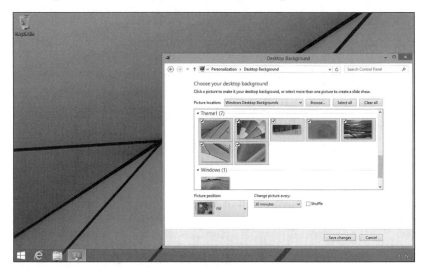

FIGURE 4.12

A number of options are available to format the Desktop background.

3. The Picture Location drop-down list includes different locations on your computer where pictures to use as a desktop background are located. Select the list to display the locations. Then select each item in the lists to see the pictures at each location. Of course, if you see a picture you like, there is no need to look further!

4. If you want to use just one picture or a color as your background, select the picture or color; then select **Save Changes**. At this point, you are done and can select the **X** on the top-right corner of the window to close it. If you want your background to rotate through a number of pictures, continue with the next step.

5. Select the check box in each picture you want to use.

6. At the bottom of the Desktop Background window (you should be there), select **Picture Position**, and then select how you want the pictures you chose in step 5 to appear.

7. Select the **Change Picture Every** drop-down list; then select the interval at which the picture should change, as shown in Figure 4.13.

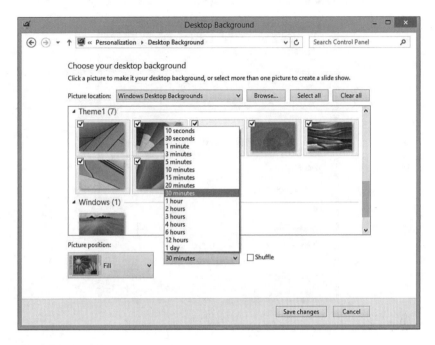

FIGURE 4.13

Select how often the Desktop background image will change.

8. Select **Shuffle** to randomly choose the order in which pictures appear.

9. Select **Save Changes**.

10. Select **Close** to close the Personalization window.

Changing the Mouse Pointers Used on the Desktop

You may want to customize the mouse pointers you use in Windows. You can adjust the pointers to reflect your personality and taste, or you might need to switch to pointers that are larger than normal to make it easier to see them. There are 10 pointers you can customize, such as the selection pointer and the double-arrow pointer. You can customize one or more of the pointers individually, or you can switch to a full set of 10 pointers.

To change the mouse pointers, follow these steps:

1. Right-click or press and hold a clear spot on the Desktop; then select **Personalize**.

2. Select **Change Mouse Pointers** near the top-left corner of the window. The Mouse Properties dialog box appears, as shown in Figure 4.14.

FIGURE 4.14

You can change many aspects of the mouse, including the pointer appearance, how fast the pointer moves across the screen as you move the mouse, and more.

3. To use a predefined set of pointers, scroll through the schemes at the top of the dialog box. Select a scheme to inspect the pointers. If you find a scheme you like, select **OK**. Select **OK** again to close the Personalization window.

4. To customize a pointer, select it in the Customize list.

5. Select **Browse** to open the Cursors folder, which contains a complete list of pointers available in Windows.

 NOTE You can change the way the selection of mouse pointers appear in the dialog box used to select a new pointer. Select the View Menu button from the toolbar, and then select the view you want. The Medium Icons view presents the most useful arrangement of icons.

6. Select the pointer you want to use from the list; then select **Open**. You should be returned to the Mouse Properties dialog box.

7. Select the next pointer you want to customize, and then repeat steps 5 and 6.

8. Select **OK** to close the Mouse Properties dialog box.

9. Select **Close** to close the Personalization window.

Change the Desktop's Color Scheme

You can change the color of the taskbar and window borders. You can choose from a preset palette of colors. To change the Desktop color scheme, follow these steps:

1. Right-click or tap and hold a clear spot on the Desktop; then select **Personalize**.

2. Select the **Color** button at the bottom of the window. A window appears with a palette of color swatches.

3. In the Color and Appearance dialog box, choose the color you like, and then select **Save Changes**.

4. Select **Close** to close the Personalization window.

Setting Up a Desktop Screensaver

Screensaver programs became popular with the introduction of Windows as a means to prevent images from the new-at-the-time highly graphical software applications from creating a ghosted image on the display. This action came to be known as *burning in*. Display technology has advanced, and the risk of burning in is negligible for modern displays, yet screensavers remain popular. If you want to use one, you can always find a screensaver that reflects your mood and personality. Follow these steps to configure a screensaver in Windows 8.1.

1. Right-click an empty spot on the Desktop, and then select **Personalize**.

2. Select **Screen Saver** at the bottom of the window. The Screen Saver Settings dialog box appears, as shown in Figure 4.15.

3. Select the **Screen Saver** list to display the list of screensavers installed on your computer.

4. In the Screen Saver list, choose the screensaver you want to use. Notice that the monitor image at the top of the dialog box shows you a preview of the screensaver you selected.

FIGURE 4.15

You can choose from the six screensavers that come with Windows.

5. Depending on the screen saver you selected, there may be options for you to set. For example, the 3D Text screensaver has a number of options. Select the **Settings** button to customize the screensaver. Click **OK** when complete.

6. Select **Preview** to review your screensaver as it will appear in use. Select anywhere on the screen to close the preview.

7. In the **Wait** box, enter the amount of time during which there is no activity on your computer before the screensaver starts.

8. If your computer is in a location where there are people that you would prefer not to potentially access your computer, enable the **On Resume, Display Logon Screen** check box. This requires a user to log on to clear the screensaver after it starts.

9. Select **OK**.

10. Select **Close** to close the Personalization window.

THE ABSOLUTE MINIMUM

Here are the key points to remember from this chapter:

- You can change a number of preferences and options in Windows 8 to suit your personality and mood. You can apply these preferences to any computer you sign in to with your Microsoft account.

- Nothing says "This computer is mine" more effectively than a custom color choice and personal photos used in various places. You can specify the color scheme to use throughout Windows, as well as the pictures that appear on the sign-in screen and the Lock screen. The pictures can be anonymous, such as a setting sun or another landscape or view. Or the pictures can be personal, showing you, family, friends, pets, or whatever.

- Many applications display information periodically without your having to open them. These messages, known as notifications, can be suppressed. For example, if you do not want to see the new email notification, preferring to check email status when you open the app, you can suppress this notification. You can suppress all notifications or individually choose which ones appear.

5

IN THIS CHAPTER

- Learn Windows Store Apps' Basic Information
- Change a Windows Store App's Settings
- Manage Windows Store Apps
- Shop at the Windows Store

USING WINDOWS STORE APPS

You have probably noticed that Windows 8 is different from previous versions of Windows. Much of the new look—colors, appearance, layout, and even placement of buttons and lists—in the new Windows comes from a set of design principles know as *Windows 8 style* (also *Metro* or *Modern*, depending on who you ask), developed by Microsoft. All the programs and tools that Microsoft and other companies build for Windows 8 also follow the Windows 8 style. Given that, it's not surprising that the new Windows 8 programs are as different from Windows 7 programs as Windows 8 is from Windows 7. The goal of this chapter is to bring you up to speed as quickly and clearly as possible on these new software programs, covering everything from starting up an app to using two apps together on the screen.

This chapter introduces you to a number of new concepts and techniques, all intended to help you manage the kinds of apps you'll find in the Windows Store. Many of these techniques are dependent on some of the skills presented earlier in the book. Be sure to review Chapter 2, "Interacting with Windows," and Chapter 4, "Making Windows Your Own," if you are confused while reading the step-by-step procedures. In particular, review the sections related to the Start screen and the Charms bar in Chapter 1, "Your First Hour with Windows 8."

Learning Basic Windows Store Apps Info

Windows Store apps are software programs developed by Microsoft and other software companies specifically for use in Windows 8; for that reason they are sometimes referred to as Windows 8 apps. The term Windows Store apps refers to applications that have been specifically designed to run on Windows 8 devices, allowing for many screen sizes and orientations.

In this context, Windows 8 isn't just an operating system. It refers to the set of design principles and philosophies about building software for users that was used to build Windows 8. Although a majority of the software used in previous versions of Windows, especially Windows 7, can run in Windows 8 (on the desktop), the opposite does not hold true—Windows Store apps cannot run in older versions of Windows. Here is more basic information you need to know about Windows Store apps:

- Windows Store apps run full screen, and only in certain conditions can two apps be viewed on the screen at the same time.

- Windows Store apps are sold in the Windows Store, which is built in to Windows 8. I cover the Windows Store at the end of this chapter.

- The Windows Store also handles the installation of Windows Store apps, saving you the confusion of installing new software into a new operating system.

- Windows Store apps leverage the Charms bar consistently for printing, setup, and search. The Charms bar is described in Chapter 1. This requires a bit of a change in thinking on your part, because you traditionally look *inside* of your app for important tools, such as for printing. Now, you should check the Charms bar first for everyday tools and functions.

Unfortunately, much of what you know about Windows programs from your experience with older versions of Windows doesn't mean anything with Windows Store apps. Programs that were built for the prior version of Windows can still run from the Desktop, but if you look for some of the standard Desktop features you're used to when running Windows Store apps, you're not going to find them. Some of these include

- Resizing windows
- Haphazardly arranging multiple windows on the screen
- Minimizing windows
- Using standard menus, such as File New, File Open, File Print

In the rest of this chapter, you can find enough hands-on instruction to make you a near-expert with Windows Store apps before you charge off on your own working with them. Here's what's covered:

- Starting and stopping Windows Store apps
- Managing Windows Store apps
- Arranging multiple Windows Store apps on the screen
- Shopping for Windows Store apps

Running Windows Store Apps

Starting an app probably seems like a basic topic, perhaps one that doesn't merit its own section in a book. But innocent situations, such as if another app is running when you start a new app, deserve some explanation. So this section explains what happens when a Windows Store app starts up, what happens when a Windows Store app is running when you start a new one, as well as how to close a running app.

Starting a Windows Store App

To start a Windows Store app, select the tile from the Start screen that represents the app you want to start. Figure 5.1 shows a representative set of Windows Store app tiles. Immediately after you select a tile, you see a bit of fancy animation that quickly transitions to the open app, which fills the screen.

FIGURE 5.1

Windows Store apps are started by selecting a tile from the Start screen; the tiles can be formatted with colors and graphics.

You'll notice Windows Store apps appear flat, borderless, and broad. There are no buttons, sliders, or other controls that appear to be raised off the screen, as shown in Figure 5.2, which presents the Internet Explorer browser built for Windows 8. Most controls are hidden until you follow the app's instructions to reveal any controls the app requires. An app's settings likely can be revealed by opening the App bar, which is covered later in this chapter. A Windows Store app typically does not have borders because the app fills the entire area of the screen.

FIGURE 5.2

Notice how Windows Store apps, like Internet Explorer, fill the entire screen and how controls appear flat against the screen.

Starting Additional Windows Store Apps

If you are already using an app and want to use another, just return to the Start screen and start the additional app. You don't need to close the app you are working with before starting another app. When you start a Window Store app, it opens full screen, replacing whatever was on the screen previously. The app you previously had open doesn't actually close. It's just hidden, so you can always switch back to it or to any other app that you started. You'll learn more about that in the section, "Managing Windows Store Apps."

Stopping a Windows Store App (If You Must)

You generally do not need to close or exit an app when you are done with it. Windows handles the housekeeping with apps it believes you no longer are using. But if you are instructed to close an app, perhaps for troubleshooting purposes, or you simply want to impress your friends, here are a few ways to close an app:

🖐 Be sure you are in the app you want to close. Slowly drag your finger on the screen down from the top of the screen. By the time you reach the bottom of the screen, the app should disappear from view. When you start this gesture, be sure your finger or stylus is close to the edge of the screen that borders the rest of your device.

◉ Press Alt+F4.

◉ If another app is open (or a few apps are open) in addition to the one you are stopping, point at the top-left corner of the screen. A portrait of the most recent app you started appears. If that is the app you want to close, right-click and then select **Close**. Otherwise, move your mouse down from the top-left corner until the app you want to stop appears. Right-click it, and then select **Close**.

◉ Point to the top-middle border of the app. Adjust the position of the mouse pointer until it changes to the shape of a hand. When it changes shape, click and drag down as if you were dragging the border of the app. The app reduces to a size not much larger than that of a large tile on the Start screen. The app follows your mouse cursor as you drag down. When you reach a point about two-thirds down the screen, the app closes down and disappears.

TOMBSTONING IN WINDOWS 8.1

To improve performance and enhance the user experience with certain applications, Windows 8.1 allows apps to hold on to memory resources that had previously been closed when using the method of dragging from the top to the bottom of the screen. Rather than completely closing the app, it is *tombstoned*. Although it will be removed from the app switcher, it still appears in the Task Manager with allocated memory resources.

Although this certainly allows a tombstoned app to start up again faster than one that has not been started in quite some time, the real reason for tombstoning has to do with apps that stream content from the Internet. If you are listening to streamed music or watching a video and the app is tombstoned by dragging it down to the bottom of the screen, it will be able to continue playback when you reopen it.

To completely close an app, if you think this is necessary, use the same method of dragging down to the bottom of the screen and hold it there for a second or two. You see the thumbnail of the app rotate, and a generic icon for that app appears. You can then release the app because it has now been completely closed.

Using the App Bar to Change an App's Settings

Almost all Windows Store applications have at least one setting that you can adjust. For example, the Photos app enables you to use one of your photos as the app's tile on the Start screen, as shown in Figure 5.3.

You summon the settings for all apps in the same way. App settings appear on the App bar (see Figure 5.3). Although the App bar appears at the bottom of the App in the figure, the App bar also can appear above the app. The developer of the app determines whether the App bar settings appear above or below the app.

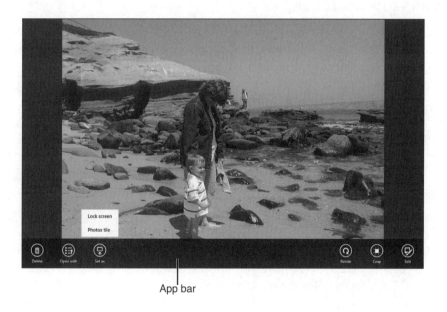

App bar

FIGURE 5.3

The links on the bottom left of the Photo app enable you to set the picture as the app tile or use it on your lock screen.

To open the App bar, do one of the following based on the device you use:

👆 Swipe in from the bottom of the screen.

⌨ Press Windows+Z.

🖱 Right-click any empty area of the Start screen.

Managing Windows Store Apps

With the new design of Windows 8, applications also have been redesigned to be more engaging and efficient. One way is to keep the screen organized and clutter-free. Restricting the number of apps that can appear at once on the screen is a helpful step toward that goal. But there are always exceptions. In this section, you learn how to switch between open apps, how to organize multiple apps on the screen at once, and how to use the app switcher to quickly get to the app you want.

Using the App Switcher

One of the important tools you use to navigate between open apps is the app switcher. The *app switcher* displays a list of open apps and apps you opened recently. You select an app from the app switcher, and Windows brings that app to the foreground.

To use the app switcher, as shown in Figure 5.4, do the following:

👆 Swipe in from the left in the middle of the screen. When the portrait for the last-used app appears, swipe back to the left. The app switcher appears. Tap the app you want to use.

🖲 Press Windows+Tab. The app switcher appears immediately. Keeping the Windows key depressed, tap the Tab key until the app you're interested in is selected. Release the keys and your app opens.

👆 Point to the top-left corner of the screen. When the portrait for the most recent app appears, move your mouse pointer down slowly and deliberately. The app switcher appears. Click the app.

List of open apps

FIGURE 5.4

The app switcher enables you to quickly switch to any app.

Configuring App Switching with the Mouse

The capability to use the corners of your screen to engage the charms or reveal the app switcher is actually a setting that you can disable if you so desire. You may have experienced this behavior at unexpected times when working with some applications where your cursor inadvertently summons the app switcher, thereby disrupting what you were working on in the currently active app.

To change this setting, follow these steps:

1. Click the Desktop tile on the Start screen to open the Desktop.

2. Right-click (or touch and hold) the taskbar and, from the menu that appears, select **Properties**.

3. In the Taskbar and Navigation Properties dialog box, select the **Navigation** tab, as shown in Figure 5.5.

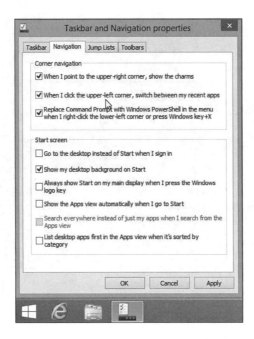

FIGURE 5.5

Use the Navigation tab to enable or disable how your mouse pointer works with the app switcher.

4. In the section labeled Corner Navigation, uncheck the box labeled **When I Click the Upper-Left Corner, Switch Between My Recent Apps**.

5. Select **OK** to save this setting and close the dialog box.

The result of disabling this setting is that your mouse cursor will have no effect at all on the app switcher when it is in this upper-left corner. (You can do the same for the upper right corner and the charms.)

Switching to the Previous App

You might be involved in a task that requires you to work with two applications, switching back and forth between them. Windows makes this kind of task easy with a gesture that switches you to the previous app you were working with.

To switch to the previous app, do one of the following based on the device you use:

👆 Swipe in from the left.

⌨ Press Windows+Tab.

Point to the top-left corner of the screen. A thumbnail of the previous app appears, as shown in Figure 5.6. Click the thumbnail.

FIGURE 5.6

The most recent app you used appears in the top-left corner of the screen when you point or tap there.

Showing Multiple Windows Store Apps on the Screen

As you use Windows 8, you'll encounter all sorts of instances in which it's useful to have two or more apps visible on the screen at once. For example, suppose you are creating a presentation or perhaps designing a thank you card with one of those snappy greeting card programs, and you'd find it helpful to also have Internet Explorer open to search for graphics to use. As another example, many people like to have the People app open so they can monitor the social chatter while they do their work in a different app. You can probably think of many other reasons to have multiple apps visible at one time.

SCREEN RESOLUTION AND MULTIPLE WINDOWS STORE APPS

One major improvement in Windows 8.1 is that you can more easily work with multiple apps on the screen at the same time. Screen resolution plays a big part in this because it determines how many apps you can display at once. Each docked app needs to have 500 pixels on the horizontal axis. Screens with resolutions starting at 1024×768 can display two apps side by side using the 50/50 snap view; a screen with full HD resolution, 1920×1080, would therefore allow three apps to sit side by side on the screen. Higher resolutions allow additional apps to be displayed side by side, making three and four apps available for multitaskers with lots of screen real estate.

Another related improvement included in Windows 8.1 is that you can now snap Windows Store apps side by side on multiple monitors.

Windows 8 lets you do this (see Figure 5.7). It does so by enabling you to dock one app on the left side of the screen and another app on the right side of the screen. When two apps are docked, you can adjust the space each app occupies by selecting and then sliding the vertical separator to the left or right. If you dock additional apps to the screen, you can use these vertical separators to tweak the spacing each app gets on the screen.

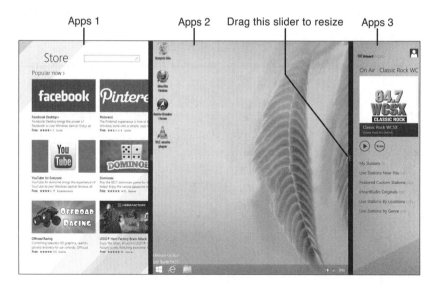

FIGURE 5.7

You can view multiple apps at once on the screen.

You can use your touch, keyboard, or mouse interface to manage your open apps. If you use your mouse or finger/stylus to place and maneuver apps onscreen, which you'll learn shortly, you can see that the apps seem to jump into the slices of the screen closest to them. This is known as *snapping*. For example, you can snap your app into place on the left side of the screen.

 TIP   The screen resolution must be at least 1024×768 to show two apps on the screen. Refer to Chapter 10, "Performing Easy Windows Configuration," for help in setting screen resolution.

Setting Up Multiple Apps on the Screen at Once

Follow these steps to arrange two Windows Store apps on your screen:

1. Start the two apps to be shown together on the screen. The order you open them doesn't matter.

2. Open the app switcher as discussed in the section "Using the App Switcher."

3. Right-click or tap and hold the app you want to share the screen with. Select **Insert Left** or **Insert Right**, depending on what side you would like to position the second app (see Figure 5.8).

FIGURE 5.8

You can insert a second app easily from the app switcher.

Following is another option for setting up two apps on the screen at once. This approach requires use of a mouse or hand/stylus via the touch interface:

1. Start the two apps to be shown together on the screen. The order you open them doesn't matter.

2. Point to the top border of the app in the middle of the screen. Move the mouse pointer carefully up and down near the border until the mouse pointer changes shape to a hand.

3. Click and drag down, which has the effect of dragging the app on the screen down with your mouse pointer (see Figure 5.9).

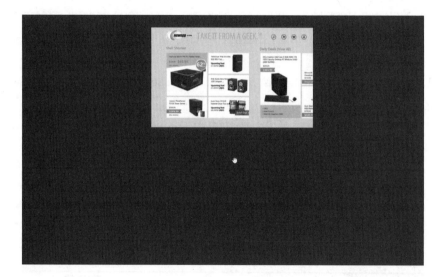

FIGURE 5.9

The mouse pointer changes to the shape of a hand as you drag the app downward.

4. At approximately the halfway point down the screen, stop dragging the app down. Instead, change direction and now drag the app horizontally to the side of the screen where you would like it docked.

5. Drag across the screen until a black vertical bar appears. Drag the app beyond the bar close to the border of the screen and release. The app should fill the smaller slice of the screen.

6. Open the other app you want to view on the screen. It should snap into the larger slice of the screen.

7. If your screen resolution allows, you can grab another app from the app switcher and drag it to the screen. Notice that it will indicate snap positions to the left or right of currently docked apps. Release the app into the desired position and adjust the separators as needed.

Uninstalling Apps (If You Can)

Some apps are considered part of the Windows operating system, and you will find that it is not possible to uninstall them. Nevertheless, you will find it to be an easy task to uninstall most apps that come with Windows 8.1, as well as apps you may install over time.

Follow these steps to uninstall Windows Store apps:

1. From the Start screen, touch and then swipe up or right-click to select an app that you want to uninstall. (It may be easier to select the down arrow and work from the Apps screen). A check mark appears on the app's tile, and the App bar appears at the bottom of the Start screen.

2. Continue to select any additional apps that you want to uninstall, as shown in Figure 5.10.

FIGURE 5.10

You can uninstall Window Store apps directly from the Start screen.

3. From the App bar select **Uninstall**. You will see a small dialog box pop up listing any apps that are selected and warning you that these will be removed from this PC or from all of your synced PCs if you have additional computers that are synced to your login credentials (see Figure 5.11).

4. Select **Uninstall** to confirm that you want to uninstall the listed apps.

FIGURE 5.11

You will be able to confirm which Windows Store apps are uninstalled.

Windows Store apps uninstall remarkably fast. In the event that you select an app that cannot be uninstalled, you will see the App bar without the uninstall option, or you will see a list of apps to be uninstalled that simply excludes the system app. Examples of system apps that cannot be uninstalled are the Store, Camera, and PC Settings apps. Additionally, if you select an app that is a desktop application, Windows switches to the Desktop, and the Programs and Features window opens so that you can proceed with the uninstall. You can learn more about Desktop programs in Chapter 9, "Working with Windows Desktop Programs."

Shopping at the Windows Store

The Windows Store is an online marketplace integrated into Windows 8 that sells Windows apps developed by Microsoft and other companies. You buy the apps at the store, and then Windows installs the apps into your copy of Windows 8, usually without a single additional step on your part.

The Windows Store organizes and provides updates to the apps you acquire from the store. This means when Windows 8 software companies release an update to an app you own you can install the updates directly from the store or let Windows install the updates automatically.

The Windows Store is a Windows Store app, so you should be as comfortable shopping in the store as you are writing and reading email in the Mail app or creating a slide show in the Photo app. The Windows Store app has been updated in Windows 8.1 to provide a better interface and easier navigation. You open the store by selecting the store's tile on the Start screen, as shown in Figure 5.12.

— Windows Store app tile

FIGURE 5.12

Enter the store by selecting its tile on the Start screen.

With the store open, you can scroll through to look at all the apps available or use the Search for Apps tool shown in the upper-right corner of Figure 5.13.

The home screen in the store presents a handful of currently featured apps as well as a list of picks for you and the current top sellers and free apps. Concise descriptions are provided, and you can see feedback ratings and price. By selecting an app, you can read more detailed overviews and specifications of the apps to help you determine if you want the app. When appropriate, a rating may be provided and the reason for the rating, as shown in Figure 5.13. Finally, you can scroll to the right to check the ratings assigned to the app by others who have acquired it, and read the reviews.

FIGURE 5.13

Select an app to see detailed information and reviews.

At any time in the store, you can open the navigation app bar by right-clicking with your mouse or swiping down from the top of the screen. As shown in Figure 5.14, you can jump easily to categories, the Home screen within the Store app, a list of your currently owned apps, or your account information.

FIGURE 5.14

You can easily navigate between categories within the Store app.

Purchasing an App

Purchasing an app should take no more than two clicks and possibly a password entry, provided you have set up your account information (see the next section, "Managing Your Windows Store Account"). To purchase an app, select its portrait in the store, and then select **Install**. You are asked to confirm, and then you may be asked to enter your password for your account to authorize the transaction, as shown in Figure 5.15. You will then see two messages appear in the upper-right corner of the Store app. The first message indicates that the app is being installed, and the second prominently indicates the app has been installed.

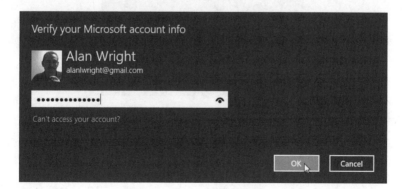

FIGURE 5.15

You may be asked to reenter your Microsoft account password to authorize the purchase of an app.

Managing Your Windows Store Account

Although some apps in the Window Store are free, most aren't. You must enter payment information into the store to purchase software. You can enter credit card information or a PayPal account number. In addition to setting up your payment option, you can also specify whether a password should be entered each time you purchase an app (refer to Figure 5.15).

To manage your account in the Windows Store, follow these steps:

1. Select the **Settings** charm. The Settings options for the Windows Store appear on the right, as shown in Figure 5.16.

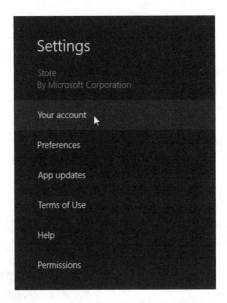

FIGURE 5.16

You manage account information, app updates, and other preferences for the Windows Store in Settings.

2. Select **Your Account**. The Windows Store Your Account screen appears, as shown in Figure 5.17. (You can also swipe down or right-click from within the Store app to choose the My Account button shown in Figure 5.14 to open this same screen.)

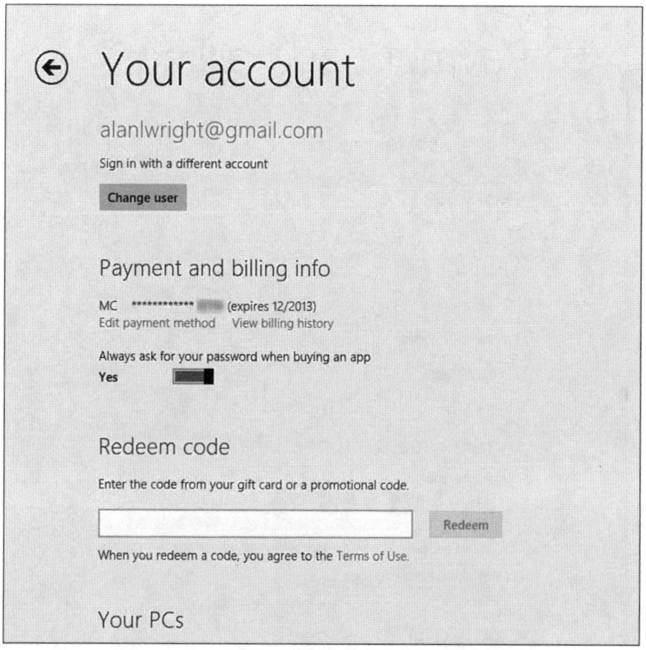

FIGURE 5.17

This screen presents options for managing your account.

3. To specify that your password is entered each time you buy an app, move the Always Ask for Your Password When Buying an App slider to **Yes**.

4. To edit payment information, select the **Edit Payment Method** link or **Add Payment Method** button if nothing has been set up previously. The Payment and Billing screen appears, as shown in Figure 5.18.

FIGURE 5.18

You enter payment instructions for all purchases in the Windows Store.

5. Enter the required information, and then choose Next. Your information is saved. You can continue shopping at this point or leave the store.

From the Payment and Billing screen you can change the default payment method by selecting from cards you have entered. From the Your Account screen you can also use the View Billing History to see details for transactions made using your Microsoft account in a web browser window.

THE ABSOLUTE MINIMUM

- Windows Store apps are software programs developed by Microsoft and other software developers that are designed to run exclusively in Windows 8. This is different from traditional Windows desktop applications that ran in Windows 7 and earlier. These programs run in the Desktop environment.

- The App bar gives you convenient access to the most important options and settings available to the app you are using.

- By default, Windows Store apps open to the full screen. You can have multiple apps share the screen at the same time by snapping apps to areas of your screen based on your screen resolution.

- A number of touch gestures, plus keyboard and mouse support, make it easy to snap apps in, out, and around the screen.

- If you do not want to view two apps at once, and you want to work with an app other than what is on the screen, switch to the other app. The app you were working with disappears from view.

- Windows Store apps are available for purchase from the Windows Store. Sometimes, apps are available at no charge or on a trial basis. You enter payment methods, such as a credit card and PayPal information, to pay for app purchases in the Windows store.

6

THESE ARE A FEW OF MY FAVORITE APPS

Windows 8 lets you add apps to your devices through the Windows Store in a way that you never could in previous Windows operating systems. In no time at all, you will find your device populated with apps that reflect your unique taste and needs. Apps choices are also influenced by your device; a desktop with a large display is usually used differently from a touch screen tablet.

This chapter doesn't necessarily list the *best* apps or even the highest selling; rather, this is offered as a list of Windows Store apps that are our *favorites* from the store.

Apps generally fall into one of several categories, and I point out what makes these apps popular and useful. I think you'll find that a few of these make it into your list of favorites, too. Also, we would love to know if you have a favorite app that we should know about or that you think we overlooked.

Email, Calendar, People

The Microsoft Mail app, shown in Figure 6.1, has been improved in Windows 8.1 and now includes improved tools for managing your email account(s). To learn more about using this app see Chapter 14, "Setting Up and Using Email." If this app does not appear on your device, you may need to install the Mail, Calendar, and People app from the store. Although this is the email app most people use on their Windows 8 device, it is possible that you are looking for an alternative.

 NOTE If you have a Windows 8 RT device, it is worth mentioning that Microsoft Outlook is included with Windows 8.1. This is a desktop application that was made available through the 8.1 update to RT devices that cannot otherwise install desktop applications. As a desktop application it is only mentioned here in passing because it is a very powerful email client that should not be overlooked if you have an RT device.

FIGURE 6.1

When you are connected to your Outlook.com email, you see many tools for managing your email.

Yahoo! Mail is a very nice free app that will appeal to anyone with a Yahoo email account (see Figure 6.2). You can add multiple Yahoo accounts, and new emails can be addressed using either your Yahoo contacts or contacts listed in the People app. The interface is clean and streamlined.

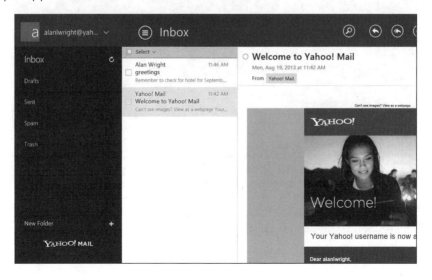

FIGURE 6.2

Yahoo! Mail is a nicely designed app targeted to anyone with a Yahoo email account.

You need a reliable calendar to keep track of personal and professional activities. You may have shared calendars that you work with for office or collaborative needs. Chapter 15, "Managing Your Calendar," delves into the Microsoft Calendar that you likely already use on your device. It is not always possible to sync your various calendars, which can be frustrating if you rely on Google- or Apple-based calendars.

A few apps promise to sync your calendars into one place, but have mixed results. The best one I have tried to date is WinPIM Calendar (see Figure 6.3). This app currently costs $4.99 and has a free trial. It allows you to sync iCloud, Google, and Yahoo calendars, and it can send notifications. I have noticed odd discrepancies, and I hope the developer continues to improve the app, which certainly fills a need. Use the 7-day trial to put it through its paces to see if it will work for you.

 TIP   One common workaround for accessing a shared Google calendar is to pin a website link to your Start screen for that calendar. Another method that offers good results is to subscribe to other calendars from your Microsoft account calendar. You will need to experiment with these alternative solutions to determine which best fill your needs.

FIGURE 6.3

WinPIM Calendar offers to keep your calendars all in one place.

Social apps are another big part of our life. The People app tries to help keep all your social connections organized for you. With updates made for Windows 8.1, it has become a very solid app, even allowing you to post comments right from the People app. Check out Chapter 13, "Managing Your Contacts," for more information on working with the People app. If you are looking for alternatives, several good apps provide live tiles, notifications, and sharing options. Several more official social apps are in development, such as Facebook and Foursquare, and may already be available in the Microsoft Store by the time you read this. Some apps you might want to check out are the following:

- StumbleUpon is an interesting app that allows you to discover seemingly random information and web pages based on your likes and dislikes. (Free)

- The official Twitter app allows you to keep up with tweets as you do other stuff (see Figure 6.4). The interface is sometimes disparaged for its simple design, but it works well. (Free)

- OpenTable is an app that you can use to find restaurants, check out menus, view pictures of dishes, and make reservations. It can be especially handy when traveling.

- For messaging apps, Skype is an obvious choice on a Windows device, especially if you use video conferencing. I also like IM+ for keeping up with multiple accounts, such as AOL, Google, and Skype, all in one place.

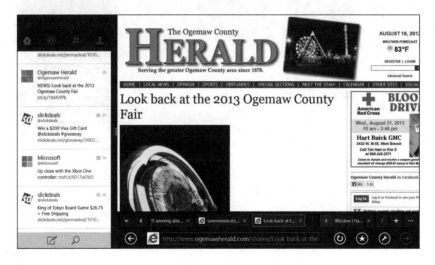

FIGURE 6.4

The Twitter app snaps to a sliver of the screen as shown here on the left, leaving the rest of the screen to other apps.

Maps

If you already have a separate GPS device or a smartphone for travel, you might not use a map on your Windows 8 device. Even with a tablet you may not use it for turn-by-turn navigation, so you might wonder if an app for maps is something you will use very often. Although smaller devices and screens are great for sticking to a windshield with their little suction-cup holders and their little power cables, using a map app on a larger screen is a pleasure when you want to get your bearings or explore.

The Microsoft Maps app shown in Figure 6.5 does a very nice job, relying on Bing map services to render your maps and show route information and traffic information. You can search for locations, businesses, and addresses from the Search charm or the Apps bar. Searches bring up locations you can select with additional links for phone numbers and nearby locations, like parking or hotels.

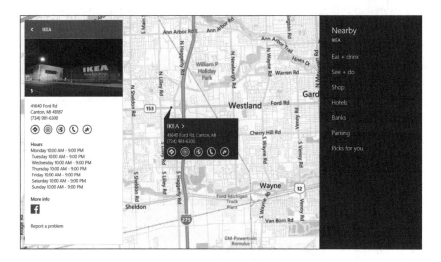

FIGURE 6.5

Microsoft Maps provides many additional details for locations found on a map.

If you are looking for an alternative to the official Maps app, take gMaps for a spin. Although this is not made by Google, it gives you access to Google's map system rather than Microsoft's, and it's been available as a Windows Phone app for many years. Many features are concealed behind its clean interface (see Figure 6.6), including a Street View so you can see what a location looks like from the street. It is free in the Microsoft Store.

Both apps allow you to print map and route information. One thing I wish they offered is the option to download state or regional maps for those times when you are away from an Internet connection with your device.

FIGURE 6.6

The gMaps app has an easy-to-use interface for both touch and mouse users.

News

The Microsoft News app is a solid news app leveraging Bing to bring the top news stories under standard categories. It is an app I still use to keep up with current news. CNN has a very nice app as well that allows you to navigate top news stories and watch video clips of news stories.

Although I think it is important to stay on top of general news, I find that I prefer to spend my time looking at news that catches my interest. Many apps are designed to do just that through the use of RSS feeds. A couple that I really like are Nextgen Reader and News Bento.

Nextgen Reader, shown in Figure 6.7, is currently $2.99 in the Microsoft Store, and it allows you to search and select the news sources that interest you. It is very easy to set up and then read your news feeds in the Nextgen Reader app. The interface has two layouts, one favoring touch and the other for a mouse.

FIGURE 6.7

Nextgen Reader has a mouse-friendly interface and makes it easy to keep up with personalized news feeds.

News Bento, shown in Figure 6.8, also allows you to personalize the news feeds that appear in a very polished interface. It features news feeds with live tiles that makes it seem an extension of the Windows 8 Start screen. Best news? News Bento is free in the Microsoft Store.

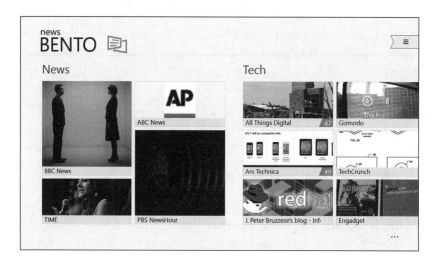

FIGURE 6.8

News Bento is a very polished news reader that is well worth installing.

Sports

Windows 8 offers a Sports app that is fine for casual sports news. I think that ESPN has done a remarkable job in creating an app that is visually attractive and very well designed. The app is free, and you can create an account in a couple of minutes with your favorite teams and sports. The result is that your choices are front and center when you open the app, as shown in Figure 6.9. When you open the app bar, you find a very well-thought-out navigation tool. Finally, you can pin tiles to the Start screen for your favorite team.

FIGURE 6.9

The ESPN app will be sure to satisfy diehard sports fans.

For baseball fans you might want to try the MLB.TV app. Subscribers can stream live out of market games in HD. The app offers up team stats, schedules, and archived games. You can choose your favorite teams to keep their information front and center.

Food and Drink

With the update to Windows 8.1, a new Microsoft app has been introduced named Food and Drink. It has some interesting things going for it, including a built-in search tool as well as a nice Browse Recipes tool that connects to allrecipes.com. If you are a fan of one of the featured chefs, such as Wolfgang Puck, you have access to some of their featured recipes, extras like chef tips, videos, restaurant pictures, and links to other media from that chef.

The drink portion of this app provides a nice wine guide and lots of cocktail recipes. One of the coolest features is the Hands-free mode, shown in Figure 6.10, available when working with a recipe in the kitchen. Using your video camera (if available on your device) you can make swiping gestures in the camera's view to advance or back up through the steps in a recipe without actually touching your computer with food-flecked fingers.

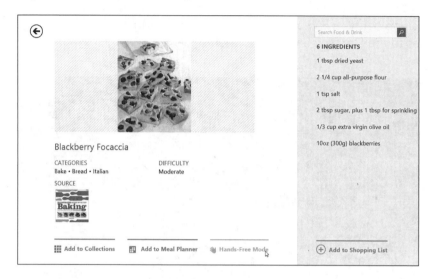

FIGURE 6.10

Food and Drink is an impressive app; try out the Hands-free mode to enable navigating a recipe using your camera.

The Allrecipes app itself is a favorite that has rescued our family from a few boring meals. It is a free app that has a nice interface. I like that you can search for recipe ideas based on available ingredients. It is worth mentioning that most of the features that make the Allrecipes app a favorite have been incorporated into the Microsoft Food and Drink app. I still recommend trying this app out based on its interface.

Weather

The Weather app that is included with Windows 8.1 is a pretty polished app in its own right. It uses Bing to provide weather for any of the places you may have selected. Besides your Home location, you can add cities to your favorite places to keep tabs on weather where friends or relatives live. Open the app bar as shown in Figure 6.11 to jump between your favorites or even pin live tiles for other cities to your Start screen. A wealth of additional information is available—from forecasts to current maps with radar or cloud cover.

FIGURE 6.11

The Weather app provides all the basic features you expect, including the ability to pin favorite cities.

I have also used the Weather Channel app and AccuWeather. I tend to favor AccuWeather which provides a nice moving background, and I like the calendar that allows me to see past and future weather for about a month all in one screen. Both well-designed apps are free and worth a look.

Photographs

A Windows 8 device is incomplete without a way to view photos and do basic editing. Chapter 16, "Enjoying Your Digital Photos in Windows," looks at the Photos app, freshly updated in Windows 8.1, and explains how to use it to view and edit your digital photos.

If the built-in Photos app doesn't provide enough features for you, there are a lot of photo apps in the Store. Many offer the same basic editing functions, and the difference comes down to the way the tools are put together to make it easy for you to use them. A couple nicely designed photo apps you should check out are Fhotoroom and Fotor.

Fotor uses the Windows file picker to navigate to select pictures stored in network locations, SkyDrive, Dropbox, and storage on your device. When you have selected a photo you want to edit, you can choose from a nice array of tools, including basic enhancements, lighting effects, borders, and tilt-shift effects (see Figure 6.12). The controls work well for both touch and mouse, and it is a free app.

FIGURE 6.12

Fotor has a nice interface and an impressive selection of tools.

Fhotoroom is more than an editing tool; it also allows you to share with other Fhotoroom users and browse pictures that others have shared. Select a photo to edit and you will see a large selection of very nice tools for editing. Fhotoroom is free, but some tools are available only to users who have purchased the Pro version (see Figure 6.13).

FIGURE 6.13

Fhotoroom includes many tools for editing, adding styles, and adding frames.

Reader

I have never been a fan of reading on a desktop computer or even a laptop. A backlit screen that you can easily hold or prop-up in a comfortable position is altogether a different story. I have read many a book on my smart phone and more recently on tablets. I have used many ebook readers over the years, and there are some obvious favorites like Kindle (see Figure 6.14) and Nook. Both are well designed and do well what they set out to do. With the capability to purchase, sync, share, and read books from within the app, both of these are good choices.

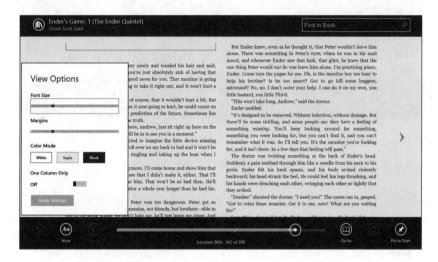

FIGURE 6.14

Kindle has an excellent interface for reading, allowing you to control font, size, layout, and even pin a book to the Start screen.

OverDrive Media Console is an app that you need to try if you enjoy books. This app allows you to "borrow" digital books and MP3 audiobooks from your local library and access them on your Windows 8 device for a period of time. The app and book lending process are all free as long as you have a library card. The best part is you no longer need to worry if someone ripped a page out of the library book you just checked out.

I have accumulated ebooks in different formats over the years; sometimes, books that I could read on a previous device (does anyone remember Palm?) I want to read on my Windows 8 device. Also, many websites offer epub formatted publications that require an epub reader. Nook now offers the capability to side-load PDF and ePub files, which makes it one of my favorites.

Freda is a free ebook reader that also allows you to find books from a multitude of sources (see Figure 6.15). You can open ePub, HTML, and TXT formatted files and adjust how text appears on your screen.

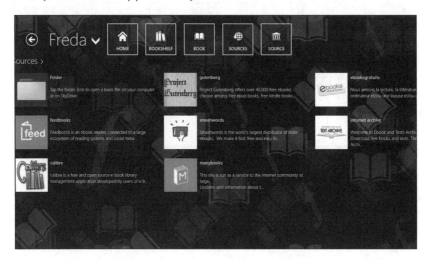

FIGURE 6.15

Freda enables you to read DRM-free ePub books you may have.

Comixology, shown in Figure 16.16, is another killer app that is aimed at reading comics. It is well designed and the Guided View technology adds a lot to the comfort of reading comic books on a digital screen. You can make purchases in the app and download your purchases when you want to read them.

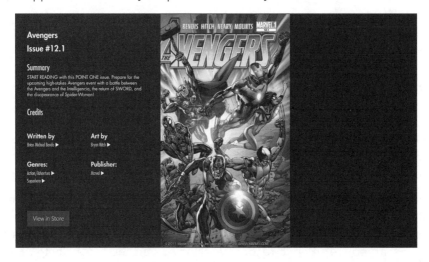

FIGURE 6.16

If you like comics, you need to check out Comixology.

Music, Games, Video

Windows 8 includes apps for listening to music and watching videos, which you learn about in more detail in Chapter 22, "Enjoying Music," and Chapter 21, "Having Fun with Movies and Video." Chapter 23, "Having Fun and Playing Games," looks at how you can take full advantage of your Xbox game system with a Windows 8 device. In this section we focus on additional apps that you can check out to enhance the way you find music and videos, as well as some noteworthy games.

Music

In the past you may have purchased MP3 songs or ripped music from CDs to amass a collection of music files. There are many ways to play these files that you have stored somewhere on a hard drive. With an Internet connection, you have some incredible alternatives offering streaming music and radio.

Slacker Radio, shown in Figure 6.17, is a free streaming music app that has a deep music library and allows you to choose from stations that are playing music according to genres or listen to news and comedy stations. To unlock additional features, such as song lyrics, on-demand songs and albums, or unlimited skips, you need to purchase a monthly subscription. To log in, use the Settings charm and then select Slacker Settings.

FIGURE 6.17

Slacker Radio provides many genres to listen to and additional information about the songs and artists playing.

Songza is a pretty cool app (see Figure 6.18). Rather than select music by genre, you can indicate the type of music using the Concierge, selecting from choices like "Drinking gourmet coffee" and "Enchanting Brazilian" or "Working to a Beat" and "Locked into a Groove: Funk." What I enjoy about this way of selecting music is that I am constantly finding new music, and it certainly is a nice way to set a mood. This free app is worth downloading.

FIGURE 6.18

Use the Concierge feature in Songza to find just the right kind of music for any activity.

Listening to radio stations is a nice way to keep up with news, sports, and happenings for an area. The free TuneIn app allows you to select from more than 70,000 radio stations. I have been surprised at how easy it is to listen to radio from rather remote locations, and it is fun to listen to radio stations from places I have lived in the past.

Shazam earns a place in this list not because of playing music, but because it enhances the way you might listen to music. Currently you can use your microphone to allow this free app to identify a song that is playing on the radio or TV. The app identifies music with amazing reliability and offers information about the music and artist, offers to search on YouTube for video and concert clips, and in some cases, it may even dig up lyrics. In the future, you can expect links to Xbox music to purchase the song right from Shazam. If you've never tried Shazam, go and install the app now. Do it.

Games

I enjoy unwinding with a good game on my laptop or tablet from time to time. Some games are fun for a while and then get stale, whereas others seem to be addictive, absorbing way too much time. I usually look for games that are not too involved to pass a few minutes here and there. It is harder for me to find the time required to play an involved game. Even so, a couple have snuck onto my list of a few current favorites.

Microsoft Solitaire Collection is in my list of favorite apps I can play for a few minutes and easily abandon it until later. Windows and solitaire have a long history, so it is nice to see that this latest iteration has kept up with the eye-candy factor that we expect from an app made for Windows 8.1. I enjoy the Daily Challenges and the option to select from several types of solitaire and deck styles.

Sudoku Free is another favorite app that I enjoy spending time on when I have just a few minutes to kill (see Figure 6.19). It feels great to conquer a puzzle rated as "Evil."

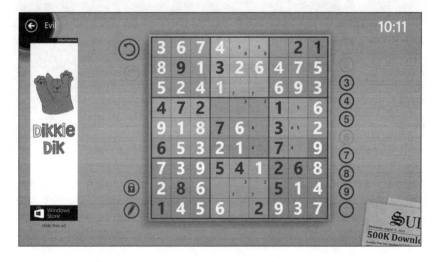

FIGURE 6.19

Sudoku Free provides a great way to pass a few minutes.

Angry Birds is almost a staple for anyone with a touchscreen device, although it also works great with a mouse. I am in the been-there-done-that camp when it comes to Angry Birds. Even so, I could not resist installing the latest Angry Birds *Star Wars* version, and I have to admit that it is as fun as always and with the added geek factor of customized *Star Wars* characters thrown in, it is a current favorite.

Adera is an early Windows 8 app that offers an interesting story that uses a variety of puzzles to advance the story line (see Figure 6.20). The story advances by means of chapters that you need to purchase to play. I generally do not like games that charge you to play additional chapters; however, Adera is very well made with some amazing graphics and very intuitive puzzles that are just fun to play with. (They offer a collection of all five chapters for the "season" for $5.99, which is not too bad considering the quality of the content). Because it's free, I recommend that you try the first chapter.

FIGURE 6.20

Adera is a beautiful puzzle game with a chapter-based story line.

If you like shooters, Halo Spartan Assault, shown in Figure 6.21, is unlikely to disappoint. The game is currently priced at $6.99 with no trial offered. This app has amazing video and music with very smooth game play, an impressive feat with such an action-packed game.

FIGURE 6.21

Halo Spartan Assault brings the huge action game to your Windows 8 device.

Video

The Windows Store provides some of the expected apps from established sources of online streaming video content. These are all well-designed and make it easy to find additional content.

- The Netflix app is a subscription-based service that allows you to watch movies and TV on your devices. The app is free, and you get a free month to try out the service. However, you need to maintain a monthly subscription to continue to see content.

- HuluPlus is another app that allows you to watch popular TV programs with some movies to choose from. As with Netflix, the app is free, and you can try the service for free for an introductory period. To continue accessing your favorite shows, you need to maintain an active subscription.

- Hyper for YouTube, shown in Figure 6.22, is a free app that allows you to search and find YouTube videos. It does this well and even allows you to download.

- Vevo is an app that enables you to look for music videos. You can search by genre and artist, and there is a lot to choose from. This app is free.

FIGURE 6.22

Hyper for YouTube is a great app to use to browse and watch videos from YouTube.

Additional Notable Apps

Some apps do not fit easily into the categories in this chapter but deserve a mention because they have a wow factor or are very well made and have become favorites.

- Audible is an awesome app that allows you to purchase and listen to audio books. The capability to navigate between chapters and the sound quality makes this a hands-down choice for listening to audio books. You can download and listen later. The app is free, the audio books are not.

- iBirds is an impressive guide to North American birds with the capability to search its database for birds based on characteristics, listen to recorded bird calls, browse pictures and illustrations, and learn all you need to become an expert birder. I was impressed with how much information is contained in this app. There is a free version with limited content; however, you need the full version if you plan to use it.

- FlightAware is a free app that allows you to track flights that are shown on a map near your location or from airports or airlines. Track flights by flight number or tail number. Check that flights are on time or delayed, and get weather alerts. The next time you see a plane flying overhead, you will be able to tell your friends all about the plane and where it is going; that is pretty cool.

- Bing Translator is a free app that has a very simple interface that allows you to translate from and to the languages you select. You can type in words and phrases or allow it to try to translate printed words using your device's camera. The concept is cool. I have not seen this to be as effective yet. You can listen to the translation, which will help you to nail the pronunciation.

- Star Chart, shown in Figure 6.23, always makes friends say "Wow" when they first see it. Impressive on a desktop or laptop, it becomes amazing on a tablet, allowing you to pan around with your device and identify the stars and planets in the sky. There is a lot of information in this free app.

FIGURE 6.23

Star Chart is an amazing app that makes it fun to learn about the stars and planets.

THE ABSOLUTE MINIMUM

Keep the following points in mind after you read this chapter:

- Apps are always being developed and tweaked to bring desired features to you as a user. Let developers know what you like and don't like about an app. Many developers appreciate this and make it easy to provide feedback.

- Most of the apps that are included with Windows 8.1 are pretty good. If you like the way another app is designed, go ahead and use it. Try other apps and ask other people what they like in that category.

- Although some apps are simple and straightforward, take the time to explore the features in an app. Sometimes they can appear to be hidden, like editing tools in the Windows Photo app or the commenting tools hidden in the People app that allow you to post to Facebook and other social sites.

- Let us know which apps are your favorites!

SETTING UP SEARCH, SHARE, AND NOTIFICATIONS

Search is important to all of us, whether we are looking for a picture, song, or some document we know we saved somewhere. With Windows 8, the Search charm leverages Bing, and your search now extends far beyond your device, making it easy to look for things both near and far, right from the Start screen. Share is another important feature in Windows 8 because you like to let others know about things you have found or done. Although using notifications may be less familiar, Windows 8 makes it easy for you to control this very useful feature.

Using Windows Search

You have no doubt used some brand of search in the past. You may have used a web browser to search for a restaurant or prices for a new flat screen TV. Perhaps you have searched on your computer for a resumé you used a couple years ago or a manual you downloaded, and now you don't know where you saved it. Perhaps you have fallen into the habit of saying "Google it" when someone asks a question you don't know the answer to. With Windows 8.1, these common tasks and much more are all rolled into the Search charm which has been greatly improved since it was first introduced in Windows 8.

The easiest way to search for something in Windows 8 is to start typing when the Start screen is open. Type a word or phrase to bring up the Search charm automatically, as shown in Figure 7.1. With a touch screen, swipe in from the right and select the Search charm to enable you to type your text. Results instantly appear based on text you have entered. Select one of the offered searches to see the search results. Search will not only offer Internet search results, but also local results from files and apps that you have on your device and in your homegroup, as well as system settings.

 TIP If you are in a different application, or even in the Desktop environment, you can still open the Search charm using the Windows+S or swiping in from the right.

FIGURE 7.1

Search by entering text from the Start screen.

Performing Search

One of the types of searches that you will really like is for well-known places, people, and artists. Microsoft created Hero pages based on how popular or highly ranked the object of your search is. A city like Chicago has a hero page with map, temperature, attractions, and links to relevant apps, such as the Travel app. A music group, such as the Black Keys, brings up different information about their songs, video clips, and a wealth of additional websites and articles.

To search for information on a well-known person, follow these steps:

1. From the Start screen open the Search charm and type in the text **tom hanks**. (Remember, you can also just start typing.)

2. Select **tom hanks** from the searches offered or press **Enter**.

3. Figure 7.2 shows the search results, which in this case opens to a hero page for the actor. Scroll to the right to play clips, see images, read articles, and access links to Xbox Video as well as related searches.

FIGURE 7.2

Some searches bring up hero screens for well-known people and places.

Besides basic Internet searches, the Search charm reveals local results first. For example, if you type in **video** as your search term, you might see results that look like Figure 7.3. Notice the Video app is listed; then there are related system settings, some video clips on the device itself, and, finally, Internet results.

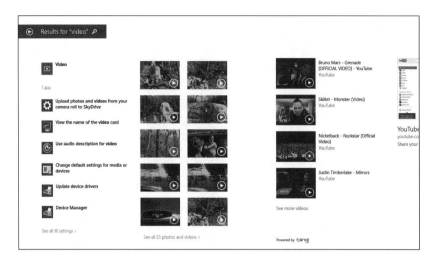

FIGURE 7.3

Search can find local resources and apps as well as results from the Internet.

You may have guessed you can use Search to quickly launch an app that may not be pinned to your Start screen or Desktop taskbar; just type in its name and launch it from the Search charm. Searching for system settings is also a very practical way to use search, and it can save you a lot of navigating through menus. For the next section, try searching for the term **Search** to bring up the indicated system configuration tools.

Setting Search Options

There are a couple of ways to refine how you search in Windows 8. By default, Search looks everywhere. To refine your search you can use the drop-down arrow to the right of Everywhere and narrow the target to search for settings, files, or web-based content, as shown in Figure 7.4. This change is a temporary one; the next time you use the Search charm it opens with the default parameter.

 TIP When you are working in an app, you can often search using the Search charm. Select the app from the Everything drop-down arrow to specify the app as your search target. An example is the Amazon app, which has its own search tool. Using the Search app produces the same results as if you typed your query into the Amazon search field. Other apps, like AllRecipes, do not have a visible search tool, and you need to use the Search charm.

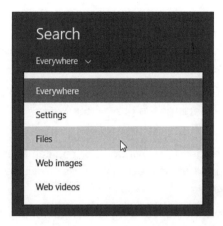

FIGURE 7.4

Change your search parameters by selecting from the drop-down menu in the Search charm.

To make permanent changes to your search parameters and settings, follow these steps:

1. Open the Settings charm and select **Change PC Settings**.

2. Select **Search and Apps** from the menu to the left. You see the screen shown in Figure 7.5.

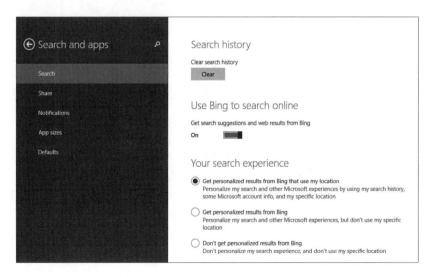

FIGURE 7.5

Navigate to Search and apps to modify your Search settings.

3. You can clear your search history by selecting the **Clear** button. You may see a pop-up alerting you that this will clear not just the local history but also history Bing has for you that is used to personalize your searches. Select **Clear** to delete this data.

4. Use Bing to Search Online is enabled by default. If you choose to disable this option, all other settings are grayed out.

5. Your search experience may be set to use your location if that was chosen the first time you logged in to Windows 8. You can change that here by selecting one of the option buttons. Using your location is helpful if you are looking for something nearby.

6. Figure 7.6 shows the next setting labeled SafeSearch. Choose from the option buttons to filter search results based on what is considered adult content. This can be a very nice feature when you have children using your device or if you want to avoid surprises when searching the Internet. By default it is set to Moderate.

7. Metered connections refers to connections that measure your data usage and penalize you for using too much data. This setting allows you to limit Bing search suggestions to unmetered connections. To learn more about metered connections see Chapter 11, "Connecting to the Internet."

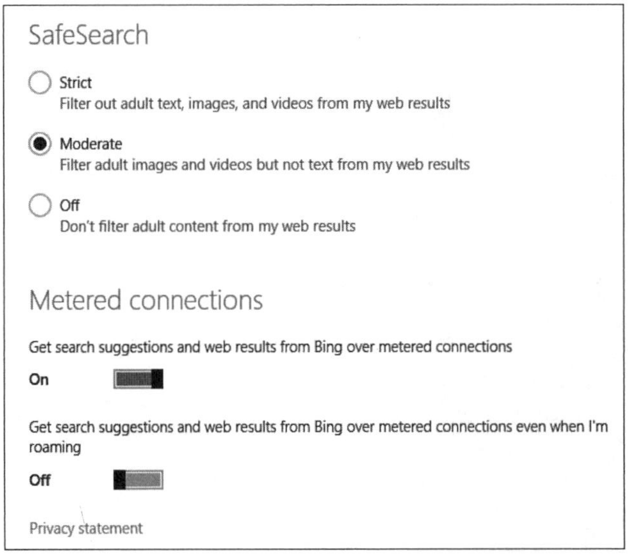

FIGURE 7.6

Use SafeSearch and Metered Connections settings to control search results and avoid unnecessary data consumption.

Some people feel uncomfortable with their search information being saved and used to provide targeted advertising. Privacy is certainly something we should value. Some of these settings allow you to protect your privacy at the cost of getting generic search results. Others like getting results that reflect an awareness of brands and product preferences. The setting you select here influences the results Bing provides for Internet searches.

Using Windows Share

You have likely found some news story or video clip on the Internet that you just had to share with a friend. It is not uncommon to see tools built right in to web pages to make this easier to do. Otherwise, you may have had to copy text or a link to the web page, open an email application, and then paste what you copied. The Share charm makes this much easier, and it contains a few bonus features that will certainly change how you share in Windows 8.

Because it is a charm, you can open Share from any app you have open, and often you see different share options based on the app. Figure 7.7 shows a traditional way to use Share by sending an email with a link to a website that is currently open. No need to copy and paste; by using the Share charm, a link and thumbnail of the website are automatically placed in the email.

FIGURE 7.7

Share a website by email using the Share charm.

You can also share things in new ways. Figure 7.8 shows an open app named Songza. After you open the Share charm, notice the small drop-down arrow to the right of Songza in the Share pane. You can change what you are sharing from a link to a screenshot to a link to the Songza app in the Microsoft Store.

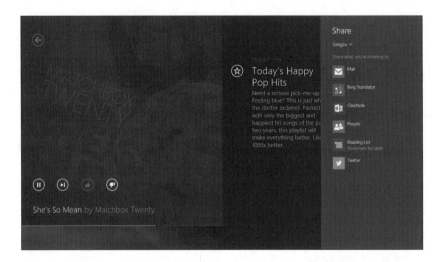

FIGURE 7.8

You can also share pictures and music from apps using the Share charm.

An app that makes an appearance with Windows 8.1 is the Reading List app. This is a convenient way to keep track of news, blogs, and other information you want to read later. To use the Share charm to add a website to your reading list, follow these steps:

1. From a website that you want to visit later, open the Share charm.

2. Select **Reading List** from the list of apps, as shown in Figure 7.9. The screen is shared with the Reading List app, which opens beside your web browser.

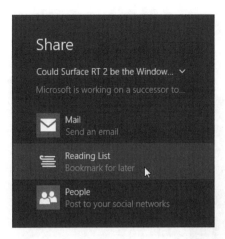

FIGURE 7.9

Share web pages with yourself by sharing a bookmark to the Reading List app.

3. Select **Add** to add the site to your reading list.

4. At a later time, open your Reading List app and you can jump to this article to read it.

 NOTE If you have more than one app open on a screen and you select the Share charm, the charm considers the last app you were using as the active app.

Setting Share Applications

Although Windows 8 does a good job of guessing which apps you may use for sharing, it is likely that you will want to edit the list of apps that are used with the Share charm. To make changes to this list, follow these steps:

1. Open the **Settings** charm and select **Change PC Settings**.

2. Select **Search and Apps** from the menu at the left.

3. Select **Share** from the menu at the left. You see the screen shown in Figure 7.10.

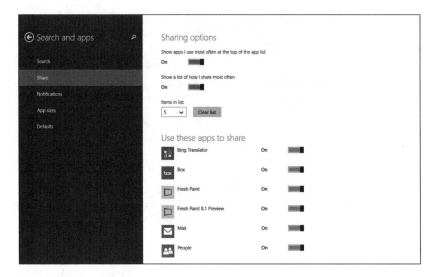

FIGURE 7.10

Change which apps you share with through the Settings charm.

4. Under Use These Apps to Share, scroll down the list and turn apps off that you do not expect to use when sharing content.

Setting Share Options

You can further fine-tune the way you share using the Share options. By default, Windows 8 keeps track of which apps you use most often and with whom you share. These choices will appear in the future when you open the Share charm, as shown in Figure 7.11. This can be convenient if you often share with the same friends or like to update the same social app.

FIGURE 7.11

The choices you select most often for sharing appear in a convenient list.

You can turn these features off and manage the list of previous choices by following these steps:

1. Open the Settings charm and select **Change PC Settings**.

2. Select **Search and Apps** from the menu on the left.

3. Select **Share** from the menu on the left. You see the screen shown in Figure 7.10.

4. Under Sharing options are two slider switches. If you would rather not filter your app list based on how often you select an app, turn the option to Off for Show Apps I Use Most Often at the top of the app list.

5. If you would rather not have Share track with whom you share, turn the switch to Off for Show a List of How I Share Most Often.

Additionally you can select Clear List to remove any history of your sharing choices that Windows 8 might have recorded. There is also an option to maintain a list of five popular share options based on your usage. You can use the Items in List drop-down list to choose a different number.

Fine-Tuning Notifications You Receive

Notifications can be a nuisance, or they can enhance your experience with apps you have installed. These can be updates that appear in the upper-right corner regarding new emails, game updates, messaging, and much more. You can disable notifications globally, or you can be selective about which apps can push notifications to you. You can even establish quiet times that respect your sleep or work schedule.

To make changes to this setting, follow these steps:

1. Open the Settings charm and select **Change PC Settings**.

2. Select **Search and Apps** from the menu on the left.

3. Select **Notifications** from the menu on the left. You see the screen shown in Figure 7.12

4. Under Notifications, make changes to the way notifications behave in general. For example, you can turn notification sounds to Off from here.

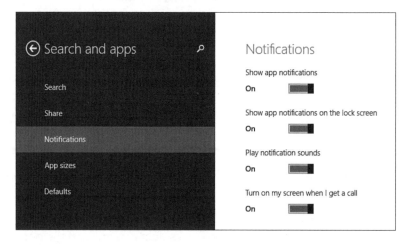

FIGURE 7.12

You can change settings globally for notifications.

5. Under Quiet Hours, make sure this is enabled and select a start and end time that suits your needs. This suppresses notifications during your designated quiet time. Turn Receive Calls During Quiet Hours to Off to prevent interruptions from Skype or other types of calls to your device (see Figure 7.13).

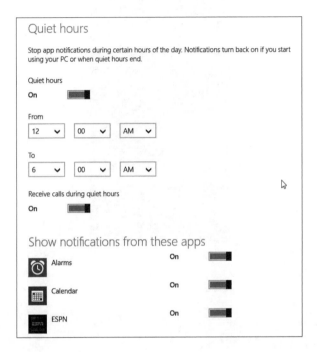

FIGURE 7.13

Configure Quiet Hours to suppress notifications.

6. Under Show Notifications from These Apps, you can scroll down and turn apps off individually to prevent notifications from select apps.

Yet another way that you can work with notifications is a temporary suppression of all notifications, which you can select from the Settings charm. Figure 7.14 shows how you can select Notifications and choose from 1, 3, or 8 hours to hide notifications. This option is useful if you need to suppress them when working or doing a presentation.

FIGURE 7.14

Notifications can be suppressed temporarily when needed.

THE ABSOLUTE MINIMUM

Keep the following points in mind after you read this chapter:

- The Search charm is capable of much more than Internet searches. Spend some time experimenting with search results and notice the difference between local file, app, settings, and web-based results.

- You can configure settings to control how search works and whether your searches are saved by Bing.

- Use the Share charm to let others know about things you have found or to update social media apps.

- Rather than save a web page to your Favorites so that you can go back to read an article, share the web page to the Reading List app.

- Make notifications work for you by controlling their behavior. If they irritate you, you need to establish new quiet hours or change that app's ability to send notifications.

LEARNING ABOUT THE WINDOWS DESKTOP

If you have any experience with previous versions of Windows, you probably had a typical reaction after signing in for the first time: "Where is my stuff? Where is that program I used for this or that?" If you are missing something that you *just know* should be part of Windows, it's probably hiding on the Windows Desktop. The Desktop is the kind-of (but not really) secret place where Windows 8 keeps many of the tools and programs that were an important part of previous versions of Windows (and really still are). This chapter helps you understand when to access the Desktop, as well as how to do so, and you'll learn how to set up the Desktop so it's easy to use.

Introducing the Desktop

One of the goals Microsoft pursued in designing Windows 8 was to rebuild the user experience to support the use of touch-screen devices, such as tablets, slates, and touch-screen monitors. Microsoft had other goals, of course, but this redesign for mobile devices was near the top of the list. This new design of Windows is known as Modern (sometimes referred to as Metro or Windows 8 style).

Changing the user experience that had been a part of Windows since 1995 certainly presented a challenge to Microsoft. Thousands of programs have been built over the years that depended on Windows looking and behaving consistently. So how does Microsoft build and roll out a brand new way to interact with Windows without breaking everything that has been built to run in Windows for decades? The core of the answer is the Windows Desktop, or the *Desktop*, for short.

The Desktop, the home for all those great Windows programs, has been dropped in the middle of Windows 8, and it remains as important to using Windows as ever. Programs that run on the Desktop are cosmetically identical to past Windows versions. In addition, some of the more complicated Windows tools and features, especially those for system administrators, still run on the Desktop. This effectively gives Windows 8 two appearances: one as the Windows 8 style and another that's almost exactly like Windows 7. Figure 8.1 shows the Windows 8 Desktop, which perhaps is familiar to you if you have used previous versions of Windows. Either way, you're certain to find it different from the Windows 8 user interface (UI).

Desktop icons

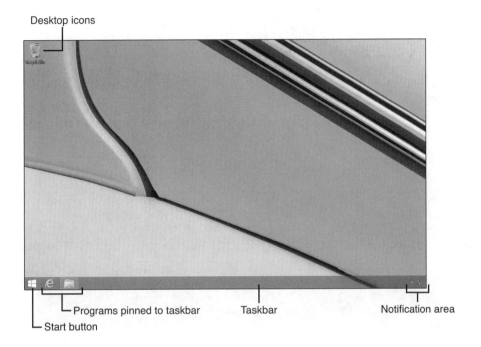

Programs pinned to taskbar   Taskbar   Notification area
Start button

FIGURE 8.1

The Windows 8 Desktop is similar to the Desktop of previous versions of Windows.

Now that you have a basic understanding of these two environments, let's dive into the Desktop, learn how to get work done, and have some fun along the way.

Getting to the Desktop

There are three methods to access the Desktop, and they each originate from the Start screen:

- Select the **Desktop** tile (see Figure 8.2).

- Change a Windows 8 setting that can only be configured on the Desktop, such as hardware and sound, appearance and personalization, clock, language, region, system and security, and more. You can enter these terms into the Search charm for settings to access the Desktop.

Desktop

FIGURE 8.2

The Windows 8 user experience is different from that of previous versions of Windows.

- Start a program from the Start screen that runs on the Desktop. When you start one of these programs, the Desktop appears. Examples of Windows programs that you might use today that run on the Desktop are Microsoft Office (Word, Excel, PowerPoint, and so on), Skype, and Steam.

Because the Desktop is still a fundamental component of Windows, you can do much more there besides run a game or save your to-do list. First, take a look at some of the tools that appear on the Desktop, as shown in Figure 8.3.

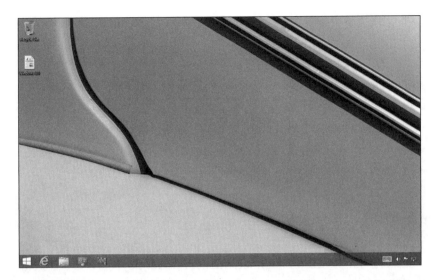

FIGURE 8.3

The Desktop is an environment almost identical to Windows 7.

Returning to the Start Screen

While you are working on the Desktop, you may need to return to the Start screen to start another application. You are not forced to exit the program you are working with or to close files you have open before switching back to the Start screen. The Desktop remains unchanged until you return to it.

To return to the Start screen from the Desktop, do one of the following:

- With your hand or stylus, swipe in from the right and tap the Start charm.

- Press the **Windows** key.

- Select the **Start** button on the taskbar.

Working with the Taskbar

An important element of the Desktop is the taskbar. Although the taskbar takes up little space, it performs a number of important tasks. Here is the full list of the taskbar's capabilities:

- Lists the programs running on the Desktop, even if a program is obscured from view

- Enables you to switch to a running program by selecting the program's portrait on the taskbar

- Shows you the status and messages from the many small programs that run silently, performing a service or waiting for you to do something

- Displays the current time and date

- Displays various toolbars that you can choose to show or hide

- Enables you to quickly jump to a website or any folder by displaying an address bar where you enter the URL or folder name

- Enables you to set up a list of the last 10 documents or sites visited

- Enables you to arrange the open windows on the Desktop

Receiving Alerts and Notifications

The Notifications section of the taskbar, often called the system tray, organizes the small icons that keep you informed about important events and the status of some Windows tasks and systems. When one of these notification icons has something it wants you to know, it pops up a small window with information about it. Although programs you install can be added to the icons listed in this area, Windows sets up some notifications of its own, such as the status of your network connection (see Figure 8.4).

FIGURE 8.4

Windows alerts you if the built-in firewall is not engaged.

The event reported on depends on the software doing the reporting. For example, as shown here, the Action Center icon notifies you if a problem develops with the security software guarding your system, or if Microsoft has released an update to Windows. To look at a notification, click or touch the icon showing the notification.

You don't need to live with a cramped notification area. You can control which notification icons are always visible and which ones appear only when they have something to report. You can also set a notification icon to be hidden all the time.

To customize how the notification items work, follow these steps:

1. In the notification area, select the **Show Hidden Icons** button (shaped like a triangle). Then, from the pop-up window that appears, select **Customize**.

2. In the Notification Area Icons window that appears, click either **Show Icon and Notifications**, **Hide Icon and Notifications**, or **Only Show Notifications** from the drop-down list for each icon, as shown in Figure 8.5.

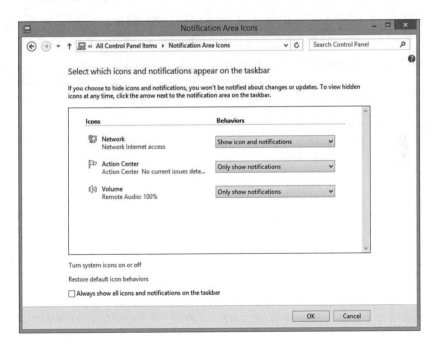

FIGURE 8.5

You can customize the behavior of each potential notification alert.

3. Select **OK**.

Adding Toolbars to the Taskbar

In Windows, toolbars are usually a set of like functions assigned to clickable icons arranged together on a bar on the screen. They're mostly common to various Desktop applications, but you can also enable a set of toolbars on the taskbar. In this case, however, the toolbar label for this feature is curious because referring to any of these five components as *toolbars* is a stretch. These features are certainly useful, though, as described here. Five toolbars are available to show on the taskbar.

To show a toolbar, right-click or tap and hold on the taskbar, and point to **Toolbars**. Then select the toolbar you want to display.

Here is a short description of each toolbar:

- **Address**—This toolbar is a box into which you can enter any address, including a website name or a folder name. After entering the address and pressing **Enter**, a window opens set to the address you entered.

- **Links**—This toolbar is a list of links to favorite websites or folders on your computer. This list mirrors the Favorites list you keep in Internet Explorer.

- **Touch Keyboard**—Launching this toolbar places a small keyboard icon in the notification area. When you need a keyboard, such as when you use the Desktop on a tablet device, touch the Keyboard icon to display the virtual keyboard.

- **Desktop**—This toolbar is a list of the files that appear on your Desktop. This list is composed of files you have placed on the Desktop and files that were placed there by Windows, such as shortcuts.

- **New Toolbar**—Windows enables you to create your own toolbars to use alongside the toolbars Windows provides. The toolbars you create are like the Desktop toolbars. You choose a folder to associate with a toolbar so that when you select the toolbar, it displays the contents of the folder.

In addition to toolbars, you can pin folders and programs to the taskbar itself to keep them handy. By default you will see Internet Explorer and File Explorer pinned to the taskbar the first time you open the Desktop. There are a few ways to add more:

- You can select Pin to taskbar from the App bar on the Start screen when you have a desktop application selected. (This is not offered for Windows 8 apps.)

- From the desktop you can simply drag-and-drop an application, file, or folder onto the taskbar to pin it. Figure 8.3 shows the Control Panel and the application Windows Defender both pinned to the taskbar.

Keeping the Desktop Organized

You can use the area of the Desktop above the taskbar much as you use your desktop in your office or at home. You can keep the files associated with a project you are working on anywhere on the Desktop. You can organize the files into folders, and the folders can also be kept on the Desktop; however, I don't necessarily recommend this because it clutters the Desktop. Back at home or in the office, when you acquire new files or folders or other items, you might drop them onto your desk to file away or store later. In Windows, when you download content from the Internet or when you create a new document, you can just as easily drop the content onto the Desktop.

With all the files potentially moving on and off of the Desktop, even organized users might find their Desktop in a state of disorder and mess, as shown in Figure 8.6.

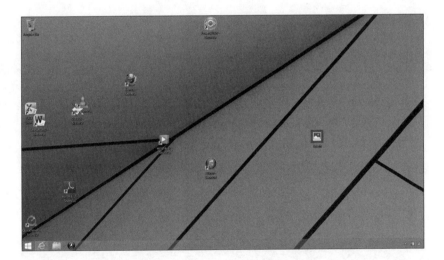

FIGURE 8.6

It's not hard to discover that your Desktop has changed into a cluttered mess.

Fortunately, it's not hard to keep the Desktop clutter under control.

Automatically Line Up Icons on the Desktop

The Desktop has an invisible grid that keeps every item positioned in uniform columns and rows. When you save, move, download, or copy a file to the Desktop, or if a program you use saves a file to the Desktop, Windows immediately snaps the file into an empty cell in the grid. Windows normally fills the grid from left to right and from the top down, but you can turn this option off. Turning this option off allows you to place an item anywhere on the Desktop, although still lined up in one of the invisible rows and columns.

To configure Windows to automatically line up icons on the Desktop, follow these steps:

1. Right-click or tap and hold an unused spot on the Desktop and point to **View**.

2. If Align Icons to Grid is checked, the invisible grid is in use. If Align Icons to Grid is not checked, select it to turn the grid on.

3. Right-click or tap and hold an unused spot on the Desktop and point to **View** again.

4. To snap icons to the first empty cell in the grid, select **Auto Arrange Icons**. To keep icons anywhere you like on the Desktop (but still lined up), select **Auto Arrange Icons** to clear the check mark and leave Align Icons enabled. Figure 8.7 shows the Desktop from Figure 8.6 with all its icons aligned using Auto Arrange.

FIGURE 8.7

Notice how with the Auto Arrange Icons settings turned ON, the icons are arranged more evenly.

Arrange the Desktop by Icon Type

If the Auto Arrange icon option is turned on (see the previous section), you can also keep the icons sorted (by rows). Windows can order the icons in the invisible grid according to each icon's name, type, size, or the date the icon was last changed.

To sort the Desktop icons by type, right-click or tap and hold an unused spot on the Desktop and point to **Sort By**. Select **Name**, **Size**, **Item Type**, or **Date Modified**.

Change the Size of Desktop Icons

You can change the size of the icons that appear on the Desktop. Your choices are Large, Medium, and Small. The default icon size is medium. Note that the size of some special objects that appear on the Desktop, such as gadgets, are not affected by this setting. Figure 8.8 shows the Desktop with this option set at Large.

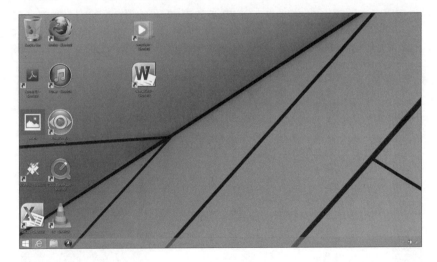

FIGURE 8.8

You can configure the Desktop to show icons in different sizes. Large is the setting used here.

To change the size of the Desktop icons, right-click or tap and hold an unused spot on the Desktop and point to **View**; then select **Large Icons**, **Small Icons,** or **Medium Icons**.

Hide All Desktop Icons

If you want a clean Desktop environment, you can hide all Desktop icons. Right-click or tap and hold an unused spot on the Desktop and point to **View**. Select **Show Desktop Icons** to clear the check mark. To make the Desktop icons appear again, repeat these steps.

Displaying Special Icons on the Desktop

You have read in this chapter how the Desktop can be leveraged to keep files and folders you're working with in a convenient, handy location. By default you will only see the Recycle Bin icon displayed on your Desktop the first time you open it. The Desktop also can keep a few more important icons readily available that give you access to some key tools and features. Although the PC Settings screen on the Start screen gives you access to a large number of settings, the Desktop, through the icons, also gives you access to a number of settings. These icons can be hidden or displayed:

- **This PC**—This PC icon opens the File Explorer window that displays the big, important, expensive parts of your system, including hard drives, network connections, and more. (In the past, This PC has been named My Computer and Computer.) Figure 8.9 shows the This PC view opened in File Explorer.

FIGURE 8.9

You can see all the elements of your computer in one window.

- **Network**—This icon enables you to see all the resources on the network, such as other computers, printers, and more. Having this icon available on the Desktop enables you to quickly locate a resource you need, such as a family member's computer, and connect to it. If you do not use your computer on a network and you don't have any devices connected wirelessly, you can hide this icon. Refer to Chapter 18, "Sharing Files and Printers," to learn more about navigating through your network at home.

- **Recycle Bin**—The Recycle Bin stores all deleted files, folders, and icons. These items stay in the Recycle Bin until the Recycle Bin is emptied, a wonderful fact for many Windows users. Having the Recycle Bin on the Desktop is a convenience. The Recycle Bin operates the same way whether or not it is displayed.

- **User's Files**—The User's Files icon, which appears as a folder with your name below it, gives you access to the set of files and folders that Windows reserves for your personal use. Selecting this item starts File Explorer, which opens to the main folder that contains all your personal files and folders. You can find a chapter's worth of information about files and folders, including the user files, in Chapter 19, "Managing Files and Folders."

- **Control Panel**—A set of small programs exist that help you set up some part of Windows. This collection of programs is called Control Panel. The Control Panel icon brings you to the front page of Control Panel, where you can select the tool you need.

To display (or hide) Desktop program icons, follow these steps:

1. Right-click or tap and hold an empty spot on the Desktop, and then click **Personalize**.

2. Select **Change Desktop Icons** at the top-left corner of the Personalization window. The Desktop Icon Settings dialog box appears, as shown in Figure 8.10.

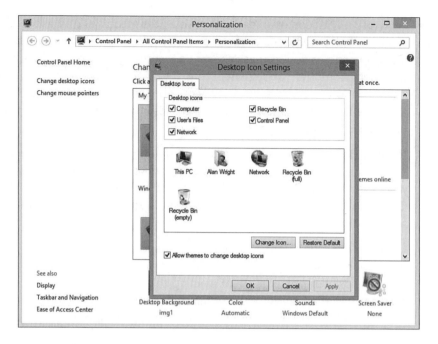

FIGURE 8.10

Display or hide icons for some important Desktop tools.

3. Under Desktop icons, select the check box for each item you want to appear on the Desktop. Remove the check mark for any item you do not want to appear on the Desktop.

4. Select **OK**.

5. Select **Close** to close the Personalization window.

THE ABSOLUTE MINIMUM

Keep the following points in mind as you work on the Desktop:

- The Desktop is a special application you can use to run programs that were built for previous versions of Windows.

- Some of the important tools and components of Windows 8 are run from the Desktop. If you are missing a program that you believe is important to Windows, check the Desktop.

- You can customize the Desktop to keep files organized on the desktop, show and hide icons, and pin programs to the taskbar.

- The notification area of the Desktop shows important information, so you should check the Desktop regularly for these updates.

- You can start the Desktop app by selecting its tile from the Start screen or by starting a program or opening a setting that runs on the Desktop.

WORKING WITH WINDOWS DESKTOP PROGRAMS

This chapter continues the learning about Windows Desktop first touched on in Chapter 1, "Your First Hour with Windows 8," and then expanded on in Chapter 8, "Learning About the Windows Desktop." As you learned in Chapter 1, the Desktop is an environment in which traditional Desktop applications and some administrative programs run. Chapter 8 covers the Desktop from a broad perspective, not focusing on one specific task and instead helping you find your way around. This chapter has a more specific goal—teaching you how to start and then manage programs that run on the Windows Desktop. You'll learn how to organize program windows and install and remove programs. If you are comfortable working with programs in Windows 7 or earlier versions of Windows, you might have less to learn in this chapter than others; however, it pays to review the troubleshooting section at the end of the chapter.

Introducing Windows Desktop Programs

For many Windows 8 users, the Desktop remains the core of their experience. Sure, there's been a host of new software applications built specifically for Windows 8, known as Windows 8 apps, but applications specific to the Desktop—ranging from Microsoft Office to financial software, such as Quicken to iTunes, to a host of games—all operate in the Desktop environment just as they always have. Windows 8.1 even lets you boot directly to the Desktop, forgoing the Start screen altogether.

 TIP A lot of people don't like the Start screen or the native Windows 8 apps designed to operate within it. If you're one of them, don't think of the Start screen as Windows 8. Think of it as the old Windows 7 Start menu, exploded and given broader functionality. Depending on what programs you want to use, you can easily spend 99% of your computing time on the Desktop, going to the Start screen only to launch an application or access a system setting.

Booting directly to the Desktop is a new feature in Windows 8.1 and one that many users like if they do not often use Windows Store apps. To enable this preference, follow these steps:

1. From the Desktop, right-click the taskbar and select **Properties**. The Taskbar and Navigation Properties dialog box will open.

2. Select the **Navigation** tab.

3. Under Start screen, enable the first option as shown in Figure 9.1, When I Sign In or Close All Apps on a Screen, Go to the Desktop Instead of Start.

4. Select **OK**. The next time you reboot you will see the Desktop rather than the Start screen.

Whether you boot to the Start screen or the Desktop, it is important to know how Desktop applications work in Windows 8.1. To start a Desktop program from the Start screen, select its tile. If it's a Desktop program, it automatically opens the Desktop. Figure 9.2 shows Microsoft Excel open on the Windows 8 Desktop. Notice that an icon for the program, known as a *portrait*, appears on the taskbar.

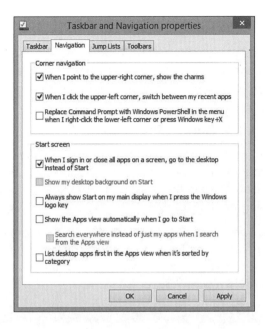

FIGURE 9.1

With Windows 8.1 you can choose to boot right to the Desktop if that is your preference.

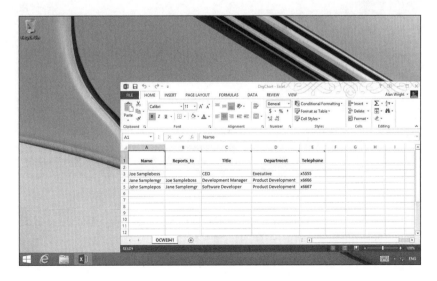

FIGURE 9.2

Microsoft Excel running on the Desktop.

Running Programs on the Desktop

This section helps you understand how programs operate in the Windows 8 Desktop environment. You learn how to manage a single program and how to organize the Desktop with multiple program windows open.

Running Multiple Desktop Programs

As you become more proficient and comfortable with Windows, it is likely you will run multiple programs on the Desktop at the same time. For example, you might need to read instructions in the Adobe Acrobat Reader for a software program you are also using on the Desktop.

You can start a Desktop application from the Start screen, results from the Search charm, or a shortcut on the Desktop or taskbar itself. When the program starts, it appears on the Desktop in a window on top of the other programs that are running, as shown in Figure 9.3.

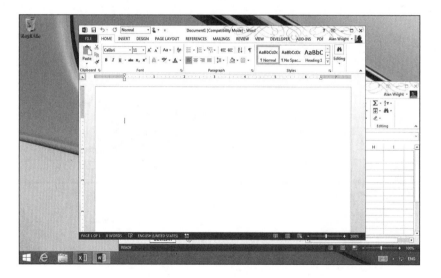

FIGURE 9.3

Notice how Microsoft Word opened on the Desktop, obscuring Microsoft Excel that was running there already.

In addition, an icon representing the program appears on the taskbar. After starting a number of programs, the taskbar starts to fill up with an array of colorful icons, as shown in Figure 9.3.

To switch from one program to another, select the program's icon on the taskbar. When you do so, the program you selected appears on top of any other windows on the Desktop.

 NOTE A quick way to switch to a program or document without moving the cursor is to use a keyboard shortcut. Press and hold the Alt key and then press the **Tab** key. A screen appears showing portraits of each program or app window open in Windows 8. While holding down the Alt key, tap the **Tab** key repeatedly to move the highlight to the next window on the screen. Release both keys when you have selected the window you want to switch to.

Certain applications enable you to work on more than one file or workspace or project at one time. In Microsoft Word, you can have your resumé open in one window, a cover letter you are writing in another open window, and a table detailing your work experience in a document in a third window. In Windows-speak, regardless of the type of program being referred to, these files you create are known as *documents*.

When you have more than one document open in a program, the taskbar behaves a bit differently than when you have just one document open. When you move the mouse pointer over the program icon, a row of portraits—one for each document—appears above the main portrait (see Figure 9.4). To switch to a different document, select the portrait you want to display.

FIGURE 9.4

The taskbar displays a portrait for each of the documents you have open in a program.

Making It Easy to Start Your Favorite Desktop Programs

You can save trips to the Start screen to start your favorite or most-used Desktop programs by pinning an icon of each of your favorite programs on the taskbar.

To pin a program to the Desktop taskbar, follow these steps:

1. Return to the Start screen.

2. Right-click or tap and hold on the tile representing the program you want to pin to the taskbar.

3. Select **Pin to Taskbar** from the App bar when it appears at the bottom of the screen.

To start one of your pinned programs, select its portrait on the taskbar.

 TIP   You can pin as many programs to the taskbar at one time as you like from the Start screen. If there are a number of programs you use frequently on the Desktop, right-click each of them before you select **Pin to Taskbar**. If you mistakenly select a tile, right-click it again to remove the check mark, which signifies the tile is selected.

Saving Files to the Desktop

Windows creates and reserves a private set of folders where each user can save his or her own files, such as documents, music, and pictures. One of these private folders is named "desktop." Each user has a desktop folder, and the contents of the folder are always displayed on the Desktop when that user is logged in, as shown in Figure 9.5.

Saving to the Desktop is convenient, especially when you are working with one or more specific files for a specific project. Storing the files on the Desktop while you are working on the project can save you time that you would normally spend sifting around your hard drive retrieving the file from its regular location.

To save a file to the Desktop, choose Desktop from the list of folders presented in the program where you created the file, as shown in Figure 9.6.

Files shown on Desktop   Desktop files listed in File Explorer

FIGURE 9.5

Items that appear on the Desktop are stored in a special Desktop folder that you can also see in File Explorer.

FIGURE 9.6

The Desktop is presented as a choice where you can save a file.

Exiting Desktop Programs

Windows does not require you to shut down a program when you finish working with it. But there are a few reasons why you should consider routinely closing Desktop programs when you finish. If you have a number of programs running concurrently, your computer's speed may be negatively impacted. If your computer seems to be running more slowly than normal, consider shutting down some programs.

To close a program running on the Desktop, follow these steps:

1. On the taskbar, locate the icon for the program you want to close.

2. Right-click the icon.

3. From the menu that appears, select **Close** Window (or **Close All Windows** if you have multiple windows open). The program disappears from the Desktop, and the program's portrait disappears from the taskbar. Note that a program that you have pinned to the taskbar remains pinned even after you have closed all its document windows.

Working with Windows

You don't necessarily need to be a Windows expert to work with multiple programs at once with several windows open on the Desktop. You may be working in an Office program, such as Microsoft Word or Excel; you might have Internet Explorer open to check in at some of your favorite social media sites; and you might have a File Explorer window open to organize a folder. So, innocently, you might have three windows fighting for screen real estate. It's easy, though, to arrange, move, and resize windows to leverage all the room on the Desktop. Figure 9.7 shows the basic controls at the top of a typical window with the important parts pointed out. When you select the icon from the title bar, you will reveal additional options from a system menu as shown.

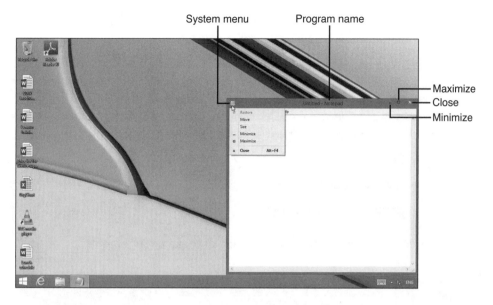

FIGURE 9.7

These controls are common to virtually all Desktop app windows.

The following list summarizes the various methods available to manage windows on the Desktop:

- You can easily **resize** and reshape a window. You can't change the window's shape from rectangular to circular, but you can make the window short and wide, narrow and tall, perfectly square, or anything in between. To resize a window using a mouse, point to any border of the window you want to resize. When the pointer becomes a double-headed arrow, click-and-drag the pointer to move the border.

- You can enlarge a window so it fills up your entire screen space (known as maximize), obscuring every other window you have open. To do so, click the **Maximize** button on the window's title bar.

- You can also remove a window from view without closing the program. Select the **Minimize** button to hide the window.

- You can minimize all open windows simultaneously, exposing the Desktop. To do so, click the taskbar between the time and date and the edge of the screen. You can also right-click the taskbar and select **Show the Desktop**.

- To return a window to its most previous state, select the **Restore** button. You can also restore the window by choosing **Restore** from the Control menu on the top-left corner of the window. The Restore command works only when the window is in a maximized state.

- You can move a window around your Desktop by dragging the window by its title bar.

- When you start multiple programs on the Desktop, or if you open several documents, it can become difficult to arrange and size the windows so that you can work efficiently. You can move and resize the windows manually, but Windows provides a few quick commands to arrange the windows on the Desktop. Right-click the taskbar to find these choices:

  - Cascade Windows

  - Show Windows Stacked

  - Show Windows Side by Side

Figures 9.8, 9.9, and 9.10 show you each of these arrangements.

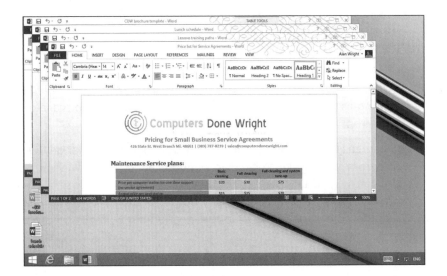

FIGURE 9.8

This Desktop has been arranged using Cascade Windows.

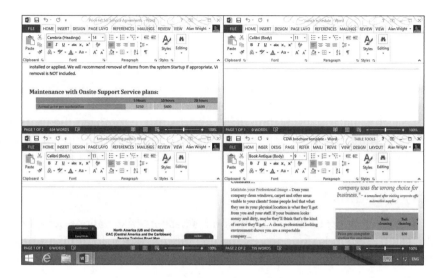

FIGURE 9.9

This Desktop has been arranged using Show Windows Stacked.

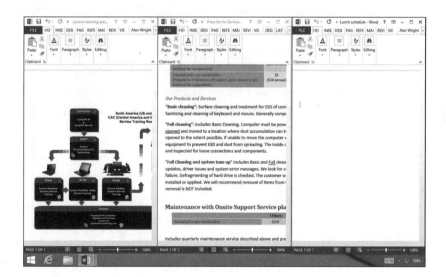

FIGURE 9.10

This Desktop has been arranged using Show Windows Side by Side.

Installing and Removing Programs

Windows Desktop programs are not installed from the Windows Store, like Windows 8 apps are. If you decide to purchase or install a Desktop app that you find in the Microsoft Store you will be redirected to the website for that software to purchase and download it. Desktop applications that you choose to install come with their own installation utility. Programs are removed the same way, although you kick off the uninstall process from a central location in Windows. You learn about the Windows Store in Chapter 5, "Using Windows Store Apps."

Installing Programs

The installation process for new programs has lots of variations. Keep in mind that the setup process is designed by the company that developed the software you are installing, meaning anything can happen:

- For software installed from a CD or DVD, the installation program usually starts as soon as the disc is inserted into the drive. If a program does not start, you should navigate to the disc using File Explorer. Look for a program named install.exe, autoplay.exe, or setup.exe. Double-click the file to start the installation program.

- Setup programs are not perfect. You may need to uninstall a program if the setup stops unexpectedly so you can try to run the setup program again.

- Setup programs sometimes require that the person installing the software have administrator rights. To run the setup program as an administrator, locate the setup program (possible names are setup.exe and install.exe), right-click the program, and select **Run as Administrator**.

Removing Windows Programs

You may need to remove an installed program for a number of reasons, including the following:

- You are running out of free disk space.

- There seems to be a problem with the software, and you need to reinstall it.

- You no longer use or plan to use the software.

- You plan to install new software that is incompatible with an installed program.

There is no harm in leaving a program installed if you have enough free disk space and if the program does not interfere with another program. If you need to remove a program, however, follow these steps:

1. Save any unsaved work.

2. Open the Add or Remove Programs dialog box. To do so, select the Search charm. Enter **Add or Remove Programs** in the Search box.

3. From the results below the Search box, select **Add or Remove Programs**. The Programs and Features dialog box shown in Figure 9.11 appears.

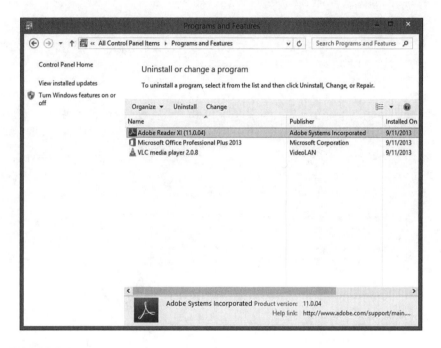

FIGURE 9.11

Programs are uninstalled from the Programs and Features dialog box.

4. Select the program and then select **Uninstall**. The program's own uninstall process starts. Follow the instructions and answer any prompts that appear.

You may be prompted to restart Windows to complete the uninstall process.

THE ABSOLUTE MINIMUM

Keep these points in mind after you've completed reading this chapter:

- The Desktop operates as a separate entity from the Windows 8 Modern UI (where the Start screen exists). Windows 8 apps designed for the Modern UI do not operate on the Desktop.

- You can run multiple Desktop programs at one time. Start subsequent programs on the Start screen or from the taskbar.

- To switch to a different program, click the icon representing the program on the taskbar. Alternatively, press and hold the **Alt** key and then press the **Tab** key. A screen appears showing portraits of each program or app window open in Windows 8. While holding down the **Alt** key, tap the **Tab** key repeatedly to move the highlight to the next window on the screen. Release both keys when you have selected the window you want to switch to.

- To arrange the open windows on the Desktop, right-click the taskbar to reveal a menu. Select **Cascade Windows** or one of the three Show Windows commands to arrange the open windows.

- Windows 8 Desktop programs are installed and removed from the Desktop (and not the Start screen).

10

PERFORMING EASY WINDOWS CONFIGURATION

Although hardware setup might not seem like a beginner topic, it is essential to getting the most out of Windows. With the information in this chapter you'll find plenty of success. Windows makes it easy to tweak some of the most important settings of the hardware connected to your computer. Although setting up some aspects of your hardware might require help from someone with more experience in Windows, or you might acquire another book from Que covering more advanced topics, the tasks covered in this chapter are doable. In this chapter, you learn about setting up your mouse, keyboard, display, sound, power, and accessibility options.

The Control Panel

You can access a lot of Windows configuration settings from the Settings charm. You will find, however, that some settings and configuration options are more detailed if accessed through the *Control Panel*. The Control Panel is the Desktop environment interface to all of the settings for Windows and its many devices such as mouse and keyboard, display, language, etc. You can make configuration changes by selecting icons in the Control Panel which are often referred to as *applets* because they're small programs that allow you to make specific changes to settings in Windows. This chapter refers to the Control Panel frequently as you explore the basic configuration choices available to you. The Control Panel on your device will have the same basic set of applets, and it will have some unique to your device depending on the hardware or software your device uses.

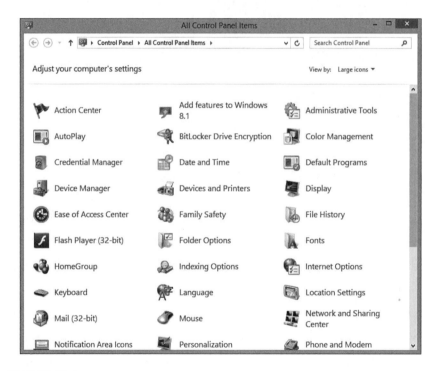

FIGURE 10.1

The Control Panel is the comprehensive center for changing how Windows and your devices operate.

To open the Control Panel follow these steps:

1. From the Start Screen select the Search charm. Enter the text **Control** and select **Control Panel** from the results. This opens the Control Panel on the Desktop.

2. The initial view in the Control Panel is to View by Category. In the upper right corner of the Control Panel, select the drop-down arrow to change View by: from Category to Large icons to get the view shown in Figure 10.1. This view makes it easier to locate specific tools rather than guess which category they might be found in.

 TIP A faster way to locate specific tools when you know their name is to simply use the Search charm. Use the search parameter of Settings rather than searching Everywhere. If you were to then search for **Date and Time**, which is an applet in the Control Panel, you will see results that point to the Settings charm (which uses a gear as the icon in the search results) or the Control Panel applet. Changes in either the Settings charm or the Control Panel applet accomplish the same thing. You will find yourself using the Settings charm more often. However, for missing features or more detailed choice, the Control Panel applet is a good tool to know about.

Setting Up Your Mouse or Touchpad

A number of settings are available for you to customize exactly how your mouse operates. Some of these settings control basic functions, such as determining which of the buttons on the mouse is the primary button, and some permit you to express your personality with your mouse.

Although basic settings can be configured from the PC Settings pane using the Settings charm, we will focus primarily on the more robust settings that are available through the Desktop's Control Panel.

Mouse Settings

Here is a list of the settings you can change for your mouse:

- **Primary button**—Mice are shipped typically with the left button configured as the primary button. You can change this configuration to make the right button the primary button.

- **Double-click speed**—Several Windows commands require you to double-click. You can slow the double-click speed to give you more time to make the second-click.

- **Click for drag**—If you have difficulty dragging items in Windows, the ClickLock option can help you. This option enables you to drag an item without holding the mouse button down while you drag the item. Instead, you click the item to be moved, hold the mouse button down over the item for a few seconds, and then release the button. To drop the object you're dragging, you click once where you want the item to be moved to.

- **Pointer speed**—You can configure your mouse pointer to keep pace with you, moving swiftly across the screen as you work. This setting is known as *pointer speed*. However, when you move the mouse, if you find that the pointer tends to fly out of control across the screen, forcing you to search for the pointer after you stopped moving the mouse, you may want to slow down the pointer.

- **Snap to default button**—Windows does a good job of asking you to confirm actions that have permanent consequences, such as deleting a file or saving a document with the same name as an existing file. Windows confirms your actions with a small window, usually with some text (Are You Sure?) and two buttons (OK and Cancel). Windows can move the pointer to the button it expects you to answer with, making it faster to either click it or select the other button.

- **Display pointer trails**—You can add some excitement to your screen by using pointer trails. This option resembles a snake trailing behind the mouse pointer as you move it across the screen and enhances its visibility. Figure 10.2 shows you an example of pointer trails in use.

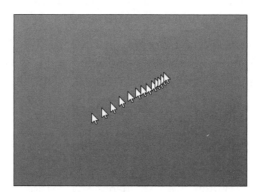

FIGURE 10.2

Mouse pointer trails help you locate the mouse pointer on the screen, plus they add some fun to the display.

- **Hide pointer while typing**—You might find you are distracted by the mouse pointer when you stop scrolling to type into your computer. Windows provides an option to hide the pointer while you type.

- **Reveal location of pointer**—Some users have difficulty locating the mouse pointer on the screen, especially when they use large monitors. By enabling the Show Location of Pointer option, you can flash an easy-to-spot signal locating the pointer by pressing the **Ctrl** key, as shown in Figure 10.3.

FIGURE 10.3

The Show Location of Pointer option helps you locate the pointer simply by pressing the Ctrl key.

- **Scroll wheel**—Most mice come with a scroll wheel or some form of touch-enabled strip that is positioned near the front of the mouse, enabling you to access it as easily as you can the mouse buttons. You turn the wheel (or drag your finger) when you need to scroll up or scroll down. The vertical scrolling setting controls the sensitivity of the wheel. The setting is measured in the number of lines scrolled for every notch you spin in the wheel. Some mice even provide a horizontal wheel, enabling you to move left to right and vice versa without moving the mouse.

To change any of the preceding settings, follow these steps:

1. Open Control Panel. Select the **Devices and Printers** category and select **Mouse**. This opens the Mouse Properties window, as shown in Figure 10.4.

FIGURE 10.4

Change many of the settings controlling how your mouse works in the Mouse Properties dialog box.

2. Choose the mouse control you want to change. There are three tabs that include all the options I just described: Buttons, Pointers, and Pointer Options.

3. When you're done making changes, select **OK** to close the dialog box and save the various changes you made to the mouse settings. Select **Cancel** to discard the changes. Select **Apply** to save the changes without closing the dialog box.

You might want to customize the mouse pointers you use in Windows. You can adjust the pointers to reflect your personality and taste, or you might need to switch to pointers that are larger than normal to make it easier to see them. See Chapter 4, "Making Windows Your Own," to learn how you can customize your mouse pointers.

Touchpad Settings

Your Windows device, especially if it's a laptop, may have a touchpad. Touchpad settings are often configured using software provided by the hardware manufacturer; therefore, you may see software on your device that has been included for this purpose. Windows also includes some general settings for touchpads. These may be grayed out or missing if you have touchpad controls available to the

Desktop that override these settings; in that case you should consult the instructions your device manufacturer provided. Often these settings can be located in
the Mouse applet of the Control Panel as a tab.

To adjust these settings follow these steps:

1. Select the Settings charm and then select **PC Settings**.

2. Select **PC and Devices**.

3. Select **Mouse and Touchpad** as shown in Figure 10.5.

4. From the Touchpad settings, you can adjust tap sensitivity, swiping gestures,
   reverse scrolling, and even enable or disable the touchpad itself.

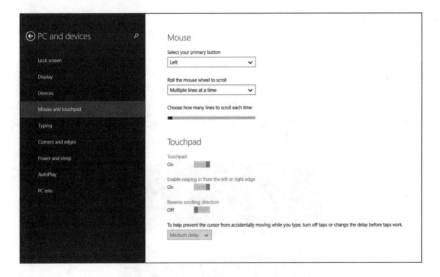

FIGURE 10.5

You can adjust basic settings for your mouse and touchpad from the Settings charm.

Setting Up Your Keyboard

Although the keyboard is an important part of your computer, there are only a few
settings you can change:

- Setting how rapidly characters repeat across the screen

- Setting when a character starts repeating across the screen

- Setting the cursor blink rate

- Using the keyboard in place of a mouse

Two settings control what occurs when you depress a key on the keyboard to repeat the key's character on the page. These settings might not be useful for your everyday work unless you design a form or a document that includes underlines to enter information or characters to create a border. The settings are

- **How long a key is depressed before the character begins repeating**—If this setting is too short, the slightest delay in moving your finger off of a key causes the character to begin repeating across the screen (depending on the program you use).
- **How rapidly the character repeats**—This rate can span from a steady pulse to a staccato spray of the character across the screen.

Changing Keyboard Settings

To access the screens where the repeating character rates are set, do the following:

1. Use the Search charm to search for **keyboard**, as shown in Figure 10.6. Narrow your search to Settings instead of Everywhere if you do not see the Control Panel applet. Select the **Keyboard** tile to display the Keyboard Properties dialog box, as shown in Figure 10.7.

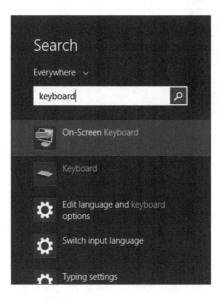

FIGURE 10.6

Use the Search charm to quickly locate settings for your devices.

FIGURE 10.7

Set the character repeating rate in the Keyboard Properties dialog box.

2. Drag the pointer on each of the two sliders to the desired speed. Try your set-
    tings in the box in the middle of the dialog box.

3. You may also adjust the rate the cursor blinks across all Windows 8.1 apps in
    the Keyboard Properties dialog box. Drag the pointer along the Cursor blink
    rate slider to the desired speed.

4. Select **OK** to save your settings and close the dialog box.

Personalize Language, Keyboard, and Date Formats

One of the most personal aspects of Windows 8.1 you can set up is your
language and other locale settings. You can customize the number, currency,
time, and date formats to match your nationality and cultural preferences.

The first phase is to set your language in Windows:

1. Open the Settings charm and select **Change PC Settings**.

2. Select **Time and Language** from the list on the left side of the screen, and
    then select **Region and Language**. The languages currently added to this
    device are indicated, as shown in Figure 10.8.

FIGURE 10.8

You can select language and other aspects of your locale from the Region and Language pane.

3. If the language you want to switch to is shown, skip to step 6. If not, select **Add a Language**. A dialog box like the one shown in Figure 10.9 should appear, displaying a list of languages.

FIGURE 10.9

You can select from a long list of base languages, as well as select a dialect.

4. Scroll down the list and locate the base language you want to select. For example, if you want to select Mexican Spanish, for now, locate Spanish and select it.

5. A list of the regional variants of the language you chose should be on the screen. Select the dialect you want, and it will be added.

6. You should be back to the Time and Language pane, shown in Figure 10.9. If there is more than one language in the list, the first language in the list is the one used. Select the language you wish to use to reveal additional buttons then select **Set as Primary**. You may also see Options for a language. Select **Options** to review possible spell checking and keyboard options.

If you need to adjust your locale's time and date formats, follow these steps:

1. Open the Settings charm, and select **Change PC Settings**.

2. Select **Time and Language** from the list on the left side of the screen; then you will see your current Date and Time settings, as shown in Figure 10.10.

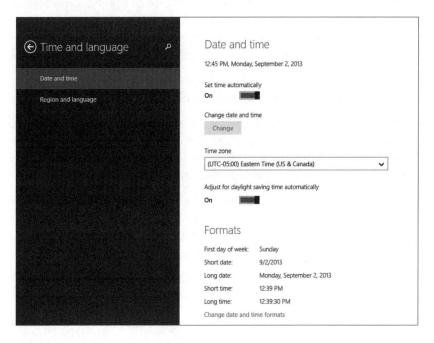

FIGURE 10.10

You can customize how dates appear based on your language of choice.

3. Under Formats, you see examples that show you how the different date fields, such as long date, short date, and so on, will appear throughout Windows (based on the language you selected). If you want to change any of the fields, select Change Date and Time Formats. A new view opens that allows you to select for any of the dates you want to customize using drop-down arrow buttons; just select the desired format from the list.

Setting Up Your Display

The computer component you work with the most is the display. The display interfaces with one of the most delicate parts of your body: your eyes. For this reason, you should set up the display the right way. Although Windows usually sets it correctly by default, Resolution is the key setting for a comfortable but efficient set up with your computer. In addition, Windows 8.1 has improved the way it works with multiple displays, which can make your work (and play) experience a more productive one. In this section, you learn how to set your resolution and how to set up a second monitor.

Adjusting the Resolution (Making the Screen Bigger or Smaller)

Resolution is one of the most important *and* one of the most misunderstood aspects of computer use. The resolution determines the level of detail of the image you see on a computer screen. Don't confuse detail with quality. Other hardware on your computer contributes to the quality of the images, such as the richness of colors.

Here is what you need to know about resolution:

- Displays on the screen are of pixels. Each pixel has the same size and shape (usually square or rectangular, but can be any shape). If you are of a certain age, you might remember a toy called Lite-Brite from Hasbro. The toy is a small version of the concept of resolution. Go ahead and Google it!

- Resolution is specified by a size. The size is the number of pixels used to create images on the screen. This size is expressed as row and column counts, such as 1024×768, which specifies that the grid pattern is 1,024 pixels across and 768 top to bottom.

- The greater the resolution, the more detailed images onscreen will be. Just think of connect the dots. Your drawing can be much more detailed if you use 500 number dots rather than 50. If you are unfamiliar with connect the dots, you can Google it, too!

- There is a trade-off when choosing a high resolution. Most monitors are not large enough to display higher resolutions at a normal size, so images appear smaller at high resolution to accommodate all the detail. You trade away some usability because some print and text might be too small to see for the sharpness of a high resolution.

- An LCD monitor has a native resolution—that is, a resolution at which it's designed to operate. Although LCD monitors can operate at different resolutions, using a nonnative setting incurs a considerable hit to image quality, so if you're planning to buy a new LCD monitor, you should note the resolution you prefer to work with and make sure the one you pick is designed to operate at that resolution. A typical HD LCD monitor operates at 1920×1080, which is a full HD display.

Follow these steps to adjust resolution:

1. Select the Settings charm and then select **Change PC Settings**.

2. Select **PC and Devices** and then select **Display** from the list to the left. The Customize Your Display pane shown in Figure 10.11 appears. If you have more than one screen attached to your computer, you see each of them represented and numbered. Be sure to select the monitor you want to work with in the Display field (or by clicking its representation on this screen). If you aren't sure which monitor is identified in the list, select Identify to tell Windows to flash a number on your screen identifying each monitor.

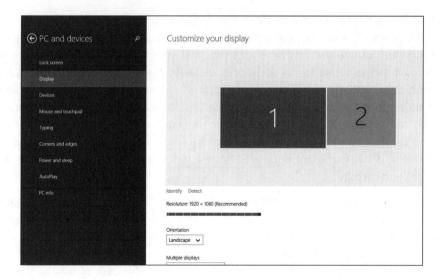

FIGURE 10.11

You can control your screen resolution through the Settings charm.

3. Select the resolution you want for each display by selecting it on the horizontal slider. You will generally see a recommended resolution, which will probably already be selected as the default.

4. Select **Apply** to see immediately the resolution you chose at work. The screen updates to the resolution you selected.

5. If you are happy with the new resolution, select **Keep Changes**. If you want to select another resolution or stick with the original resolution, select **Revert**.

TIP You can select a resolution your display doesn't support, resulting in a blank screen when you attempt to change it. If this happens, just sit tight for a few seconds. If you don't click Keep Changes on the confirmation dialog, Windows reverts back to the previous resolution.

6. To select a different resolution, repeat steps 3–5.

NOTE To snap at least two Windows Store apps to the screen at the same time or to snap an app to one side of the screen, the screen resolution must be set to 1024×768 or higher.

Setting Up Multiple Monitors

You can set up a second monitor if your computer has the capability. Look at the back of your computer near where your monitor is plugged in. If you see a second plug like the one the first monitor uses, you are in good shape. If you are not sure, it makes sense to ask someone, because there are a few different plugs for monitors. Virtually all laptops manufactured in the last few years have an external monitor port that can work at the same time as your laptop's built-in display. So you can take advantage of the extra screen real estate a second monitor provides even if your everyday machine is a laptop. Microsoft's Surface tablets, as well as those of other manufacturers, also have a video out port you can use for attaching a second display.

There are a number of advantages to having a second monitor. You can extend Windows to the additional screen. You can extend your screen horizontally, so you have more room across Windows. You can also extend your screen vertically to have more room top to bottom. You can open several programs at the same time and arrange them on your extended display. You can also have the same image generated on both displays (duplicate), something that can come in handy for presentation purposes.

When you add a second screen to your computer (having done so according to its supplied documentation), you can configure it for use with Windows by following these steps:

1. Select the Settings charm and then select **Change PC Settings**.

2. Select **PC and Devices** and then select **Display** from the list to the left. Under Customize Your Display, look for the Multiple Displays setting shown in Figure 10.12. Use the drop-down arrow to choose from duplicating or extending your display. You can also select to display only on one display screen.

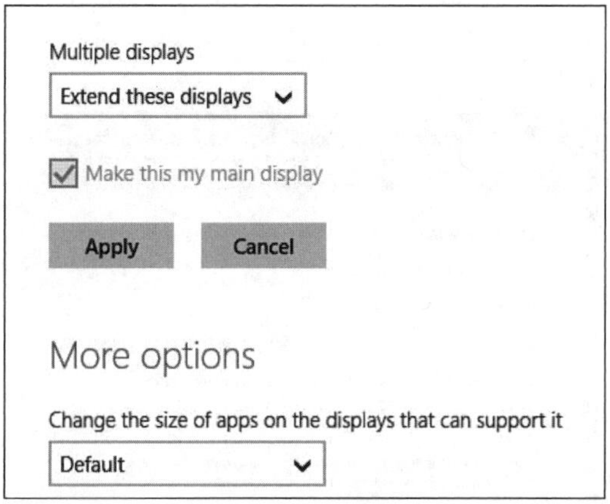

Multiple displays

Extend these displays ∨

☑ Make this my main display

Apply   **Cancel**

More options

Change the size of apps on the displays that can support it

Default   ∨

FIGURE 10.12

In Windows 8 you can change the behavior of multiple displays through the Settings charm.

3. If you need to change the position of your displays relative to one another, you can select and drag a screen (refer to Figure 10.11) to show its position to the right, left, above, or below. This will determine how your mouse cursor moves between extended displays and affects panoramic wallpaper choices.

4. Select **Apply** to make changes.

 NOTE Another way to quickly change how your Windows 8.1 device uses a second display is through the Device charm. Select **Project** from the Devices list, then choose **From PC Screen Only, Duplicate, Extend,** or **Second Screen Only**. This can be especially useful when working with a projector for a meeting.

Windows 8.1 has enhanced the way multiple displays are used by enabling many variations and configurations to meet diverse technology and usage. Consider some of these enhancements:

• Show different backgrounds on each display or extend the same background across several displays.

• Have taskbars set to display just the applications that are on each screen (see Figure 10.13).

- Use screen corners on any display to access the charms or Start button.

- Use Windows Store apps on any display.

- Dots per inch (DPI) scaling can optimize how apps are displayed on ultra-high-resolution screens. This can be set the same for all displays, or a unique setting can be used for each display. This addresses a huge problem for Surface Pro tablets running multiple displays prior to Windows 8.1.

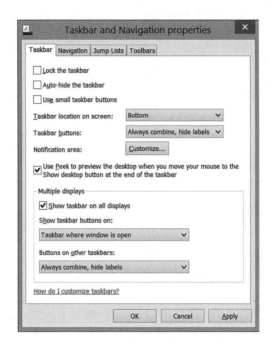

FIGURE 10.13

Control how the taskbar behaves across multiple displays.

Adjusting Brightness

Brightness is often taken for granted. Windows devices that rely on batteries benefit from settings that dim the display while on battery power, thus extending how much time the battery can power your device. Also, many devices can adjust screen brightness using a setting called adaptive brightness, which is intended to adjust display brightness based on ambient light.

Basic adjustments to display brightness can be made using the Settings charm. Select Brightness to reveal a slider that you can use to manually change the current display brightness. Although the next section deals with power plans in more detail, two specific settings may deserve your attention if you feel your device is not as bright as it should be; these are the display brightness and the adaptive power settings buried in your current power plan.

To make permanent changes to the brightness on your screen, you need to follow these steps:

1. Open the Search charm, and search for **power**, then select the **Power Options** tile.

2. The Power Options window opens in the Desktop environment. One of two default power plans will likely be enabled. Figure 10.14 shows the Balanced plan is enabled. **Select Change Plan Settings** (to the right of Balanced).

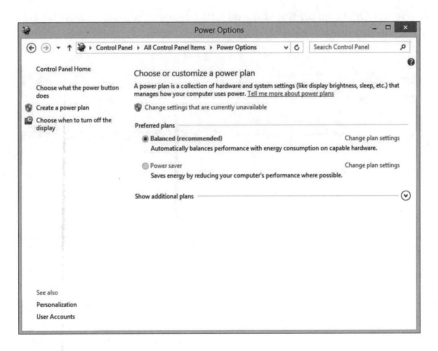

FIGURE 10.14

Brightness settings are part of your power plan.

3. The Edit Plan Settings window appears. Select Change Advanced Power Settings (at the bottom of the window).

4. The Power Options dialog box appears as shown in Figure 10.15.

5. Scroll down in the list of settings to find Display. Expand the menu by selecting the plus sign and scroll down to find Display Brightness. Select the plus sign to see the current settings for On Battery and Plugged In. Adjust the setting if needed by selecting the current number and use the up and down arrows to change the number. 100% when plugged in is normal; if you want the brightest display even while using battery power, change this to 100% also.

6. Expand the Enable Adaptive Brightness settings. This is generally On by default. You can disable this feature when on battery or when plugged in. Disable this feature here by selecting **On** and selecting **Off** from the drop-down list.

7. Select **OK** to apply the settings and close this window. Close all other windows if you are done changing your settings.

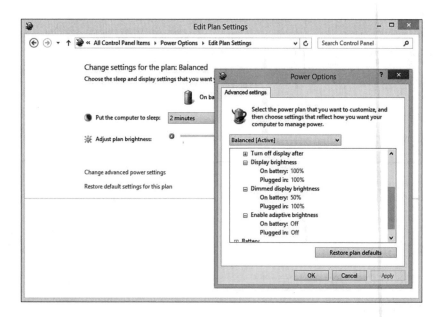

FIGURE 10.15

Tweak display settings from the Power Options dialog box.

CAUTION   Balanced power plan settings are meant to give you the best performance while on battery with the longest time possible. Changes to these settings may significantly cut your battery time. Also, the Adaptive Brightness is a great feature when it is working correctly. You may need to update your drivers if you are experiencing problems with this feature. Make changes here with caution. After making changes to these settings, you can always go back by selecting **Restore Default Settings for This Plan** in the Edit Plan Settings window shown in Figure 10.14.

Setting Up Power Use

Windows 8 and 8.1 come at a time when more people than ever are aware of the cost and effect of power consumption. That's why Windows comes loaded with options enabling you to minimize or control power consumption, but these options are helpful beyond wanting to be a good citizen of the environment. If you tend to keep your computer running continually, you may want to consider options to automatically reduce the brightness of your screen after a period of nonuse, as well as other options to reduce wear on your computer. If you travel with Windows installed on a laptop, you may be interested in putting the computer to sleep when you close the laptop lid, which makes it easy and quick to restart your computer.

Windows enables you to customize how power is managed on your computer in extreme detail. There are more than 20 settings you can tweak. The various methods for setting power options fall into three groups:

- Easy Method
- Really Easy Method
- Manual Method

You learn the Easy Method and the Really Easy Method here. Before getting into the details, there are a couple terms you should know:

- **Sleep mode**—When your computer goes to sleep, which happens in a second, rather than in an hour, Windows saves any unsaved work and reduces power to the monitor, hard drives, fan, and network connections. Windows takes notice of your system when it goes to sleep, and it retains those settings in a memory where the settings can be accessed and applied quickly. This mode protects your work while the computer sleeps but returns the computer to full power in the same state that you left it in just a few seconds.

- **Hibernate mode**—Hibernate mode is much like Sleep mode. Hibernate mode also captures the state of your computer so that it can restore it on request, but in Hibernate mode, your computer is powered down. This means restoring a computer from hibernate takes longer because it has to write all this information to your computer's hard drive.

The Easy Method to Set Up Power Use

The most useful power use settings are the following:

- Specify whether a password is required to unlock your computer after it has been awakened.

- Choose what happens when you press the Power button on your computer.

- Specify the length of time at which you're not at your computer before the display turns off.

- Specify the length of time at which you're not at your computer before the computer goes to sleep.

These options probably give you all the control you need over power use. Here is how to set these up:

1. Open the Power Options dialog box. To do so, use the Search charm to search for a setting named **power**, and then select **Power Options** from the list of results (refer to Figure 10.13).

2. Select the option you are interested in from the frame on the left. The options are self-explanatory.

The Really Easy Method to Set Up Power Use

The Really Easy method requires you to choose one of a group of *power plans*. A power plan is a prebuilt set of approximately 15 options, each of which manages some aspect of power or energy consumption, such as preventing a slideshow from running when the computer is low on battery life. Windows includes one or more power plans, and the company that built your computer might have loaded a plan onto the computer. You can create a plan from scratch, change one and give it a new name, or delete one.

Here are some sample power plans:

- **Balanced**—Conserves energy when the computer is not used but uses full power when you are actively working at the computer, such as using multiple applications.

- **High Performance**—Uses full power all the time and will drain power quickly for laptop computers running on a battery.
- **Power Saver**—Reduces power consumption as much as possible, which causes applications to run a bit more slowly, reduces the display's brightness setting, and more.

Follow these steps to select a power plan:

1. Open the Power Options dialog box. To do so, search for a setting named **power**, and then select **Power Options** from the list of results on the left side of the screen.

2. Select the plan you want to use from the list of plans. To review the settings for a plan, select the corresponding **Change Plan Settings**. Select **Cancel** when you have finished reviewing the plan's settings.

3. Close the **Power Options** dialog box. The power settings in the plan you selected should be active.

The Manual Method to Set Up Power Use

The manual method calls for you to specify a value for each of the 20 or so settings. It takes time to do so, but the payoff is a power plan configured to your exact requirements. To do so, select a plan, as previously described in step 2 under "The Really Easy Method to Set Up Power Use." Before you close the Power Options dialog box, as instructed in step 3, select **Change Plan Settings** and then **Change Advanced Power Settings**. Change settings as needed, select **OK**, then **Save Changes**. This updates the plan you selected. Review the steps in the "Adjusting Brightness" section of this chapter for an example of this manual method.

Customizing Corner Navigation

Windows 8 introduced us to corner navigation. The idea is to preserve your screen space by hiding powerful navigation tools in hotspots that are triggered by touching or hovering a mouse cursor over a corner. This can be frustrating at times if you are using an application or playing a game that is suddenly interrupted by accidently bringing up the charms or jumping to the last-used app.

To disable corner navigation in the upper corners, follow these steps:

1. Open the Settings charm, and select **Change PC Settings**.

2. Select **PC and Devices** and then select **Corners and Edges** to reveal the screen shown in Figure 10.16.

3. Disable either or both of the hotspots in the upper-left or upper-right corners of your display by sliding the appropriate selector to Off under Corner Navigation.

FIGURE 10.16

You can easily turn off corner navigation for the upper corners.

Setting Up Sound

Setting up how sound works in Windows might seem like a task that should not be required. Shouldn't your computer play your music and ding and chime at all the appropriate occasions without you having to do anything? The answer, of course, is yes. In this section, though, you learn a few things that are not quite obvious, such as how to get the best sound from the speakers you just purchased and how to specify what sounds you hear when certain events occur.

Setting Up Your Speakers

If you play videos or music on your computer, having a set of speakers, or at least headphones, is a requirement. Most computers today can take advantage of a set of surround speakers configured for movies and games—all the way down to two little desktop speakers.

These days, plugging in speakers is easy. Each of the plugs from your speakers are colored, and the jacks in the back of your computer also are colored. Just match the colors and you're good to go. Follow the instructions provided with your hardware to be sure your speakers are set up correctly. After everything is plugged in correctly, follow these steps to set up the sound quality and configuration:

1. Open the Sound dialog box. To do so, open the Charms bar and select **Search**. Select **Settings** and enter **sounds** into the Search box. Select **Change System Sounds** when it appears in the results. The Sound dialog box appears in the Desktop environment.

2. Select the **Playback** tab.

3. Select Speakers and then select **Configure**. The Speaker Setup dialog box appears, as shown in Figure 10.17.

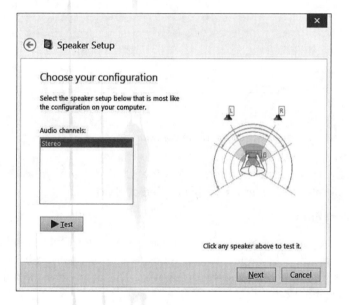

FIGURE 10.17

You must indicate to Windows 8.1 how to configure your speaker setup.

4. Select your speaker setup from the list. The diagram shows you the configuration. Select **Test** to hear a test sound rotate through each of the speakers, or click a speaker to hear just one. Select **Next.**

5. On this screen, you can add or remove speakers from the configuration you just picked (see Figure 10.18). Select **Next.**

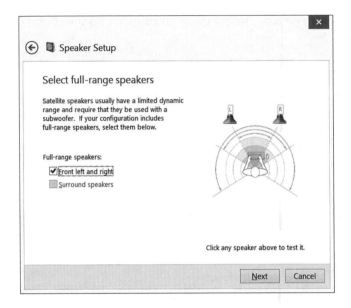

FIGURE 10.18

You can add full-range speakers to the configuration.

6. You may have the option to select the relative size of your speakers, whether small satellites or larger speakers. Select **Next**.

7. Select **Finish**.

8. Try out your configuration with music, videos, and DVDs. Feel free to run through the steps again to fine-tune the setup. Finally, don't be afraid to select a configuration that sounds great even if it doesn't match your real setup. You're the boss!

Selecting Sounds for Windows Events

Windows is set up to play certain sounds when various events occur, such as when it needs your attention, when an email message arrives, when your battery reaches a low level, and many more. You can change the settings that are set up with Windows, such as using the start up sound when email arrives. Or you can use your own sounds, such as gag sounds or short excerpts of music, with Windows events.

Individual sounds are stored in small files that end in .WAV or .MP3. If you have sound files stored elsewhere on your computer, such as if you downloaded sounds from the Internet (certain websites enable you to download famous quotes and sounds from popular movies), you can use them in place of the sounds Windows provides.

To set up your own sounds for Windows events, follow these steps:

1. Open the Sound dialog box. To do so, open the Charms bar and search for **sounds** in the Search box. Select **Change System Sounds** when it appears in the results. The Sound dialog box appears.

2. To use a prebuilt list of sounds already assigned to Windows events, select the Sounds tab, then select a scheme from the Sound Scheme list, as shown in Figure 10.19.

3. Select the event in the Program Events list.

4. Select the sound to associate with the event you select from the Sounds drop-down list. To use a custom sound, select **Browse**, and then navigate through your file system to find the sound file you want to use. Refer to Chapter 19, "Managing Files and Folders," for assistance in navigating the file system.

5. To hear the sound, select the **Test** button.

6. If you are happy with the sound, continue selecting sounds for other events as instructed, starting with step 3. When you finish selecting sounds, continue with the next step.

FIGURE 10.19

You can select a Sound Scheme, which is a prebuilt list of sounds assigned to specific system events, or create your own.

7. To save these new sound settings as a scheme, select **Save As**. Then enter a name for the scheme, such as **Paul's Favorite Sounds**, and select **OK**. If you want to save your new sounds without committing them to a scheme, select **OK**.

Your new sound setup should be ready to go.

Ease of Access

With Windows 8.1, the accessibility options, known as Ease of Access, have been improved and now offer even more options. Accessibility options are of use both to folks with disabilities and folks without. You might find it easier to work with the display configured in a high-contrast format, and hearing a voice confirmation of commands also can be helpful. Larger mouse pointers or thicker cursor lines are other settings you can modify here to make things easier to find on the display.

Figure 10.20 shows the screen where you set up the Ease of Access settings with the High Contrast option on, and you can also see the same screen with the option turned off. Figure 10.21 shows the Ease of Access settings screen with the Make Everything Bigger on Your Screen setting turned on.

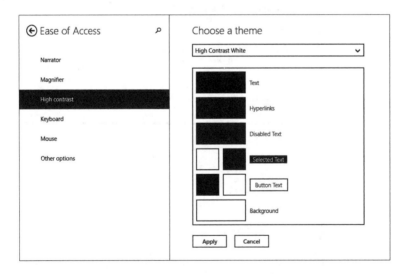

FIGURE 10.20

The image shows the Ease of Access screen with the High Contrast setting turned on using High Contrast White, which is previewed below.

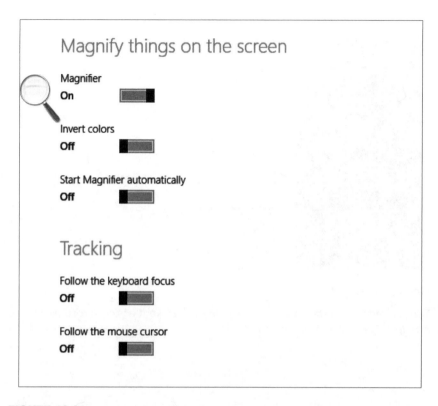

FIGURE 10.21

This image shows the Ease of Access settings screen enlarged with the Magnifier option turned on.

To use the Ease of Access settings, follow these steps:

1. Open the Settings charm and select **Change PC Settings**.

2. Select **Ease of Access.**

3. To use one or more of the following options, select from the categories to the left, such as **Narrator**.

4. Enable the feature as shown in Figure 10.22 by moving the slider to the right to the On position. Scroll through the options and turn additional options on as needed. You can even select the voice you want to hear by using the drop-down menu.

5. Select other options from the left to enhance readability and usability by using the Magnifier, High Contrast, Keyboard, Mouse, or Other options.

FIGURE 10.22

You can enhance certain aspects of Windows to make it easier to read and respond to prompts by enabling tools like the Narrator.

THE ABSOLUTE MINIMUM

- Use the Control Panel to access configuration settings that are not available in the Settings charm. Consider pinning the Control Panel to your Start screen or even to your Desktop taskbar for easy access.

- Use the Control Panel applets for Mouse and Keyboard to change how these peripherals work with Windows.

- Use the Settings charm to change language and date settings.

- To change the resolution of your display, you can access the Display settings through the Settings charm.

- Windows can accommodate multiple monitors if your computer has the capability. You can specify whether the image from the computer appears on one screen, appears on both screens, or extends across the screens—in effect, doubling your screen real estate.

- You can apply a few built-in, ready-to-use power schemes. You can also build your own power scheme that leverages up to 50 settings.

- Use Ease of Access settings to enhance your Windows experience by enabling visual and audible features or by enabling how your mouse and keyboard work with Windows.

11

CONNECTING TO THE INTERNET

Although Windows is jammed with cool and fun features, most of its power comes from its integration with the Internet. For example, your personal contacts are developed and maintained through social media, email, and messaging on the Internet. These contacts are the fuel that powers the sharing capabilities throughout Windows. And the information you work with every day is a combination of content you have stored on your computer merged with content Windows finds on the Internet. It's fair to say that Windows has limited functionality without a connection to the Internet. Fortunately, Windows makes it easy to connect to the Internet regardless of your location.

To help you connect wherever you are, this chapter provides several step-by-step lists of instructions. So that you understand a bit of the fundamentals, following is a brief review of a number of key topics on Internet connections.

Reviewing Important Internet Connection Basics

Connecting to the Internet from your desktop, laptop, or tablet usually runs smoothly after everything is set up properly. But there are lots of moving parts in the process, any of which can stop working or become dated as new capabilities are developed. One way to anticipate problems, as well as to be on the lookout for faster and better ways to connect, is to know the basics of connecting to the Internet. You won't necessarily become an Internet engineer after reading this section, but you can certainly gain a better understanding of what happens when you fire it up.

Learning About Internet Service Providers

The devices you use today to browse the Web, send and receive email, play videos, and more cannot connect to the Internet on their own. Whether you are at home, in an office, on a plane, or in a coffee shop or another public place, you need a go-between to connect to the Internet. This go-between is known as an *Internet service provider*, or *ISP*. The ISP keeps a pipe open to the Internet. You pay your ISP to connect you to that pipe. Even large companies that provide their employees fast Internet access do so by working with an ISP. Figure 11.1 illustrates how your computer works with the ISP.

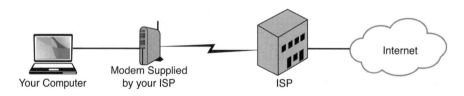

FIGURE 11.1

The ISP provides access to the Internet. Your connection does not run through your ISP's headquarters. The picture expresses your ISP managing your connection.

Checking the Hardware Required to Connect

Although Windows is powerful, connecting to the Internet usually requires some hardware, all of it usually (but not always) provided by the ISP, including the following:

- **Modem**—The modem is a device that bridges the Internet to your computer or home/office network. Each type of Internet connection—cable, DSL, and such—uses a different type of modem. If you'd prefer not to lease or purchase a modem from your provider, you can usually purchase one compatible with most providers from your preferred home electronics retailer. Many newer modems include Wi-Fi capability.

- **Ethernet cable**—Except for dial-up and mobile broadband connections, you need an ethernet cable to connect your computer to the modem or to connect the modem to a router and your computer to the router. If an ethernet cable was not provided by your ISP, you can purchase one at any store that sells electronics, especially computer equipment.

- **Wireless antennae**—If you want to connect wirelessly but your device does not have a wireless network adapter already built-in, you can purchase and connect one easily.

 NOTE Another common device you may have is called a *router*, which is discussed in this chapter in the section "Understanding Routers for Internet Connection Sharing." Routers are essential if you want to share your connection across multiple devices.

Learning the Internet Connection Services Typically Available

Each ISP uses a specific technology to connect your computer to the Internet. The technology the ISP provides, plus the price the ISP charges, the availability of the service, how to use and configure the technology, and how convenient and reliable the technology is, all combine to define a service offered by the ISP. It may be that you have a number of services available at your home. If that is the case, review each option carefully to make a decision. Price is important, but be sure to research the reliability of the service. Reliability is defined by how often the service is down and whether the connection that you pay for is provided at the speed advertised. There may be just one ISP doing business in your neighborhood, and that ISP might provide just one service. In that case, your options are obviously limited.

Here's a list of the most popular services used to connect users today, as well as a short explanation of how you connect to the service:

- **Cable**—Technology companies have learned to piggyback Internet traffic on the cable and hardware that provides cable TV service to their customers. Your ISP, which with this technology is the company that provides your cable TV services, provides you a modem that connects, using coaxial cable, to one of the cable ports in your home. If you want the modem in a particular room in your home, you may need to have a new plug installed in that room.

  You connect your computer to the modem with an ethernet cable. You usually do not need a user ID and password to access the Internet with a cable modem, but be sure to ask if one is needed when you have cable modem service installed.

   NOTE Many cable companies provide a choice for speeds of Internet service. Many services start at 3Mbps, which stands for 3 megabits per second, or *3 million bits per second*. At 3Mbps, a song available on the Internet would take about 14 seconds to download (assuming the song is 5MB). Cable companies often offer services (at a higher cost) up to 30Mbps and some offer even faster speeds.

- **DSL**—A broadband service is DSL, which, because it uses the same lines that support your regular telephone service (if you still have that), is provided exclusively by telephone companies. The ISP provides a small device that splits the signal so that the phone signal goes to the telephone and the Internet signal goes to the modem. The modem is another piece of hardware provided by the ISP.

  You need access to a telephone port close to the location, ideally in the same room, where the modem is installed. Like the cable modem, you connect your computer to the modem with an ethernet cable. You usually do not need a user ID and password to access the Internet with a DSL modem, but be sure to ask if one is needed when you have the service installed.

- **Satellite**—DirecTV, the largest television and music satellite company, also provides Internet access through its satellite service. The signal is delivered to your home or home office from the satellite dish mounted on a building or based on the ground.

  The signal is then delivered by a cable from the dish that connects to a modem, which is used to convert the signal for use with your computer, as shown in Figure 11.2. You connect your computer to the modem with an ethernet cable. You usually do not need a user ID and password to access the Internet with a cable modem, but be sure to ask if one is needed when you have cable modem service installed.

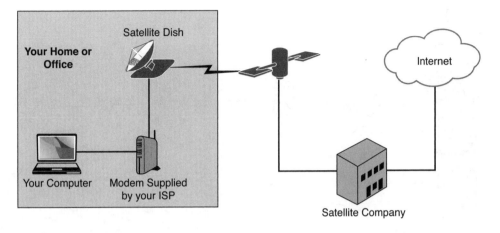

FIGURE 11.2

Satellite service is an option for locations that can't be served by cable or telephone companies.

The benefits of DirecTV Internet service is its availability where DSL and cable service is not available. You might also save money by bundling satellite entertainment service with Internet service. The disadvantage of satellite service for Internet is that under overcast skies the satellite signal is easy lost. The service is also considerably slower than cable service. It's reasonable to say that you should use satellite service only when no other service is available.

- **Dial-up**—Dial-up Internet access is still in use where broadband access is not available. With this service, a dial-up modem is used to send and receive Internet traffic over telephone lines. Many computers have a built-in modem, but it's far less common than it used to be, so it's important to check if one is installed before you commit to using dial-up service. Dial-up service is slow, but using this technology may be your last resort when other services are unavailable. Your local telephone company may offer dial-up service. If you can get online, you'll find a popular and useful site that lists dial-up services at http://www.freedomlist.com.

Understanding Routers for Internet Connection Sharing

To extend an Internet connection to several computers in your home or home office, you can use a router. A router is a piece of hardware (costing usually less than $75) that helps share the Internet connection with computers connected to the router. Routers today can provide both wired and wireless access. A router suitable for home or home office use can usually accommodate 4–10 wired devices. You connect your router to the Internet modem, as shown in Figure 11.3.

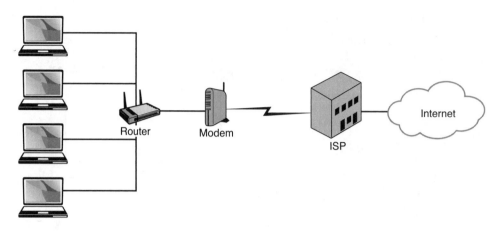

FIGURE 11.3

A router is used to share a single Internet connection with several computers.

 TIP The modem provided by your ISP might also double as a router by providing support for sharing the connection with multiple computers, including permitting wireless access to the modem.

Understanding the Network Adapter

The network adapter is the piece of hardware used to connect to a network. Don't worry—it is extremely unlikely that your PC or tablet, if purchased in the past four years, does not have a built-in network adapter. Often these adapters are internal, meaning you can't see them unless you open your computer (which is not recommended), although you can see the port (wired) or sometimes the antenna (wireless).

To view the network adapters set up in Windows, so that you can make sure Windows recognizes them and they are functioning, follow these steps:

1. Open the Charms bar and select **Search**.

2. Type **view network connections** into the search box.

3. Select the **View Network Connections** setting, which should appear at the top of the list of results.

4. The Network Connections dialog box shown in Figure 11.4 will open on your Desktop, showing available connections and their current status.

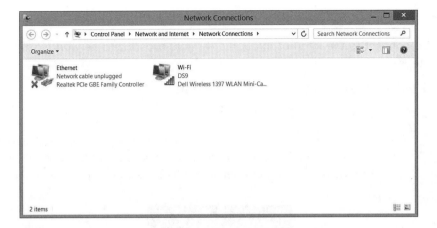

FIGURE 11.4

You can check your connections using the Network Connections dialog box.

Connecting to the Internet

Following are some of the most common Internet connection scenarios. You can follow the step-by-step procedures to connect to the Internet for each scenario in the following list:

- Connecting to a wireless network

- Connecting where free Wi-Fi is advertised

- Connecting where Wi-Fi access can be purchased

- Connecting to a wired network at work or home

- Connecting after you upgrade to Windows 8

- Connecting if you have been forced to restart

Before diving into the individual connection scenarios, it's important to understand that after you install Windows 8 and connect to the Internet initially, you may not need to make any changes to your setup or to even purposely connect to the Internet. Windows automatically connects to the Internet on startup unless you use a manual connection method, such as dial-up.

Unless you want to change how you connect—for instance, if you bring your computer to a new location or if you change your network or connection setup at home (that is, you change your hardware or Internet service provider), you might not need the information provided in the rest of this section.

Connecting to a Wireless Network

To connect to the Internet through a wireless broadband network, follow these steps:

1. Open the Charms bar and select **Settings**.

2. Select **Change PC Settings**.

3. Select **Network**. If the Network option does not appear, you are already connected, and you should see a graphic for your connection, as shown in Figure 11.5. To switch to a different network, select your network connection.

FIGURE 11.5

You can review all the network connections in one place in Windows.

4. Select the network to which you want to connect. The pane opens to display the Connect button, as shown in Figure 11.6.

5. If you want to connect to the network automatically the next time you sign in to Windows, enable the **Connect Automatically check box**.

FIGURE 11.6

You are able to easily connect to other available networks.

6. Select **Connect**. You are prompted to enter the PIN of the router your wireless adapter connects to, as shown in Figure 11.7.

FIGURE 11.7

You confirm you have access to the network by entering the PIN of the router.

7. Enter the PIN and click **Next**. Skip to step 10.

   Alternatively, if you know the security key (passphrase) for the network, select **Connect Using a Security Key Instead**. The screen shown in Figure 11.8 appears.

FIGURE 11.8

You confirm you have access to the network by entering the security key set up on the router.

8. Enter the security key and click **Next**.

9. If you have not configured security on this network yet, you can specify whether sharing is allowed. You may answer Yes here and then control which items are shared, as well as with whom, with the Homegroups feature. See chapter 18, "Sharing Files and Printers," to learn more about Homegroups.

10. Click **Close**.

Connecting Where Free Wi-Fi Is Advertised

There's little doubt that you have come across a store, a coffee shop, or another public location advertising Wi-Fi. If the place offers free Wi-Fi, follow the previous steps under "Connecting to a Wireless Network." At step 8, you may need to provide the network passcode, although many public Wi-Fi hotspots aren't secured. If a password is required, presumably someone at the location can provide you with the passcode.

NOTE Some sites do not require a passcode; however, they may require you to read an agreement or watch an advertisement to connect.

Connecting to Pay-as-You-Go Wi-Fi

Most airports and many small coffee and snack shops offer Wi-Fi today, which is almost always provided by a national service. You can usually tell which type of Wi-Fi is offered from advertisements or notices on the walls. Or you can ask someone. Most ISPs charge a fee based on the time you connect. If you connect from this location frequently, you may consider signing up for a plan that gives you access for a longer period at a reduced price.

If Wi-Fi is offered for a fee, you need to enter credit card information to pay for the access.

Follow these steps to connect to a Wi-Fi hotspot:

1. It might seem like a hassle or a waste of time, but if your device was powered on when you entered the store or shop that offers Wi-Fi, shut it down completely and restart when you are at the location.

2. You need to first connect to the wireless service in place at your location. This does not provide you access to the Internet yet. You are simply joining the network at your location. Follow the instructions in the previous section, "Connecting to a Wireless Network." Someone working at or supporting your location can identify the network you should connect to; however, the name of the network (Paul's Bagel Shop Network) might make the selection obvious.

3. Open Internet Explorer. You should be brought to the sign-up page for the ISP in use at the location. Enter the information requested. You should connect shortly.

Connecting to a LAN/Wired Network

You might be at an office, a school, or a place of business where Internet access is not advertised, but you have access to the local area network (LAN). Most corporate and school networks connect to the Internet over a LAN. This is no different than using a wired network connection in your home.

At an office or school, look for an unused ethernet port. There is only one type of port that accommodates the ethernet plug, so you should determine quickly if a port is available. At home, simply connect to one of the ports in your modem or router.

After you connect, wait a few seconds and then start Internet Explorer to verify you are connected. If you are not connected to the LAN, it's a good idea to shut down your computer and restart. After you sign on again, open Internet Explorer to confirm you are connected to the Internet. If an error message appears, meet with a member of the information technology team or contact the support desk.

Connecting After Upgrading to Windows 8

If you upgraded your computer from Windows 7, and you could connect to the Internet before you upgraded, you should connect without issue in Windows 8. If you installed Windows 8 on a new drive or partition, you were probably prompted to connect to the Internet to complete the setup. You definitely need to connect to the Internet if you want to sign in with a Windows account.

Connecting After You Restart Your Device

Windows automatically reconnects to the wireless network you have been using. If you intentionally disconnected from a network, Windows no longer automatically connects you to that network. Wi-Fi networks always have priority over mobile broadband networks.

THE ABSOLUTE MINIMUM

- You must connect to the Internet to complete the initial configuration and installation of Windows. The connection type you use—wireless, wired, and so on—becomes the default connection type, and Windows attempts to automatically make the same connection each time it starts.

- A number of technologies are in use today to connect people to the Internet. Because typically just one ISP serves a neighborhood, you might not have a choice of Internet connection technologies.

- You may specify that Windows should connect automatically if you are using a wireless adapter. Doing so requires you to enter your wireless connection password the first time you connect.

- Windows permits you to use the PIN assigned permanently to your router to authorize you to use the Internet connection. This use of a PIN supplements the traditional use of a password or passphrase.

12

SURFING THE WEB

Surfing the Web probably is the most popular activity in Windows, more so perhaps than checking email, and definitely more so than doing work! If you think the same way, you'll also agree how important it is to like your web-surfing tool.

Microsoft thinks it's important, too—so important that Windows 8 comes with two versions of Internet Explorer. One version uses the Modern UI style and launches from the Start screen; it's slick, modern, and simple to use. The other Internet Explorer is the Desktop version, which is much like the Internet Explorer you are accustomed to using in earlier versions of Windows. The version you use most will likely depend on where you spend the bulk of your PC time. Are you primarily on the desktop or do you stick with Modern UI apps like those found in the Windows Store? This chapter helps you understand how to use the new Windows 8 browser, as well as when you may need to use the Desktop version.

FIGURING OUT WHICH BROWSER TO USE

You can use whatever version of Internet Explorer you prefer. The main reason cited for the two different browsers is that people sometimes find themselves working in the desktop environment and they like to have a more mouse-friendly browser. If you are using a touchscreen, you will find the Windows 8 version to be much easier to navigate with. On rare occasions you may be directed to the desktop version if it has add-ons that will display better from the Desktop, which has a more robust set of features that are generally not needed for casual web browsing. The differences between the two probably won't lead to a permanent choice. You might switch between the two browsers based on the kind of browsing you want to do. Table 12.1 points out the major differences between the two browsers.

TABLE 12.1 Windows 8 Browser Versus Desktop Browser

Capability	Windows 8	Desktop
Perform downloads	✓	✓
Run Flash content	✓	✓
Maintain list of favorites	✓	✓
Show most popular sites	✓	
Maintain list of sites you visit most frequently	✓	
Organize open websites in tabs	✓	✓
Pin sites to the Start screen	✓	
Use toolbars	✓	

To start the Windows 8 browser, from the Start screen, select the Internet Explorer tile, as shown in Figure 12.1. Figure 12.2 shows the Windows 8 browser open to Microsoft's website.com. Notice that there are no onscreen controls—all you see is the website.

The Internet Explorer tile

FIGURE 12.1

Start Internet Explorer from the tile on the Start screen.

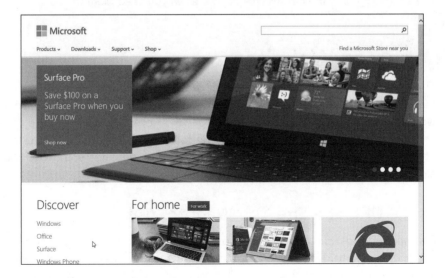

FIGURE 12.2

This screen shows Microsoft's home page in Internet Explorer.

As you can see in Figure 12.2, no buttons or other controls display in the Windows 8 browser. To display the buttons, tabs, and other widgets that you need to operate the browser, do one of the following based on the computer or device you use:

- 👆 Swipe up from the bottom or down from the top of the screen.
- 🖱️ Right-click anywhere on the page you are viewing. Avoid right-clicking any text, pictures, buttons, or links.
- ⌨️ Press Windows+Z.

Doing this displays the address bar and the tab switcher, as shown in Figure 12.3.

FIGURE 12.3

The address bar and the tab switcher appear when you need them to.

Navigating to Websites

The Windows 8 version of IE has lots of great features. But none of the new features that, for example, help you pin your favorites to the Start screen are worth anything if you can't perform a browser's core function—browse the Web and stop at sites you're interested in. The following sections demonstrate a variety of ways you can get to your favorite websites or to websites you never knew existed.

Entering the URL of a Site You Want to Visit

Perhaps the most direct way to navigate to a site is to type in the name of the site you want to go to. Don't worry, you don't have to memorize complicated website addresses. Many times, just the main part of the address will do. For example, to visit Microsoft's website, you don't have to enter http://www.microsoft.com, because just **microsoft** will do.

As you visit more sites, the browser begins to recognize the site you want to visit after you enter just a few characters. As you enter characters into the address bar, the Windows 8 browser tries to match your input with sites on these lists, as shown in Figure 12.4:

- The sites you visit the most

- The sites you hit most recently

- The most popular sites

FIGURE 12.4

*Internet Explorer suggests sites as you enter characters into the address bar. In this example, the characters **c l i p** are entered, and a number of matching tiles appear.*

To enter the URL of the site to visit, display and select the address bar by swiping in from the top or bottom or with a right-click and enter the name of the site you want to visit.

TIP   If you miss seeing the URL for web pages as a constantly displayed feature, you can enable this in the modern Windows 8 web browser. From the IE charms, select Settings and then select Options. The first item listed under Appearance is a slider labeled Always Show Address Bar and Tabs. It's Off by default, but if you slide it to On, it keeps your web address bar displayed at all times.

Searching the Web

Using Internet Explorer's search function can help you find sites on the Internet you probably never knew existed, as well as those you're specifically searching for. You can choose from a number of search engines, such as Bing or Google. Depending on the topic you search for and the engine you want to use, you might see hundreds or even thousands of results returned.

To search the Web from the Windows 8 browser, follow these steps:

1. Open the Charms bar and select **Search**.

2. Type your search terms. Notice how the browser begins to retrieve results as you type, as shown in Figure 12.5.

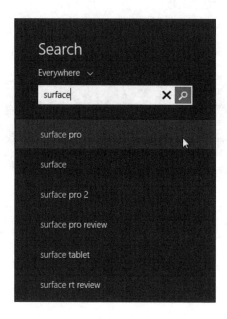

FIGURE 12.5

Internet Explorer begins searching as soon as you type text into the search terms box.

3. If any of the search results are of interest to you, select it.

4. If the Windows 8 browser did not show any early results as you typed the search terms, just press **Enter** when you finish. After a moment, your search results appear on a web page (see Figure 12.6). Select any link of interest. You can also scroll or swipe to the right to see a variety of results, including News, Windows Store, Related, Images and Video, followed by general search returns.

FIGURE 12.6

The Bing search engine provides an organized list of results on Windows 8.

Following a Hyperlink to Another Page

It's rare to come across a web page that does not have a link to another page. A link on a web page that brings you to another page is known as a *hyperlink*. A hyperlink normally has a color other than the rest of the text on the page, and often there is a line underneath the words of the hyperlink. A picture or even a word or headline larger than the other text on the pages also can be a hyperlink. On many sites, almost every element on the page links to another page.

Click or tap on a link to open the page targeted by the hyperlink. Whether that page opens in the same window or tab or in a new one depends on the website. If you want control over how it opens, right-click or tap and hold a link. This pops up a menu, as shown in Figure 12.7. From that menu, you can

- Copy the link so that you can use it somewhere else, such as in an email or another web browser.

- Open a new tab containing the page the link points to.

- Open the page targeted by the hyperlink in a new page for side-by-side viewing.

- Perform some action based on the type of link you selected, such as saving a picture on the website to your computer.

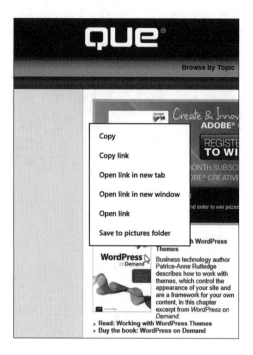

FIGURE 12.7

The target pop-up shows you the web page that will appear when the link you point to is selected.

Revisiting a Site You Visit Often

The Windows 8 browser keeps track of the sites you have visited recently and makes it easy for you to revisit any of those sites. To see the list of sites you visit frequently, as well as see your list of favorites, select the address bar. A row of frequently visited tiles should appear above it, as shown in Figure 12.8. Select a tile to visit the site it represents.

FIGURE 12.8

When you select the address bar, a row of your most frequently visited websites appears.

Opening a Tabbed Site

A feature known as *tabbed browsing* enables you to have several websites open at one time. You can easily switch from one tab to another to see pages from as many sites as you like.

To access the sites you have open in tabs, follow these steps:

1. Open the address bar.

2. Above the address bar a list of currently open tabs appears (see Figure 12.9). Switch to the site you want to browse by selecting the tab that shows the site. To use your keyboard, press Ctrl+the tab number, where the tab number refers to the position of the tab you want to switch to in the collection of all tabs. For example, to navigate to the second tab, press Ctrl+2.

FIGURE 12.9

This figure shows the Windows 8 browser with a number of tabs open.

Navigating Back and Forth

You can easily go back to the last page you opened; from there, you can move forward to the screen where you started. Just swipe with your finger to go back a page or forward to the next page. Using other input devices, use the forward and back buttons on the page you are viewing, as shown in Figure 12.10. Point to the middle point on either the left or right border. Then click or tap to move forward or backward. To use your keyboard, press Alt+right arrow to go forward or Alt+left arrow to move back.

Previous page   Next page

FIGURE 12.10

Move to the previous or next page by choosing one of the navigation buttons.

Enhancing Your Browsing

A few features can make your browsing experience better. You can magnify the page you look at, which is known as *zooming in*. You can also *zoom out* to see a broader view of the page. You can also very easily open the site you're currently browsing in the Desktop browser, which gives you access to some features not available from the Windows 8 browser, such as playing Flash movies or playing some browser-based games.

Zooming In and Out

Sometimes you come across websites in which the text and/or the graphics on the side have been formatted too small. Rather than abandon looking at the site, you can take advantage of a tool that enables you to enlarge or reduce the view used for the site.

To zoom in or zoom out of the Windows 8 browser, follow these steps:

1. Open the Windows 8 browser to the page you want to see.

2. Open the Settings charm. Select **Options**.

3. Notice the Zoom slider bar near the top of the Options pane in Figure 12.11. Tap or click the slider to zoom in or out, or drag the dark block on the slider until the browser is at a size that enables you to read the site clearly.

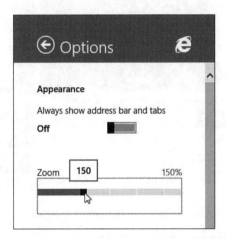

FIGURE 12.11

You can change the default zoom setting from the Options pane.

To zoom in or zoom out whenever you need to, you can also pinch with your fingers on the screen to zoom out or pull your fingers apart from the pinch gesture to zoom in. With your mouse, you can turn the mouse wheel while holding the Ctrl key.

Playing Videos and Music on the Web

You will find it easy to play your favorite media from your web browser. Popular sites like YouTube, Pandora, and other streaming video and music sites play equally well from either version of your web browser. Just navigate to a site that contains the media you want to play and use the site's built-in controls to activate it. Figure 12.12 shows a video playing from YouTube in the Windows 8 browser.

FIGURE 12.12

Video and music play easily in your web browser.

 TIP Although it is easy to stream music from the Windows 8 browser, the music pauses if you switch to a different tab. To continue listening to streaming music while you work on other things, use the Desktop browser.

Viewing Web Pages in the Desktop Browser

You learned earlier in this chapter that there are two versions of Internet Explorer in Windows 8. One is the Windows 8 version that you have been reading about in the chapter, and the other is the Desktop version, which includes some capabilities not found in the Windows 8 version. If you go to a site with features that can be experienced only with the Desktop browser, you can view the site in the Desktop browser with just one click.

To open the page you are viewing in the Desktop browser, follow these steps:

1. Open the browser command bar. To do so, swipe up or down from the bottom or top of the screen, or right-click anywhere on the page.

2. Select the **Page Tools** button that looks like a wrench.

3. Select **View on the Desktop** from the menu that appears, as shown in Figure 12.13. The page you were viewing in the Windows 8 browser opens in the Desktop browser.

FIGURE 12.13

You can choose to open a website in the Desktop browser from the Windows 8 modern browser.

 NOTE It may be that you prefer to use the Desktop browser by default. To learn more about using it, see "Using the Desktop Browser," later in this chapter.

Pinning Websites to the Start Screen

Starting the Windows 8 browser in Windows 8 is a snap. After the browser is up and running, you are just a swipe or click or two away from seeing your favorite sites. As easy as it is to visit the sites you like in the Windows 8 browser, you can make it even more convenient by creating tiles on your Start screen for each of your favorite sites. This is known as *pinning*. Figure 12.14 shows an example of a Start screen with several websites pinned to Start. Some websites include the capability to provide notifications that appear on the site's pinned tile, just like with other live tiles.

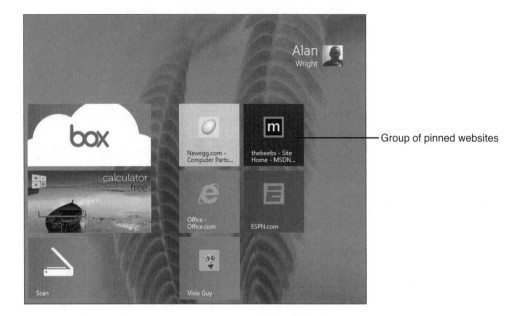

FIGURE 12.14

Pinned sites are added to the right side of the screen, but they can be added to existing groups.

To pin a website to Start, follow these steps from the Windows 8 browser:

1. Display the address bar by right-clicking a page or swiping up from the bottom or down from the top of the screen.

2. Select the **Favorites** button, which looks like a star.

3. Select the **Pin** button, as shown in Figure 12.15.

4. Select the appearance and edit the text label of the tile and then select **Pin to Start.**

FIGURE 12.15

You can see a preview of the tile to be used when a website is pinned to the Start screen, although the Internet Explorer logo may be used if a preview is not available. You can also supply your own label for the tile.

Sharing Web Pages

Right after "Wow," the first reaction most people have when they see something interesting on a website is to decide to show it to someone. Windows 8 can help. The Share charm is tightly integrated with the Windows 8 browser, making it a snap to share content with other folks.

The Share charm connects the content you want to share with any app installed in your Windows 8 that is capable of sharing. When you open the Share charm from the Windows 8 browser, you immediately see a list of those apps (see Figure 12.16). Mail probably comes to mind as the application most useful for sharing, and because Mail comes with Windows 8, it happens to work well with the Windows 8 browser. You can read more about the Share charm in Chapter 7, "Setting Up Search, Share, and Notifications."

FIGURE 12.16

Any app capable of sharing appears on the menu when you open the Shares charm. In this example, sharing from a website works with Mail and People.

The Mail app shares by sending a friend a link to the site you are looking at. However, the word *link* understates what is shared. Windows prepares a preview of the site, including the image, colors, link, and a review of the site.

Printing While You're Web Browsing

You may want to print one or more pages from a website, perhaps to keep a paper copy of a receipt, a confirmation number, or to retain interesting or valuable information. Unfortunately, the dimensions of a website don't always match those of a sheet of paper, so the print never looks as good as it does on the screen. But there are times when you are forced to print from a website regardless of how poor the formatting and print may turn out, such as printing a boarding pass for a flight.

Windows 8 makes it easy to print from any page. The Charms bar, specifically the Devices charm you learned about in Chapter 1, "Your First Hour with Windows," is the tool you use for printing from websites. It provides access to all the hardware on your system, including printers, to all the Windows 8 applications.

To print from a website, follow these steps:

1. Open the Devices charm.

2. The Devices charm shows any devices that you could potentially use with the Windows 8 browser, such as the projector you can use to display your screen or a printer, which you can then use to print open web pages. Select Print.

3. Select the printer from the list of printers. Figure 12.17 shows a typical set of options that are available in the pane for your selected printer. You can even scroll through the pages that will be printed in the preview image and selectively print pages using the Pages drop-down menu. When everything looks right, click Print.

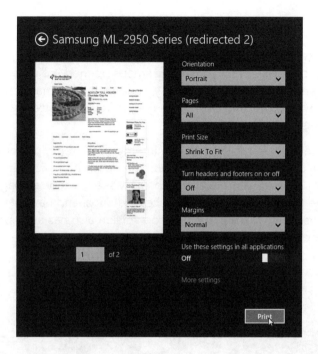

FIGURE 12.17

You can preview and customize the appearance of content you want to print from a website.

  TIP   If you need to print one or more pages from a website but you do not have access to a printer while you have the site open, you can always print to a file. You can take the file with you on a portable drive, or you can email the file to an account you can access on the Web. When you print, be sure to select Microsoft XPS Document Writer from the Devices charm. A file will be created that you can print at a later time. Be sure to either email the file or copy it from the machine before you depart!

Using the Desktop Browser

You have seen ways to open the desktop browser from within the modern Windows 8 web browser, and you have perhaps opened it directly from the desktop environment. Although the browser you use is often a matter of preference, there are times when using the Desktop browser provides better results than the Windows 8 version.

What is the difference? The modern Internet Explorer app is optimized for touch and keeps the focus on the webpage. The desktop browser appears as a traditional web browser with the ability to easily see the tabbed pages and address bar for the page you are viewing, access settings, and navigate on the page with a mouse using scroll bars. The desktop version also has an impressive set of tools for developers. Figure 12.18 shows a desktop browser with three open tabs.

FIGURE 12.18

The desktop browser provides a traditional web browsing experience

Creating Shortcuts to Websites

You have seen how easy and convenient it is to pin websites to the Start screen using the modern browser. Now you can also add website shortcuts to your Apps screen. These shortcuts automatically open in the Desktop browser. To do this, follow these steps:

1. From the Desktop browser, open a website you would like to add to your Apps screen.

2. Select the **Tools** button to open the Tools menu, as shown in Figure 12.19.

3. Select **Add Site to Apps**.

4. In the Internet Explorer dialog box that appears, click the **Add** button.

FIGURE 12.19

Select Add Site to Apps to create a link right in the Apps screen.

At the time of this writing, it is not possible to pin this from Apps to the actual Start screen. Perhaps that will be rectified in a future update. This shortcut in the Apps screen still makes it easy to open websites in the correct browser when working in the modern UI environment.

Opening All Links in the Desktop Browser

If you need or prefer to use the Desktop browser exclusively, there is a setting for that.

1. Open to the Desktop environment and open your Desktop browser.

2. Open Tools and select **Internet Options**.

3. Select the **Programs** tab.

4. Under Opening Internet Explorer, change the drop-down box labeled Choose How You Open Links to Always in Internet Explorer on the desktop as shown in Figure 12.20.

5. Enable the check box labeled Open Internet Explorer Tiles on the Desktop (refer to Figure 12.20).

6. Click **OK**.

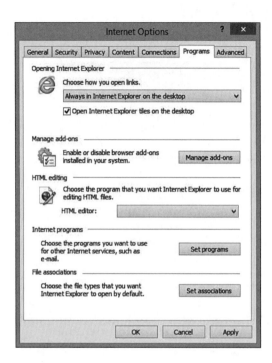

FIGURE 12.20

Use Internet Options to open all websites using the Desktop browser if you desire.

Any websites, including ones that were pinned to the Start screen, using the modern browser will now open on the Desktop browser. Use the preceding steps to change back if you want to at a later time.

THE ABSOLUTE MINIMUM

Keep these tips in mind as you work with the Windows 8 browser:

- Two Internet browsers are available in Windows 8. The Windows 8 browser is designed for a great user experience with a minimum number of buttons and other onscreen elements. The Desktop browser supports all the traditional browse requirements, such as plug-ins, toolbars, and all Flash content.

- There are no visible controls in the Windows 8 browser. To show the controls necessary to enter the address of sites you want to visit, to pin sites to the Start screen, and much more, right-click, swipe in from the bottom or top, or press Windows+Z.

- To navigate to a site, simply start typing the name of the site into the address bar. The browser presents suggestions based on the sites you typically visit, today's most popular sites, and the sites you recently visited.

- To see the list of sites you typically visit, open the address bar again and touch or click the long box where the address of the current site is shown.

- As you navigate to different sites, the sites remain open as tabs. This makes it easy to jump back to any open site you like.

- Remember to use the Share and Print charms when you want to send a link in an email or if you need to print a web page.

MANAGING YOUR CONTACTS

If you routinely visit multiple social networking sites to see what your friends, family, and co-workers are up to, those days are over if you use the People app. The People app brings together all your contacts with all the ways they communicate on the Web. This gives you an all-in-one socially aware record of your contacts infused with posts, status updates, and photos. This chapter helps you navigate through the different views of your contacts that the app provides. You also learn how to link the app to various social sites, saving you from entering your contacts by hand. Finally, you learn how to keep the app up-to-date at all times, ensuring you see the posts almost as soon as they are made.

The People app in Windows 8.1 is an updated Microsoft Store app that may have newer interface elements than you have used in the past. To be sure you can easily follow the instructions in this chapter, consider reviewing some of the content in Chapter 2, "Interacting with Windows," and Chapter 1, "Your First Hour with Windows."

Introducing the People App

The People app is the hub for all your web contacts, both professional and personal. This hub has more than just people's names, email addresses, and phone numbers. With the People app, you can keep tabs on your contacts by viewing their status, news, views, and photos from many of the various social networking sites people use today, including Facebook, LinkedIn, and Twitter. The People app is a component of the People, Mail, and Calendar bundle that either came with your computer or can be downloaded from the Windows Store at no extra charge.

To start the People app, select it from the Start screen (Figure 13.1). The People app tile also has a live option, which replaces the standard People logo with a set of randomly chosen photos.

FIGURE 13.1

The Live version of the People tile shows randomly selected photos posted by you and your friends.

The main view in the People app, shown in Figure 13.2, gives you a consolidated view of all the persons in your personal and professional life, including their contact info, status, photos, profiles, and tweets.

You can also jump to the various sections in the app:

- **What's New**—What's New provides you with events, activities, posts, and status updates, including photos and links, by all your people, as shown in Figure 13.3.

- **Me**—The Me page is all about you. It shows your updates, plus people's responses to them, and all your photos, as shown in Figure 13.4.

FIGURE 13.2

The home screen of the People app gives you a consolidated view of your personal and professional contacts.

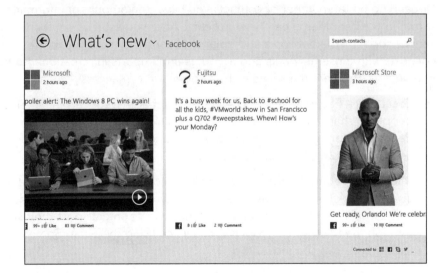

FIGURE 13.3

What's New is a view of events, activities, and posts.

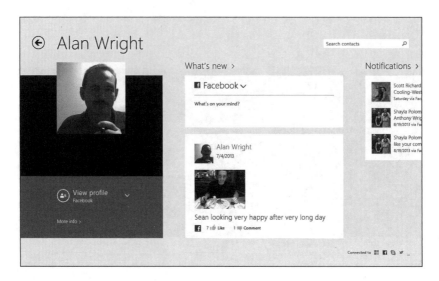

FIGURE 13.4

The Me page shows updates you've posted and more.

Depending on the number of contacts you have, the amount of information shown in the People app can be significant. After you set it up to connect with various social media networks and email and contact accounts you use, Windows connects with those networks and accounts and imports information into the People app. Here are the services the People app can access:

- **Facebook**—Facebook is the premier social media website, which enables people to share pictures, opinions, news, links, videos, and messages. The People app brings in your Facebook friends and both your posts and theirs, as well as photos, likes, and statuses.

- **Microsoft webmail**—For any webmail-based Microsoft mail account (Hotmail, Live, Outlook.com) you have, People can sync your contacts, calendars, and task list services from that account. Also, if your contacts post their statuses through the Microsoft Windows Live service using the Share Something New feature, you can see those, too.

- **Google Mail Contacts**—Gmail is Google's email service. You can maintain an address book in Google to use with your Gmail service. The People app links to your contacts in Gmail. This enables you to connect with your Gmail contacts with People.

- **LinkedIn**—LinkedIn is a web-based contact and social media service for professionals that enables its users to exchange information about their professional expertise, employment, and views. It's fair to think of LinkedIn as the professional version of Facebook. The People app link connects to LinkedIn to import your list of professional relationships.

- **Microsoft Outlook/Exchange/Office 365**—Exchange is Microsoft's email, contacts, calendar, and to-do server product. Outlook is Microsoft's number one mail client, whereas Office 365 is a new solution for providing email, collaboration, and business tools over the Internet. The People app connects with each of these three solutions to bring your contacts list to Windows 8.1.

- **Skype**—Skype is the default messaging app in Windows 8.1, and you can access your Skype contacts through the People app.

- **Twitter**—Twitter is the popular social networking application that enables you to post your views, news, photos, and comments in 140-character posts known as *tweets*. The People app links to persons you follow in Twitter, and it links to your tweets as updates, including photos.

Connecting with Your Contacts

When you start the People app, you automatically see all the people with whom you have connections through email and social media sites. You also have quick access to the people you have deemed your favorites.

From this first view of the People app, referred to as the *People page*, you can review all your people. Using the skills you learned in Chapter 2, you can swipe left and right to see all your people, or you can use the scrollbars at the bottom of the screen.

You can do a lot in the People app besides scroll through your list of people. You can filter your list of contacts in certain ways, see information about one or more of your contacts, connect with any of them, or simply keep an eye on their social media activities. Try each of the tasks in this section to see how you can both review and contribute to the social chatter with your people:

- **Browse for a contact by first or last name**—If you have a large number of contacts loaded into People, it may be time consuming to locate a particular person. The People app provides a condensed view of your contacts starting with the alphabet. Select the appropriate letter to jump to contacts that start with that letter. By default, your contacts may be sorted by first name. To change this setting, select the Settings charm and then select **Options**. Change the slider switch to Yes for Sort My Contacts by Last Name (see Figure 13.5).

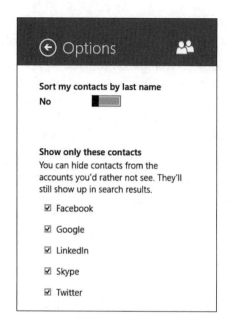

FIGURE 13.5

Your contacts can be sorted by first or last name by changing the selection in the Options pane.

- **Show contacts only from specific social media sites**—From the Settings charm, Options you can deselect contacts from specific sites if you do not want them to appear in your contacts. To enable a site, select its check box, as shown in Figure 13.5.

- **Search for contacts**—Start typing a name with your keyboard or select the Search contacts tool located in the upper-right corner of the People app to start a search for a contact, as shown in Figure 13.6. As you type letters, you see results that are filtered as you enter additional letters.

- **See a person's profile**—To see a contact's profile select the person's tile in your list of contacts. The contact's portrait appears, as shown in Figure 13.7. From here you have easy access to contact information and a What's New link for this contact. Scroll to the right to see recent photos and albums posted by this contact.

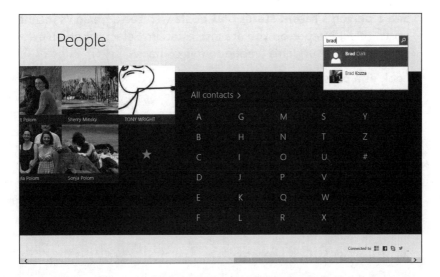

FIGURE 13.6

Search for a contact by typing a name using the Search contacts tool.

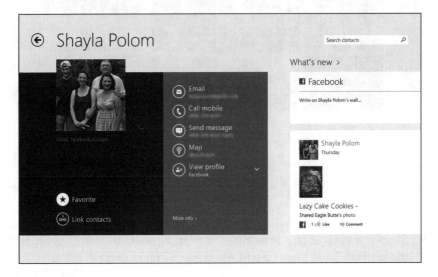

FIGURE 13.7

You can see details about any of your people. These are the details collected at the site or service where your contact is registered.

- **See a person's recent status and posts**—To see a person's recent status and posts, select the person you are interested in. Select **What's New** to jump to posts and other updates unique to this contact.

- **Look at a person's photos**—To look at someone's photos, select the person you are interested in. Scroll to the right beyond What's New to the Photos section. To see older albums, select Photos to expand the photo album gallery. Select any album (the album cover is a photo) and then select it to review the photos in it. Use the scrollbar with your mouse or pan with your finger or stylus to scroll through the photos in the album. To enter a comment about a photo, type your comment into the Add a Comment box at the bottom of the screen, as shown in Figure 13.8, and then select **Comment**.

FIGURE 13.8

You can scroll through a contact's photos in the People app, as well as post a comment about a photo.

- **Send a message to someone**—To send a message to a contact, first select the person. Then select **Send Message**. After doing so, the Skype messaging app appears where you write your message. If Select Message does not appear, your contact does not have an account with a service that provides messaging, such as Facebook. If you see a Twitter prompt for your contact, you can tweet your contact.

- **Make a person a favorite**—Your favorite contacts appear as very large tiles at the start of your people list (refer to Figure 13.2). To add a few contacts as favorites, select the **Add Favorites** star to start selecting contacts to add to your group of Favorites, as shown in Figure 13.9. Select the contacts and then select **Add** to change their status to Favorite. To add a single contact, you can also select the contact to view the person's profile. Below the contact's image you can enable or disable the status as a Favorite. You can make as many contacts a favorite as you like.

- **Pin a person to the Start screen**—To create a tile for a person on the Start screen, select the person, and then open the App bar. Select **Pin to Start**. Doing so creates a handy link to the person's details screen in the People app. If there are folks you email, message, or call frequently, selecting their tile created from the People app may be the quickest way to contact them.

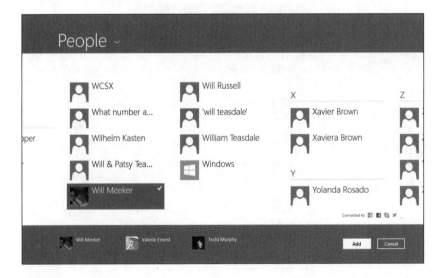

FIGURE 13.9

Add contacts to your Favorite people to make them easy to find.

Setting Up Your Contacts

One of the best features of the People app is how it brings together all the social media activity for all your contacts. To see all these posts, tweets, and photos, connect the People app to your social media networks/email accounts. Follow the instructions in the next six sections for whichever service you want to link to Windows 8.1.

Linking to Facebook

Follow these steps to link the People app to Facebook. You need the email address and password that you use to sign in to Facebook:

1. Open the People app.

2. Open the Charms bar and select **Settings**. From the Settings screen, select **Accounts**.

3. The Accounts screen appears, which shows a list of the accounts that have been set up so far in the People app. Select **Add an Account**.

4. The screen shown in Figure 13.10 appears, which presents the accounts you can link to in People. Select **Facebook**.

FIGURE 13.10

You can load information from several social media and email websites into People.

5. The screen shown in Figure 13.11 appears. Select **Connect**.

6. After doing so, Windows connects with Facebook and prompts you to sign in to Facebook. Do so and select **Log In**. If you entered your email address and password correctly, the screen shown in Figure 13.12 appears.

7. Select **Done**.

FIGURE 13.11

You may select Connect right away or read the info from Facebook by selecting the blue text.

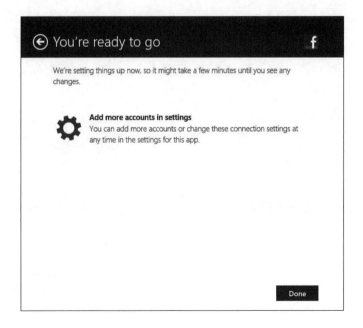

FIGURE 13.12

This screen indicates success in linking to your Facebook account.

Linking to Google, Outlook.com, and Exchange/Office 365

The steps for linking to Google, Outlook.com, and Exchange/Outlook/Office are similar. Follow these steps, and pay particular attention to instructions specific to connecting to one of the networks:

1. Open the People app.

2. Open the Settings charm and select **Accounts**.

3. Select **Add an Account**. Choose from the networks and email providers you can link to in People.

4. Select **Google**, **Outlook.com**, or **Exchange**. A screen that looks like the one shown in Figure 13.13 appears. The title and coloring on this screen can vary with the kind of account you intend to add. Select **Connect**.

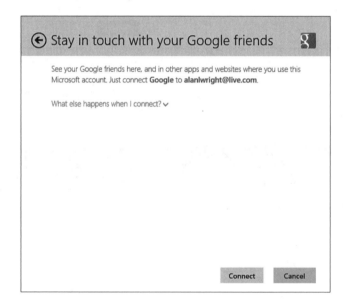

FIGURE 13.13

You can add contacts from many common social networks that you already use.

5. Enter your email address and your password in the fields provided.

6. If you want to link to Google or Outlook.com, click **Connect**. If you have entered your email address and password correctly, the link is created, and posts from your Google and Outlook.com contacts appear soon after.

    If you want to link to Exchange, Outlook, or Office 365, you have a little more work to do. Select **See More Details** to see the screen where you enter more information about your Microsoft accounts (see Figure 13.14).

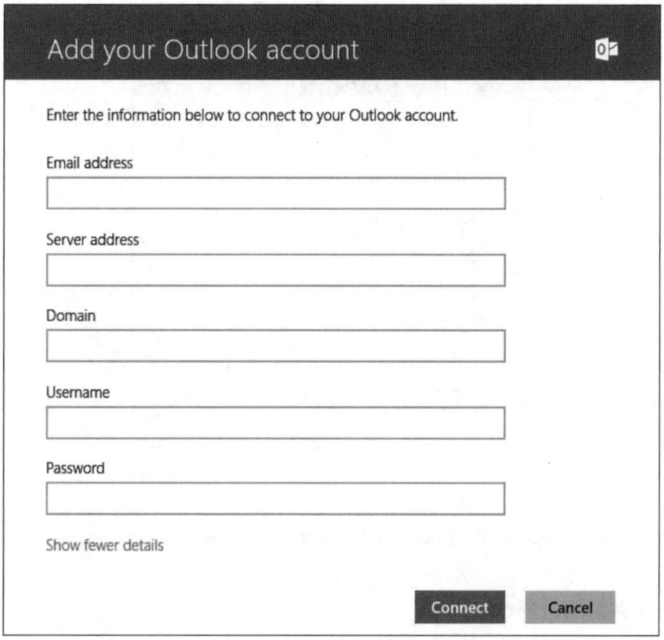

FIGURE 13.14

Additional information may be supplied to link to Exchange, Outlook, or Office 365.

7. Enter the information required. The only field that might give you difficulty is Domain. If you are unsure of what to enter for Domain, check with a member of your technical team at your office. With each field filled in, select **Connect**.

Windows attempts to connect to Microsoft based on the server information you supplied. When it is successful, your Exchange/Outlook/Office 365 contacts begin to appear on the screen.

Linking to Twitter

Linking the People app to Twitter is a simple process. Follow these six steps to see tweets from your Twitter friends in Windows:

1. From the People app, open the Charms bar and select **Settings**. The Settings screen appears on the right.

2. Select **Accounts**. A screen with a list of the accounts that have been set up so far appears (see Figure 13.15).

FIGURE 13.15

You can see which accounts you have linked to so far.

3. Select **Add an Account**.

4. Select **Twitter**.

5. Click **Connect**. The screen shown in Figure 13.16 appears, in which you enter the username (or email) and password of your Twitter account.

6. Enter the username (or email) and password of your Twitter account. Do not enter the @ symbol at the beginning of your username. Select **Remember Me** so you don't have to enter your Twitter username and password again. Then select **Authorize App**.

7. A screen stating You're Ready to Go appears. Click **Done**, which is the last step in linking to Twitter. In a short time, persons and organizations you follow in Twitter appear, and their tweets appear in What's New.

FIGURE 13.16

Enter your Twitter username and password.

Linking to LinkedIn

Follow these steps to link People to LinkedIn. You need the email address and password you use to sign in to LinkedIn. When connected, your professional contacts in LinkedIn appear.

1. Start the People app.

2. Open the Charms bar and then select **Settings**. You see the Settings screen fly out from the right.

3. Select **Accounts**. The Accounts screen appears, where you can see the list of the networks and/or email accounts that have been set up so far.

4. Select **Add an Account**. A screen appears that presents the accounts and networks you can set up in People.

5. Select **LinkedIn**. The screen shown in Figure 13.17 appears.

FIGURE 13.17

Windows offers to show you a bit more information before you connect to LinkedIn.

6. Select **Connect**. After you do so, Windows connects with LinkedIn for you to sign in, as shown in Figure 13.18.

7. Enter the email address and password you use to sign in to LinkedIn. Leave Access Duration set to Until Revoked, which means your People account will remain linked to LinkedIn until you purposely disconnect the link.

8. Select **OK, I'll Allow It**. Select **Done** from the next screen that appears, and in a few minutes, your LinkedIn contacts begin to appear.

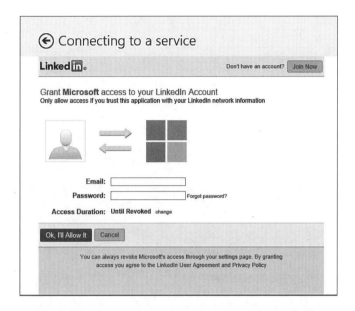

FIGURE 13.18

Windows requires your LinkedIn username and password to create the link to the People app.

THE ABSOLUTE MINIMUM

- The People app links to the social media networks plus your email accounts to show you all your posts, notifications, photos, likes, and comments, plus those of your friends and contacts, in one place.

- The People app connects to Google, Exchange servers, Hotmail, Twitter, LinkedIn, and Facebook.

- You must supply the username (or email address) and password you use to sign in to the networks and accounts you want to see in People. In most cases, you can choose to create an account that opens a web browser to allow you to create your account directly on the website.

- The People app is an address book that includes social media content. The What's New page shows you the latest content from the social media networks you connect to. The Me page shows content sent to you or from you.

14

SETTING UP AND USING EMAIL

This chapter introduces the updated Mail app in Windows 8.1. Like the People, Calendar, News, and many other apps, Mail is launched directly from the Start screen.

There are certainly email apps, many of which run from the Desktop, available in the market with more features than those found in Mail. You might find a suitable replacement in the Windows Store, or you can use an email program you used previously with an older version of Windows. But this app is free, and it is extremely easy to use.

If your primary need is to exchange email with family and friends, including sending and receiving pictures and other attachments, this app should be perfect for you. It is integrated with all the important parts of Windows, such as displaying all your contacts when you address your message. This chapter leads you through the Mail app, explaining everything you need to know to use it and to set it up.

Because Mail relies on many of the techniques covered in Chapter 1, "Your First Hour with Windows 8," you should refer to that chapter if you need help, or perhaps review the entire chapter if you need a refresher. Pay particular attention to these features, which play an important role in this chapter:

- Display the App bar, which reveals several formatting commands you can use to dress up your email.
- Open the Settings charm, where you specify the various email accounts you can consolidate in the Mail app.

Exploring the Mail App

To start the Mail app, select the Mail tile on the Start screen, as shown in Figure 14.1.

After starting the Mail app, you see a short bit of animation before the app starts. Depending on how many email accounts are set up in your Mail app, your screen will look more or less like the one shown in Figure 14.2. Your list of accounts and folders appears on the left in the Navigation bar. The middle pane shows a messages list containing the messages in the folder currently selected in the Navigation bar. The message selected appears in the message pane on the right.

FIGURE 14.1

Select the Mail tile to launch the Mail app.

FIGURE 14.2

The initial view of the Mail app shows your accounts and folders, your Inbox, and the selected message.

 NOTE If the account you use to sign in to Windows is a Microsoft account, an email account is set up automatically for you using the same credentials you use to sign in.

Setting Up Your Email Accounts

One of the best features of the Mail app is how it brings together your email from all sources. To see all your email, you need to set up the Mail app to retrieve and send mail from the different email services you use. The Mail app works with the following email providers:

- **Outlook.com**—Microsoft's web email service is known as Outlook.com (previously named Hotmail); you may at times see it referred to on the Web as Microsoft Email or Live Mail. Regardless of the name, Outlook.com is Microsoft's primary email service, and the Mail app has been updated with Outlook.com in mind.

- **Gmail**—Gmail is Google's email service. You can learn about Google's email service at www.google.com.

- **Exchange**—The Exchange option in the Mail app is a catch-all for email accounts you have in Microsoft's new online email at Outlook.com, Office 365, which is Microsoft's collaboration and business cloud solution, and email accounts through Exchange, which is used almost exclusively by corporate customers. Many users view their Microsoft Exchange email with Microsoft Outlook, which runs on the Desktop. The Mail app is one of the first apps that enable users to retrieve their Exchange email without Outlook.

- **AOL**—AOL is now supported in the Mail app.

- **Yahoo**—Yahoo is a popular email service that is now supported in the Mail app.

- **Other**—You can manually configure email accounts that use IMAP or EAS (POP is not currently supported; however, many accounts offer more than one protocol for configuring an email client).

You can create as many accounts in the Mail app as you need. If you use just one email service, and the service meets your needs, there is no reason to create more accounts. When you're ready to add an email account, follow these steps to set up any email account in the app:

1. Start the Mail app.

2. Open the Settings charm and select **Accounts**. A screen appears with a list of the mail accounts that have been set up so far.

3. Select **Add an Account.** A screen like the one shown in Figure 14.3 appears, with a list of the email services you can set up.

From here, check out the following section that applies to the type of email account you want to set up.

FIGURE 14.3

Select an email service.

Setting Up Your Google, Yahoo, AOL, or Outlook.com Account

To set up your Google, Yahoo, AOL, or Outlook.com account with the Mail app, start with the three steps at the end of the preceding "Setting Up Your Email Accounts" section and then continue with the followings steps:

1. Select **Google, Yahoo, AOL,** or **Outlook.com**. A screen like the one shown in Figure 14.4 appears.

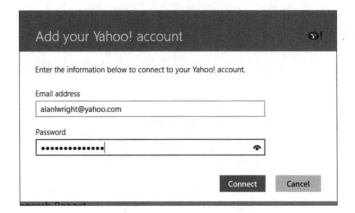

FIGURE 14.4

Yahoo requires just two pieces of information to connect to the server.

2. Enter the email address and password for your account.

   To verify you entered your password correctly, tap and hold or click and hold the **Password Preview** button at the end of the Password box.

3. Select **Connect**. The Mail app connects to the email provider to complete setting up your account. Your new account appears at the bottom of the list of accounts in the Navigation bar.

 TIP Be sure you enter your full email address in the Email Address field, including the **@yahoo.com** portion.

Setting Up Your Exchange/Office 365/Outlook.com Account

To set up your Exchange/Office 365/Outlook.com account with the Mail app, start with the three steps at the end of the "Setting Up Your Email Accounts" section and then continue with the followings steps:

1. Select **Exchange**.

2. Enter the email address and password for your account.

   To verify you entered your password correctly, tap and hold or click and hold the **Password Preview** button at the end of the Password box.

3. If you are setting up an account to pull email from Exchange or Office 365, select **Show More Details**. Fill in the domain and server fields as needed. You can learn the values for these fields from your administrator or from information on the service's site, if one is available.

4. Select **Connect**. The Mail app connects to the Exchange server to complete setting up your account. Your new account appears at the bottom of the list of accounts in the Navigation bar.

> **NOTE**   Outlook accounts enjoy a special relationship with the Mail app in Windows. In addition to the management features that can be used with any email account, you will find a few extra features. Sweep is a powerful tool when you need to delete emails. Pinned favorite contacts, social updates, and newsletters are additional tools that appear on the Navigation bar when viewing your Outlook.com account.

Manually Setting Up an Email Account Using IMAP or EAS

To set up an email account manually with the Mail app, start with the three steps at the end of the "Setting Up Your Email Accounts" section and then continue with the followings steps:

1. Select **Other Account**.

2. Select **Exchange Activesync (EAS)** or **IMAP**, as shown in Figure 14.5. Select **Connect**.

3. Enter the email address and password for your account.

    To verify you entered your password correctly, tap and hold or click and hold the **Password Preview** button at the end of the Password box.

4. If you are setting up an account to pull email from Exchange or using specific IMAP server and port settings (see Figure 14.6), select **Show More Details**. Fill in the domain, server, and port fields as needed. You can learn the values for these fields from your administrator or from information on the service's site, if one is available. ·

5. Select **Connect**. The Mail app connects to the email server to complete setting up your account. Your new account appears at the bottom of the list of accounts in the Navigation bar.

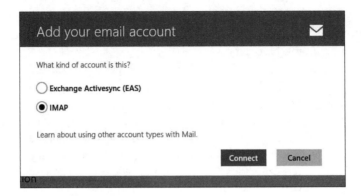

FIGURE 14.5

You can manually configure IMAP and EAS settings to bring an email account into the Mail app.

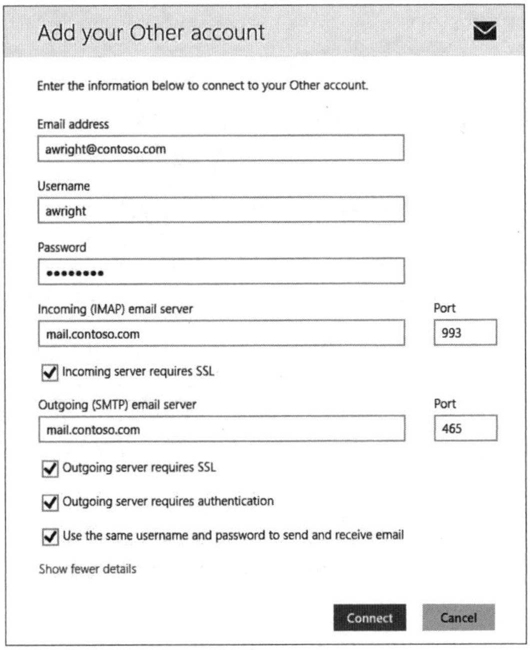

FIGURE 14.6

The Mail app provides a nice interface to configure IMAP settings.

After you have set up your email accounts, you can easily go back and tweak any settings that you need to. Select the Settings charm, and then select Accounts. Select one of the accounts you have already created to view the current settings (see Figure 14.7). Change how notifications occur, how long messages are kept locally, if external images are downloaded, the default email signature, account credentials, and server and port information. Settings that you can configure are unique to each email account.

FIGURE 14.7

Adjust settings and customize how an account is configured from the Accounts pane.

Reading Your Email

The Mail app retrieves email from your accounts every few minutes. To force the Mail app to retrieve mail right away, open the App bar and select **Sync**.

It's easy to read through email messages you receive. Return to the home screen by selecting the large back-arrow button on the top-left corner of each screen. The bottom of the list on the left side of the screen shows each of your accounts. You may find that not all email accounts display the same way. Outlook accounts provide additional features on the Navigation bar, for example, than would a Gmail account (compare Figures 14.2 and 14.8). When you select an account, the folders and features for that account appear.

To read a message, select the message from the list of messages in your Inbox. The message you select appears in the Message pane on the right side of the screen. To see the messages in a different folder, select the folder from the Navigation bar, and then select the message.

 NOTE Depending on the resolution of your screen, you might not see the Message pane, which is on the right side of the screen. If you are sharing the screen or your resolution is too low, you might see just the Navigation pane and the message list.

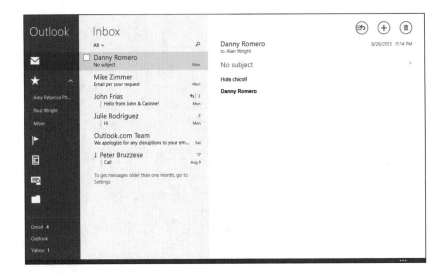

FIGURE 14.8

The home page in the Mail app enables you to see email from each account you set up.

Replying to a Message

You can send a reply to a message you receive. You can send your reply message just to the author of the message you received, or send your message to everyone who received the original message. You can attach other documents or pictures to a reply, and you can format your reply however you like.

To reply to an email, follow these steps:

1. Select the message to which you want to reply.

2. On the top-right corner of the screen, select the **Respond** button. Then select **Reply** or **Reply All** on the menu that appears, as shown in Figure 14.9.

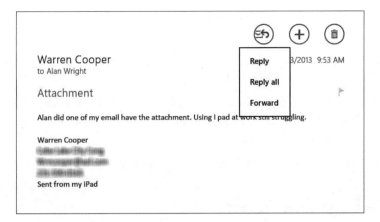

FIGURE 14.9

You can reply to only the sender, reply to everyone on the original email, or forward the message to a new recipient using the Reply menu.

3. Write your reply message, as shown in Figure 14.10.

FIGURE 14.10

Type your reply message.

4. Format the message based on the instructions in the "Formatting Your Email" section later in this chapter.

5. Address the reply message using the instructions in the "Addressing Your Message" section later in this chapter.

6. To send a file with your message, such as a photo or a spreadsheet, follow the instructions in the "Attaching a Photo or Another File to Your Message" section later in this chapter.

7. Select the **Send** button. Your message is sent.

Filing a Message in a Folder

You can reduce the clutter in your Inbox not only by deleting messages that have no value but also by filing messages that do. You can create folders to organize your email. You can usually file your messages into those folders on the email service websites, such as on Google's Gmail page, or with other email services. These folders are visible in the Mail app. Here is how the folders work:

- When you create a folder in your webmail account, the folder appears in the Mail app in that service's list of folders.

- When you file a message in a folder using your webmail account, the message appears in the folder in the Mail app.

- When you file a message in a folder using the Mail app, the message is filed in the folder with the email service.

In Windows 8.1 you can finally use drag-and-drop to move messages from your Inbox to a folder, or vice versa. You also can use the Move tool from the App bar to file a message in a folder in the Mail app. Here are the steps:

1. Select the message to file.

2. Display the App bar and select **Move**, as shown in Figure 14.11.

3. Select the folder in which you want to store the message. The message is moved to the folder you pick.

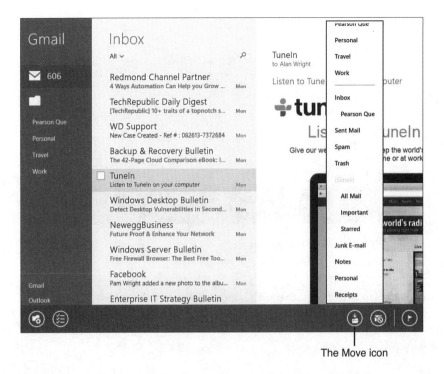

The Move icon

FIGURE 14.11

You can file a message in any of the folders created with your email service.

Deleting a Message

If you no longer need a message, you can delete it. The message disappears from your Inbox.

To delete a message, select the message to delete. Then, select the **Delete** button on the top-right corner of the screen. The button is shaped like a trash can. When using a mouse, you can also hover briefly over a message directly in the list of messages, wait for the trash can icon to appear, and click it.

When using your Outlook email account, you can also use the Sweep tool, new in Windows 8.1, to reveal additional delete options. With your message selected, reveal the App bar and look for the Sweep icon, which looks like a broom. As shown in Figure 14.12, you can choose to delete all messages from a sender, anything older than 10 days, or all but the most recent message. You can also choose to keep this choice enabled going forward.

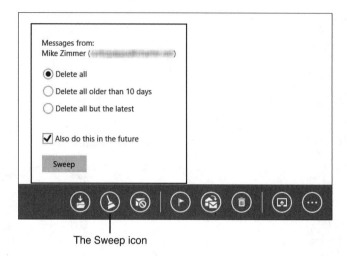

The Sweep icon

FIGURE 14.12

Use Sweep to perform quick maintenance on your email account.

Forward a Message

When you forward a message, you send a message you received to someone else who did not receive it in the first place.

To forward a message, follow these steps:

1. Select the message to forward.

2. Select the **Respond** button; then select **Forward** from the menu that appears (refer to Figure 14.10).

3. You can add your own text to the message you are forwarding. Your message appears above the forwarded message. To add your own message to the email you're forwarding, type it just as you would a normal reply. Format your message, if you choose, following the instructions in the "Formatting Your Message" section.

4. Address the message to be forwarded using the instructions in the "Addressing Your Email Message" section.

5. Select the **Send** button.

Mark a Message as Unread

When you select a message by clicking it, tapping it, or moving the focus to the message using the arrow keys, the message appears in the Viewing pane. If you don't select another message or if you don't leave the Viewing pane in five seconds, your message is marked as read (removing its bold formatting). This system of formatting messages differently for those you have read makes it easy to see quickly what messages are new and deserve your attention. Though some experts suggest that using the read/unread status is a poor method to manage your Inbox, you can easily switch a message back to unread if you know you want to go back to it later.

To mark a message as unread, select it, display the App bar, and select **Mark Unread**. When using a mouse, you can also hover briefly over a message directly in the list of messages to toggle the Read/Unread setting.

Managing Junk Mail

Spam filters have improved greatly over the years. That doesn't mean some junk won't get through, especially if it's something you've signed up for. To send an email to your Junk folder using an Outlook.com email account, just select the message in your inbox. From the App bar select the junk email icon, an envelope with a slashed circle symbol, and the message is moved to the Junk folder.

To get a message back that you accidently marked as junk, open the Junk folder from the list of folders. Select the message and open the Apps bar as shown in Figure 14.13. Select the not junk icon, an envelope with a checkmark, and your message is returned to the inbox.

Junk mail folders are a standard feature for any email service, however they may have slight differences from the Outlook.com example used here. The junk folder in Gmail for example, is named Junk E-mail and the Mail app does not seem to work correctly because of this difference.

Not Junk

FIGURE 14.13

Return an email to your inbox that you accidentally marked as junk mail.

Writing an Email Message

Writing an email is a simple process. You write your message, format it as you like, address the message, and then select the **Send** button. There are no restrictions on the type of message you send. You can attach a picture or another document to a message and send it without any text of your own. Or you can write a 20-page letter if you choose. You can write a grocery list in an email message, or you can write a resignation letter to your employer.

To write a message, follow these steps:

1. Select the **New** button, as shown in Figure 14.14.

2. If you have more than one account set up in the app, select the down-arrow button next to your name. Select the account from which you want to send the email, as shown in Figure 14.15. If you have one account, move to step 3.

The New button

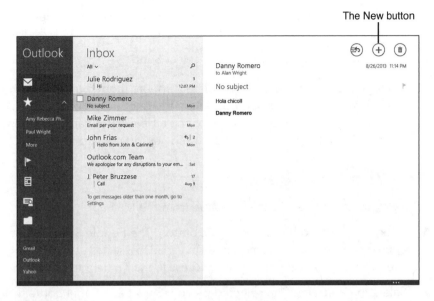

FIGURE 14.14

Select the New button to write a new email message.

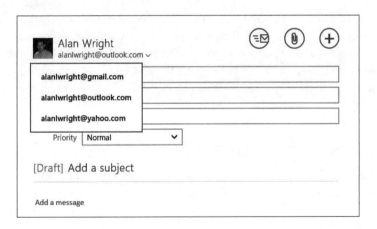

FIGURE 14.15

Select the account from which the message will be sent.

3. Type your message and subject.

4. Address your message using the instructions in the "Addressing Your Message" section.

5. Format your message using the instructions in the "Formatting Your Email Message" section.

6. To send a file with your message, such as a photo or a spreadsheet, follow the instructions in the "Attaching a Photo or Another File to Your Message" section.

7. If your message is ready to be sent, select **Send**.

Newly created email messages immediately appear tagged as a [Draft] message until you either send the message or delete the draft (refer to Figure 14.15). This means you can jump to another app or open a different email without having to retype your email. It appears as a draft when you go back to finish it up.

Addressing Your Message

Follow these steps to address a message from the Mail app:

1. Click or tap the **To** button or the **Cc** button. The People Selector screen appears. Although you can enter as many addresses as you like in the Cc list, you must have at least one email address in the To field to send the message.

2. Select the portrait of the selected person. Select additional portraits until you have selected all recipients. Then select **Add**.

3. Repeat steps 1 and 2 to select recipients for the other list.

4. To secretly add recipients to the message, select **More Details**, which appears below the addresses of the recipients you selected in steps 1 and 2. When the Bcc field appears, choose the recipients you want to include. When your message is viewed by those recipients, they will not see any of the other addresses you might have included in this list, nor will any other recipients see their address.

Formatting Your Email Message

The Mail app has a number of options you can use to format and personalize your email message. You can use colors, different fonts, and some text options, such as bold, italic, and so on. You can also use emoticons to add personality to your message.

Using Text Formatting

To format the text in your message, select the text. To select text, click and drag with the mouse or press and drag with your finger over the characters to format. The App bar opens automatically when text is selected and displays the formatting commands, as shown in Figure 14.16. Figure 14.17 shows examples of the formatting commands in use.

The App bar reveals several formatting options.

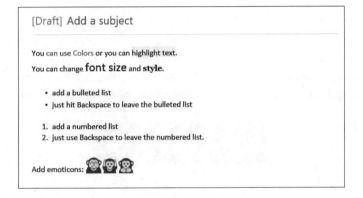

FIGURE 14.17

This screen shows examples of some of the formatting commands.

Using Emoticons

Who doesn't like a smiley face or a cheeseburger in messages they write? You can easily add emoticons to your messages. The Mail app has a surprising large library of emoticons to help you add character to your emails.

To add an emoticon to your message, do the following:

1. Click, tap, or use the arrow keys to move the cursor to the location in the message where you want the emoticon to appear.

2. Display the App bar and select the **Emoticons** button.

3. Select the category and the symbol you like. You can add as many as you like while the emoticons fly-out panel is on the screen. To select an emoticon, do one of the following:

   - Click it with your mouse.

   - Tap it with your finger or stylus.

   - Use the arrow keys to move the focus to the emoticon you want. Press the **spacebar** to select the emoticon.

4. Continue writing your email. The emoticon fly-out screen closes.

Adjusting and Removing Formatting

You can also adjust your default formatting by selecting a font, size, and color. Select the Settings charm and select **Options**. From the Message font section, make your choices for fonts from the available choices, as shown in Figure 14.18. The Sample Text shows how your text will appear by default in new messages.

FIGURE 14.18

Select your default font choices for new email messages from the Settings charm under Options.

If you get carried away with formatting, you can undo all formatting by selecting the ellipses (on the App bar) to show More Options. This reveals Undo, Redo, and Clear Formatting.

Attaching a Photo or Another File to Your Message

To send one or more files with your email, such as a photo, select **Attachments** (look for the paperclip icon) above and to the right of the address fields. The File Picker window appears, as shown in Figure 14.19. The File Picker is a tool used throughout Windows 8.1 for navigating through the folders on your system and then choosing a file.

FIGURE 14.19

Select attachments using the File Picker tool.

Find the file you want to attach by moving through the folder and drives on your computer. Select the file by clicking or tapping it once. Then select **Attach**. You can attach more than one file by selecting additional files before you select **Attach**. You can click Attachments a second time to add more files to your email.

Checking Spelling in Your Message

If you are even mildly embarrassed to have an email you sent appear in your recipient's Inbox with spelling errors or typing mistakes, it makes sense to take advantage of the built-in spell check in Windows 8.1. The spell-check features are universal in Windows, which means you don't need to turn spell check on or off in each application you use.

There are two features available:

- **Highlight misspelled words as you type them**. This feature also enables you to correct the word or add the word as you spelled it to the dictionary. These two functions are carried out by right-clicking or tapping and holding on the highlighted word.

- **Autocorrect words as you type**. This feature fixes some misspelled words as they are typed. You can try this on your own. Create a new email message and type **hte**. With the autocorrect feature turned on, you should see the word you typed be corrected to "the."

To turn the spelling features on or off, follow these steps:

1. Select the Settings charm, and select **Change PC Settings**.

2. Select the **PC and Devices** group of PC Settings.

3. Under Typing, move the slider to the left for Off or the right for On for the Autocorrect Misspelled Words and for the Highlight Misspelled Words options.

Managing Your Inbox

With the updated Mail app in Windows 8.1, you have many practical tools at your disposal for managing your email. You can create new folders in the Mail app, and these new folders will be synced and appear when accessing your email from a web browser for services like Gmail. You can pin folders to your Navigation bar to simplify access. You can choose to have emails appear grouped by conversation and choose whether to include original emails in your replies. Figure 14.20 showed you several options for the Message List. Use the On/Off sliders to make the following changes:

- **Group Messages by Conversation**—Use this switch to view emails separately based on time stamps in your Inbox or to see emails grouped that are part of the same conversation. This is On by default.

- **Show Messages from Sent Items in Conversations**—This allows you to reply to an email with the previous message included in the conversation. This is useful when time has elapsed or if important details need to be readily available to all parties in a conversation. This is On by default.

- **When an Unread Message Is Selected, Mark as Read**—This allows you to turn the default behavior Off if you would rather manually mark emails as read.

Creating Folders

Folders are often used to organize email. Creating new folders and pinning folders can be managed from within the Mail app.

To create a new folder, follow these steps:

1. Open the App bar and select the Manage folders (or in some cases Folder options) icon on the far left, as shown in Figure 14.20.

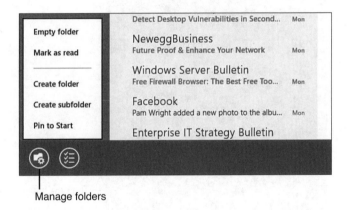

Manage folders

FIGURE 14.20

Use the Manage folders icon to create new folders.

2. Select **Create folder** (or **Create subfolder**). A pop-up appears. Type in the name of the new folder and select **OK** (see Figure 14.21).

3. Another pop-up appears, stating that the new folder has been created. Select **OK**.

4. On the Navigation bar, select the folder icon to reveal your folders as shown in Figure 14.22. Your new folder will appear in this list.

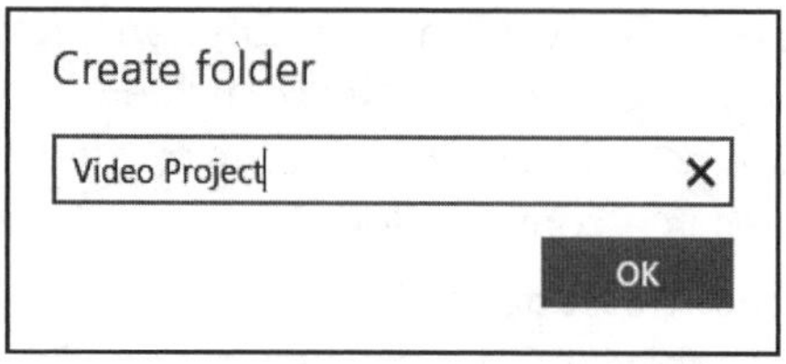

FIGURE 14.21

Type in a name for your new email folder.

FIGURE 14.22

From the Navigation bar, you can see your folders.

To pin a folder to the Navigation bar, follow these steps:

1. Select the folder icon on the Navigation bar, as shown in Figure 14.22.

2. Next to the folder you want to pin, select the star icon to add the folder to the Navigation bar. To remove a pinned folder, deselect the Add Icon from Here.

Flagging Messages

Flags can be very useful when you want to make sure you can find important mail again later. This feature may not be available for every email account you use. Outlook and Yahoo are two examples of services that work well with this feature.

To flag a message, you can do the following:

- Hover over a message in the message list using your mouse pointer to select the flag icon.

- Select the flag tool to the right of the subject line in an open email message.

- Open the App bar and insert a flag.

Flagged messages appear together on the Navigation bar under the flagged icon regardless of which folder they may be located in (see Figure 14.23). To remove a flag, select the flag again to disable it. The message will still remain in its folder; it will no longer appear with the Flagged messages when this group is refreshed.

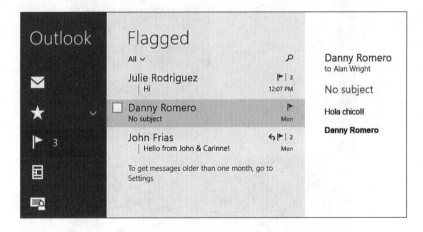

FIGURE 14.23

Flagged messages appear in a special list on the Navigation bar.

Printing Emails

From time to time, you may need to print emails as part of your management process. Perhaps you want to keep hard copies of receipts or information needs to be filed away in case questions arise later. The Mail app does not currently offer many options for printing emails; it hands the particulars off to Windows.

Depending on which printers you are connected to, you may see several printers or just a few choices. As with most things in Windows, there is more than one way to print. Perhaps the easiest way is through the Devices charm.

To print an email, follow these steps:

1. Select an email that you want to print and then open the Devices charm.

2. Select **Print**.

3. From the list of printers, select the printer you want to use.

4. You will see a preview of the print job and options that are unique to your printer for paper, color, orientation, and source settings (see Figure 14.24). Make your choices and select **Print**.

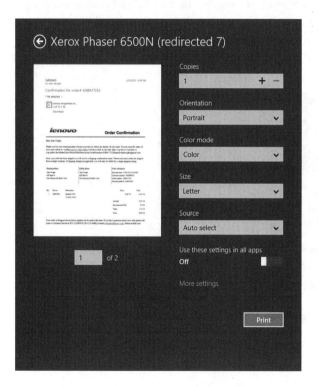

FIGURE 14.24

Make selections to control how your email will print from the Windows 8.1 Print pane.

THE ABSOLUTE MINIMUM

- The Mail app is provided for free with Windows 8.1. You probably can find email programs with more functionality, but not likely so many additional toys and features as to justify paying for a program when the Mail app is free.

- You can bring together into the Mail app your email from many of your accounts and services, including Microsoft Exchange, Google, Yahoo, and more. This means you can read email from all accounts in one place but still author and send emails from any account you choose.

- When you're writing an email, the App bar includes multiple formatting and email authoring tools, including colors, attachments, font choices, and even emoticons.

- You set up email accounts from the System Settings pane, which you reach by selecting **Settings** from the Charms bar. Settings for the message you are working on, such as formatting and folders, are reached from the App bar.

- Use Manage folder tools to create and organize your email from within the Mail app.

- Use the Device charm to print emails from the Mail app to any of your installed printers.

15

MANAGING YOUR CALENDAR

Windows 8 provides an integrated Calendar app that has been improved with Windows 8.1. The app is one of the Windows 8-style apps, which means it matches the Modern UI style used in the Mail People apps. Although the Calendar app is extremely easy to use, it has a few elements that deserve a bit more explanation. For example, you can synchronize your calendar with calendars you maintain online. You can create events and respond to invitations in the Calendar app, see those events appear in your online calendar, and invite your contacts listed in the People app.

Getting to Know the Calendar App

The Calendar app provides you a view of your calendar, as well as scheduling and event scheduling abilities. Here is a list of the things you can do with the Calendar app:

- Schedule one-time meetings and events.
- Schedule regular, recurring events.
- Set reminders so that you're notified before scheduled events.
- Review your calendar in a day view, a monthly view, or a weekly view.

To start the Calendar app, select the Calendar tile on the Start screen, as shown in Figure 15.1. When the Calendar app opens, the view you last used—daily, weekly, monthly—appears automatically, as shown in Figure 15.2.

FIGURE 15.1

You start the Calendar app by selecting the Calendar tile on the Start screen.

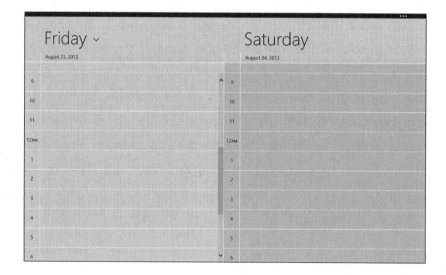

FIGURE 15.2

The two-day daily view appears automatically because it was the view last used.

Controlling the Calendar View

You can review your calendar in five different views: What's Next, Day, Work Week, Week, and Month. You can easily change from one view to another. To do so, display the App bar, and then select the view you prefer, as shown in Figure 15.3.

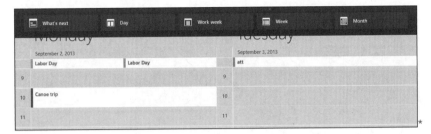

FIGURE 15.3

You change views by making a choice from the App bar.

The What's Next view is a new feature in the Calendar app that allows you to have a dashboard view of upcoming appointments and activities. You can customize the appearance of this view by selecting an image for a background, as shown in Figure 15.4. Select an upcoming meeting, for example, to view details from your calendar.

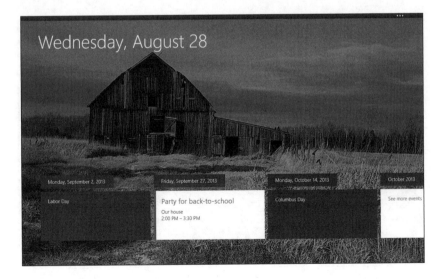

FIGURE 15.4

The What's Next view provides a dashboard display of upcoming entries in your calendar.

The Work Week view displays a traditional Monday through Friday work week with details for each day similar to the Week view. The Week view shows up to 14 hours in a day and 7 days of the week. The default setting uses Sunday as the first day of the week. The Week view is shown in Figure 15.5, whereas the Month view is shown in Figure 15.6.

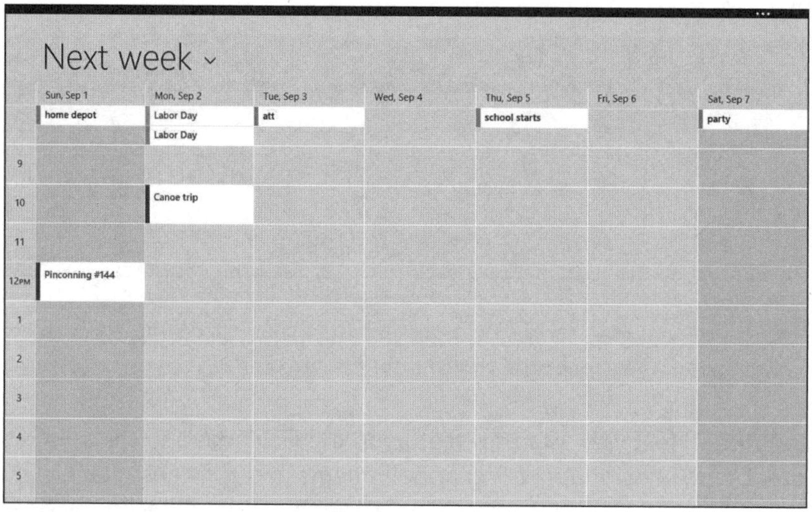

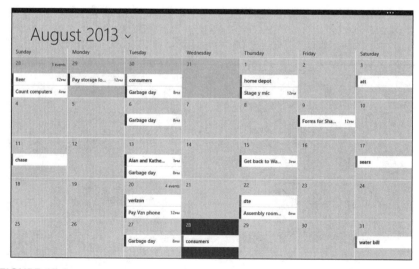

FIGURE 15.5

The Week view provides details for each day of the week.

FIGURE 15.6

The Month view shows the current month, plus a number of days from the prior and next month.

You can scroll to a different date from any day, week, or month view by swiping or scrolling with a mouse wheel. Each of these views includes arrow buttons you can select to move to the next or previous date. You can quickly switch to a different date by selecting the down arrow next to the title for the current view, as shown in Figure 15.7. This opens a calendar that you can use to navigate to a different month and select the date you want to switch to. At any time you can use this floating calendar pane to jump to the present day by choosing the Today button below the calendar (refer to Figure 15.7).

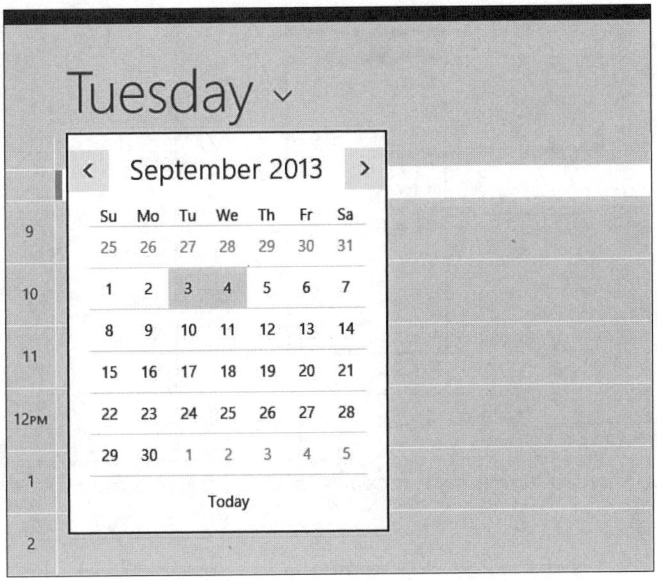

FIGURE 15.7

Use the floating calendar pane to quickly jump to a different date or to today.

Setting Calendar Colors

If you have set up just one account with the Calendar app, all events appear in the same color. A different color is used for events for each additional account you set up in the Calendar app. To set the colors used for each calendar, as well as to hide or show certain calendars, open the Charms bar and select **Settings**. Then select **Options**. The Options pane shown in Figure 15.8 appears. Select the list under each calendar to select the color. You may have to scroll down to see other calendars. To hide a calendar, move the slider left to the Hide position. You can also select whether birthdays and holidays appear from each calendar with their unique color choices.

FIGURE 15.8

You can specify a different color for each calendar you've added to the app.

Synchronizing with Other Calendars

If you maintain a calendar online using Microsoft Outlook, Hotmail, or Live, you can synchronize those calendars in the Calendar app. You can also synchronize the Calendar app with Microsoft Exchange, which is useful if you use Microsoft Outlook to read and write email at work.

When you synchronize your calendar with Outlook.com, Exchange, or Hotmail, any events scheduled on the online Calendar appear on your Windows 8 calendar, merged with any appointments or events you entered here. You can synchronize your calendar with multiple accounts, although they must be Microsoft based (Outlook, Exchange, and the like). You can see all your appointments booked on all your calendars in one place, including appointments on family members' calendars or work or corporate appointments.

Follow the steps in the next sections to set up the Calendar app to work with these services.

Connecting to Your Hotmail Account

Hotmail has been Microsoft's email, contacts, and calendar service for 15 years. It has been replaced with Outlook.com, even though you may see Hotmail branding referred to now and then. Hotmail refers to Microsoft's Live online platform. You can synchronize the Windows 8 People and Mail apps with Hotmail's email and contacts service, as well.

Follow these steps to connect your calendar to your Outlook.com/Hotmail/Live account.

1. Start the Calendar app.

2. Open the Charms bar, and then select the **Settings** charm.

3. Select **Accounts**. Another pane flies out; this one has a list of the calendars you have connected to, if any (see Figure 15.9). If you sign in to Windows with a Microsoft account, the account you used to sign in is already set up in the Calendar app.

FIGURE 15.9

The Accounts pane shows the calendars you have connected to.

4. Select **Add an Account**. When you do so, a screen appears, showing the online services you can connect to.

5. Select **Outlook**. The Add Your Outlook.com Account screen displays, as shown in Figure 15.10.

6. Enter your email address and password in the fields provided. To verify you entered your password correctly, tap and hold or click and hold the Password Preview button at the end of the Password box.

7. Select **Connect**. The Calendar app connects to Outlook to complete setting up your account. Shortly, the Calendar app synchs to your Outlook account, and you can see events and appointments on your Outlook calendar appear in your calendar in Windows 8.

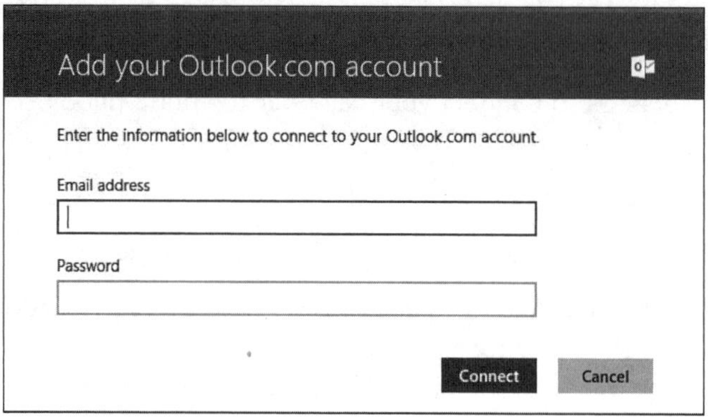

FIGURE 15.10

Outlook.com requires just two pieces of information to connect to the server.

Connecting to Microsoft Accounts

You can use the Exchange option to set up Exchange and Office 365 in addition to the new Outlook mail, which replaced Hotmail, to synchronize your calendar. Microsoft's server calendar, email, and contacts platform is Exchange, and Office 365 is a cloud-based office and collaboration platform. Almost all users integrate their Microsoft Exchange calendar with Microsoft Outlook, which runs on the Desktop. The Windows 8 Calendar app is one of the first apps that enables users to retrieve their Exchange calendar without Outlook.

1. Start the Calendar app.

2. Open the Charms bar, and then select the **Settings** charm.

3. Select **Accounts**. A screen flies out from the right showing the list of the calendars you have connected to, if any (refer to Figure 15.9).

4. Click the **Add an Account** button. When you do so, a screen appears showing the online services you can connect to.

5. Select **Exchange**. The Add Your Exchange Account screen displays (refer to Figure 15.11).

6. Enter your email address and password in the fields provided. To verify you entered your password correctly, tap and hold or click and hold the Password Preview button at the end of the Password box.

7. Select **Show More Details** to enter the server name and domain name, as shown in Figure 15.11. This information can be provided by the help information available at the account you are synching with.

8. Select **Connect**. The Calendar app connects to Microsoft to complete setting up your account. Shortly, the Calendar app synchs to your account and you can see events and appointments on your Outlook/Exchange/Office 365 calendar appear in your calendar in Windows 8.

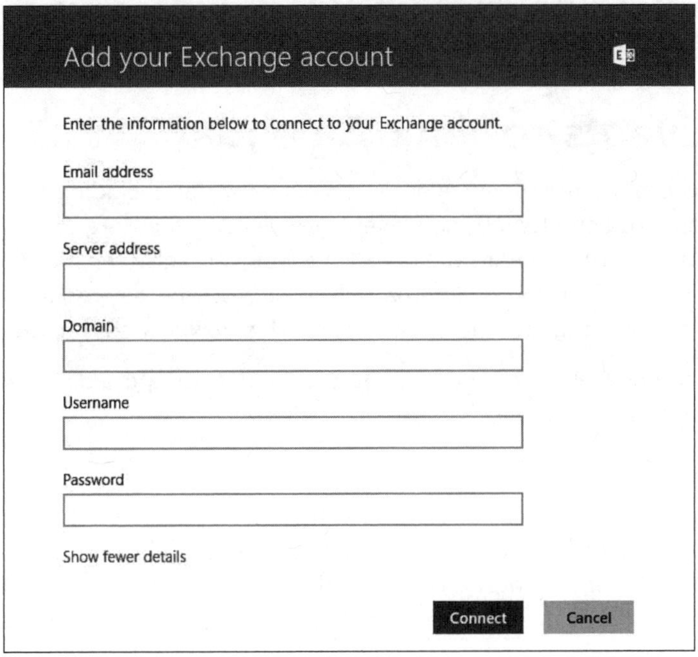

FIGURE 15.11

Outlook.com requires just two pieces of information to connect to the server, whereas Exchange may need more details.

Connecting to Your Gmail Account

Gmail is Google's email and calendar service. Google and Microsoft are rivals on many fronts, most notably involving web search (Google vs. Bing), web browsers (Internet Explorer vs. Chrome), operating systems (Windows vs. Chrome), and email with calendar support. This rivalry has created an uncooperative spirit that affects how easily you can sync with Google services from a Windows device. This is a situation that changes from month to month; at the time of this writing, there is no option to sync a Google calendar to your Calendar app. Without pointing fingers, the way the Calendar app syncs with online calendars is no longer supported by Google. This might change because consumer pressure is strong on this issue to have Microsoft and Google resolve their differences.

If you use a Gmail account as your Live ID, you will be able to see your calendar synced by default, and Google has indicated it will support individual accounts for a period of time. In the future, Windows 8.1 may be updated to allow you once again to add Google calendars to the list of online calendars you can sync to. In the meantime, feel free to let both sides know that you want to see this feature restored and an end to the dispute.

Adding Events to Your Calendar

You can easily enter a new event into your calendar, including inviting others to the event. You create your new event by selecting the date of your new event. Then you enter the details of your event. You can enter most of the details of your event by choosing from ready-made lists, such as the day, hour, frequency, duration of the event, and if the event recurs. This makes it easy to create your event.

To enter a new event directly into your calendar using the day or week views, follow these steps:

1. Open the Calendar app.

2. From any day or week view, select the date of your event in the calendar. If the event will be multiday or recurring, select the first date. Select the beginning time of your event. An entry of this type has two fields to enter: What and Where. Figure 15.12 shows that What has been replaced by the event "Return AR content."

3. If your event is one hour long, you need do nothing further. If you want to show the event for a period of several hours, you can adjust one of the two adjustable brackets that mark your event on the calendar, as shown in Figure 15.12. Just select and drag the round handle.

FIGURE 15.12

You can quickly adjust the time for an event to your calendar by dragging the start and stop handles for the event.

TIP You can select any date to start creating your new event. Use the Add Details option mentioned in step 5 to switch the date of the event from the date you clicked or tapped to the correct date of your event using the event properties discussed in the next set of steps.

4. Select the down arrow to the right of the What field of your entry (see Figure 15.13).

5. The first option is to select the calendar on which the event should appear. To configure additional details select **Add Details**; otherwise, you can click elsewhere on the screen to save the entry to your calendar as is.

FIGURE 15.13

You can quickly add an event to your calendar with minimal effort.

6. Clicking **Add Details** opens the Details pane shown in Figure 15.14. You can add and edit information using text entry and choosing from drop-down lists.

7. To display an End date, select **Custom** from the How Long field.

8. Select **Show More** to reveal additional fields for recurrence, reminders, and status.

 NOTE Don't forget this important point: The event you create will also appear in the calendar on the site of the service whose calendar you choose. So if you select, for example, your Outlook account, the event appears on all devices syncing to your Outlook calendar as well as the calendar at Outlook.com.

9. When all details are correct, select the Save icon in the upper right.

10. If you decide you do not want this event on the calendar after all, or if you want to remove an event that was entered previously, select the Delete icon located in the upper-right corner.

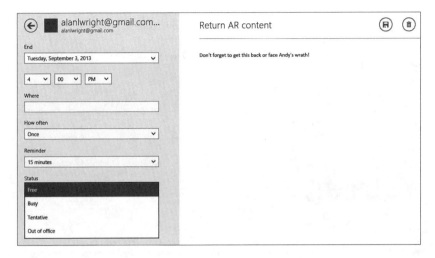

FIGURE 15.14

This screen shows the form in which you enter details of your calendar event.

From anywhere you can also select New from the App bar in the Calendar app to go straight to a blank Details pane. Select the date, the time, and enter any additional information.

Although most of the information you enter is self-explanatory, you should know about a few items as you enter information about your event:

- Any field that has a down arrow includes a list of possible values for the field. Click or tap the arrow to see the items in the list, as shown in Figure 15.14.

- If you are creating an event using Outlook or an Exchange-based calendar, you can invite others from your contacts using the Details pane. Select the Who field, as shown in Figure 15.15, to start typing in a name to select persons from your contacts to invite to your meeting. You start seeing names that match the letters you type in, and you can select from the contacts shown or keep typing to narrow the selection. Add more contacts if desired. The Save icon changes to a Send icon. Select this to save the event and send emails to your invitees at the same time. Invitees receive an email with the calendar event details, as shown in Figure 15.16 where an email has arrived in an Outlook 2013 Inbox. From your Calendar app, you can track responses from the Details pane.

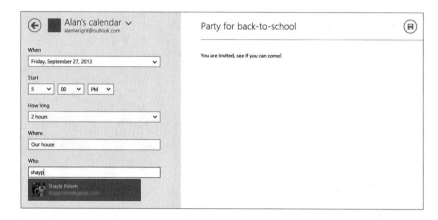

FIGURE 15.15

When using Outlook and Exchange-based calendars, you can invite contacts to an event.

FIGURE 15.16

Invitees will receive a calendar invitation, which allows them to easily update their calendar and indicate their availability.

THE ABSOLUTE MINIMUM

Keep these points in mind after you finish reading this chapter:

- You can synchronize your Windows 8 calendar with your calendar on Outlook, Live, and with a Microsoft Exchange calendar. This gives you the ability to maintain your online calendars as you always do, but bring all your calendars together in one place in Windows 8.

- You select people to invite to events you schedule from the list of persons consolidated in your People app in Windows 8 when using Exchange or Outlook calendars.

- You can schedule events in the Calendar app on the online calendars you synchronize with. This means the event appears on both the calendar in Windows 8 and on the online calendar.

16

ENJOYING YOUR DIGITAL PHOTOS IN WINDOWS

It's almost impossible to find regular people who take photos with film anymore. The moment it became cheaper and easier to snap shots on a digital camera, store pictures on a computer, make excellent prints on affordable consumer printers, and share photos on the Internet, film cameras were done. Windows 8 makes it easy to view and edit pictures you have shot, and even share photos by email or to other apps. The toolset for managing your digital photos in Windows 8.1, known as the Photos app, does not have the integrated sharing features that many people liked in the original Windows 8 release, but its new editing tools are noteworthy and worth exploring. This chapter covers the basics of the app, how to access editing tools, and how to manage your photo collection.

Before diving into this chapter, you should be familiar with the various techniques and gestures you use in Windows. In particular, it would be helpful if you understand how to open Charms, as well as the App bar. You can find instruction on these topics in Chapter 1, "Your First Hour with Windows."

Learning Photos App Basics

Everyone today likes to look at their digital photos and share pictures, too. For many, it's a race home from an event to load photos onto a computer and then upload them to a website for others to enjoy. Those with smartphones can upload photos right from the event so that the entire world can get instant visual updates of what happens! Although it's not filled to the brim with features, the Photos app provides an easy-to-use hub for your digital pictures.

The Photos app is an easy-to-use tool for reviewing your digital photographs. As shown in Figure 16.1, you can organize your pictures into folders that display a thumbnail to help you easily identify the folder contents.

FIGURE 16.1

The Photos app enables you to view your pictures stored in the Pictures library.

The span of capabilities and features in the Photos app might seem limited compared to some of the applications available in the Windows Store; you can surely find an application that creates much fancier slideshows, and dozens of sites can help you publish a stunning picture book. However, the ease of use of the Photos app can't be challenged. If you're more dedicated to photography and working with photos, perhaps the role the app can play for you is to provide a streamlined, simple, central library for your photos, enabling you to leverage other applications to do the interesting work.

To open the Photos app, select the tile shown in Figure 16.2. If you cannot locate that tile, open the **Charms** bar and then select **Search**. When the Search pane opens, enter **Photos** into the search box. Select the Photos tile from the list of results. After you do so, the Photos app opens, as shown earlier in Figure 16.1.

FIGURE 16.2

This tile opens the Photos app.

The Photos app is limited to the pictures and folders that are currently included in the Pictures folder on your device. This Pictures folder is actually a special type of folder referred to as a *library* which explains why it is labeled in the Photos app as the Pictures library. Chapter 19, "Managing Files and Folders," offers more information on libraries.

 NOTE Originally, Windows 8 offered the capability to share pictures and video from social websites. Microsoft explained that it is more practical to share photos from social apps that have been designed to work with Windows 8. Although these features may never return to the Photos app, I would be surprised if an update does not provide additional options to reach network locations or shared photos on other devices in a homegroup at the very least. After all, this can be done easily from the file picker in other Windows Store apps.

Accessing Pictures Stored on SkyDrive

Initially you will see folders and pictures of folders that you have included in your Pictures library, although it could be empty if you have not added any pictures yet. When you log in to your device using your Microsoft account, you will have access to your SkyDrive as well. To open this location, select the down arrow to the right of Pictures library, as shown in Figure 16.3, and select SkyDrive. This allows you to see pictures you may have uploaded to SkyDrive from other devices.

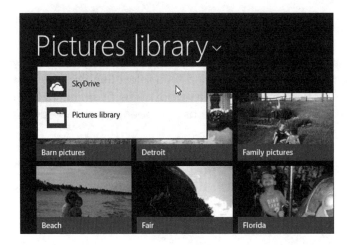

FIGURE 16.3

Select SkyDrive to browse for pictures that you keep in the cloud.

As long as you are connected to the Internet, you can open pictures stored on SkyDrive from the Photos app the same as if they were located directly on your Windows 8 device.

 NOTE SkyDrive is an online storage service designed to integrate with Microsoft products. You can read about SkyDrive in Chapter 20, "Working with SkyDrive." You can save photos to SkyDrive as easily as you can to the hard drive on your computer, and you can barely tell the difference between browsing through SkyDrive or through a local drive. As an added bonus, pictures saved to your SkyDrive are available to your other devices and are protected from unexpected loss.

Transferring Pictures from a Flash Drive

What if you want to browse through pictures stored on a USB flash drive or an external drive? At this time, you cannot browse the contents of these locations from the Photos app. If you want to edit these pictures or view them with the Photos app, you must transfer them to the Pictures folder on your device. To transfer your pictures from a USB device, follow these steps:

1. Connect your USB drive to your Windows 8 device. From the Desktop, open File Explorer to the This PC node.

2. Locate and select your connected flash drive and the folder stored on it that has the pictures you want to transfer (see Figure 16.4).

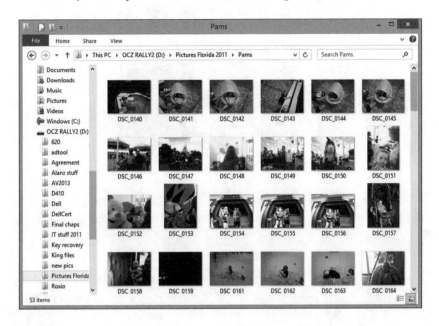

FIGURE 16.4

Locate pictures you want to add to your Pictures library using File Explorer.

3. Select the picture(s) that you want to move. To select all of them, press Ctrl+A.

4. Select the Home tab near the top of the File Explorer window and select Move To; then, from the drop-down list, select Pictures, as shown in Figure 16.5.

5. You will see a progress bar as these pictures are moved.

6. Open your Photos app and you now see these pictures in your Pictures library.

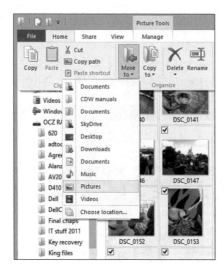

FIGURE 16.5

Use controls from File Explorer's Home tab to move or copy pictures to your Pictures library.

 CAUTION In the steps here to move pictures, you could also use Copy To in place of Move To. Copy leaves the original pictures and creates copies in the Pictures library. Move To removes the pictures from the original location, and this may not be what you wanted to do. Copy is a safer option if you are unsure.

 TIP File Explorer also lets you find pictures on network drives and libraries shared from other devices in your homegroup. Chapter 18, "Sharing Files and Printers," shows you how to share files in a homegroup.

Browsing Through Your Photos

It's very easy to browse through your photos in the Photos app. You can move forward and backward through the photo library, and you can select a photo to see a larger version in the photo gallery. Here are some tips:

- Select a folder to open it. Folders display the folder name. If in doubt, hover over the folder with your mouse pointer to reveal additional information, as shown in Figure 16.6.

- Select a photo to display the photo in full-screen mode.
- If you have opened a particular photo source in the Photos app and then drilled into one of its folders or albums, click the **Back** button to navigate back to the main Photos app home screen. If the Back button does not appear on the screen (top-left corner), click or tap once on the screen.

FIGURE 16.6

You can find out details about a folder by hovering over its tile with a mouse pointer.

You can view pictures in the gallery (a folder containing multiple photos) by swiping left or right to move back and forth in the gallery or use a scroll wheel on your mouse to navigate left and right in your folder.

The easiest way to view your photos is to launch the app's slideshow. To do so, open a picture and, from the App bar, select **Slide Show**, as shown in Figure 16.7. Your screen automatically opens each photo in the folder you are looking at.

FIGURE 16.7

Select Slide Show, grab some popcorn, and sit back to see all the photos in a folder.

The photos appear for a few seconds before the show advances to the next photo. The slideshow displays the pictures in the same order that they appear in their folder or album. There are no options to control the slideshow, such as transitions or duration.

Working with Your Photos

As you might have noticed in the App bar shown in Figure 16.8, in addition to admiring the fine photography on the screen, there are a few other easy tasks you can complete as you browse through your library. This list provides the details and simple instructions:

- Select the Set As button to select a photo to be used on the Photos tile on your Start screen, or select a picture to be used for your Lock screen.

- Select the Open With button to reveal a list of apps installed on your device that could be used to open the image, as shown in Figure 16.8.

FIGURE 16.8

Use Open With to choose from other apps to open a picture.

- Although it is less obvious, you can use the Share charm, as shown in Figure 16.9, to share a photo through email or other apps that are designed to handle the image.

- Use the Crop button to reveal easy tools that enable you to crop a picture right in the gallery.

- Use the Rotate button to rotate your picture 90 degrees in a clockwise direction. Each click rotates the picture further.

FIGURE 16.9

The Share charm enables you to send a picture as an attachment, or you can share using other installed apps.

- Select Edit to enter edit mode and reveal some very nice editing tools, several of which are new to Windows 8.1 (see Figure 16.10). Some of the things that you can do within Edit include fixing red eye, color enhancement, and selective focus.

FIGURE 16.10

Don't be fooled by the minimalistic design of the Edit window; there are a lot of tools in here.

- Controls are very intuitive; using radial sliders, shown in Figure 16.11, to apply effects makes it easy for both touch and mouse controls. To leave edit mode and save changes, open the App bar and select from Undo, Save a Copy, Update Original, or Cancel and return to the photo gallery.
- Select Delete to send the picture to your trash bin.

FIGURE 16.11

Rather than a boring horizontal slider, this new radial slider makes it easy to control the saturation level.

EDIT YOUR PICTURES WITH THE PHOTOS APP

I am really impressed with the editing tools included with Windows 8.1. There are the expected Auto Fix and Basic Fixes that are so common in photo editing apps. The minimal interface is nice compared to some apps that overwhelm the screen with tools. Of the more powerful editing tools included, fixing red eye, color enhancement, and selective focus (sometimes called tilt-shift) have often been reasons to purchase or install additional apps. These editing features are all now included in the Windows 8.1 Photos app. Take some time to experiment and familiarize yourself with the menus and tools. Although this app is not meant to replace Photoshop, you will be very pleased with the editing tools that are tucked under the hood.

Organizing the Pictures Library

Digital photography has made it so easy to take pictures and make them available on our devices that it becomes a challenge to keep things organized. You will find it to your advantage to accept the concept of keeping your pictures in the Pictures library or on your SkyDrive rather than saving folders of pictures to a desktop or other location. Although you could jump to the Desktop environment and use File Explorer to create folders and drag and drop pictures, it is also possible to organize things from within the Photos app.

To create a new folder, follow these steps:

1. In the Photos app, navigate to the location where you want to create a new folder. This could be within an existing folder or at the root of the Pictures library.

2. Bring up the App bar by swiping in from the top or bottom or by right-clicking in an open area. Select **New Folder**.

3. As shown in Figure 16.12, type in a name for the new folder and select **Create** or press **Enter**. Windows creates a new blank folder to the left of any pictures that are already located in this folder.

FIGURE 16.12

Create new folders in the Photos app using the New Folder tool.

4. Select pictures that you would like to move to the new folder, as shown in Figure 16.13. When you select the first picture, the App bar appears. Select **Cut** to move these pictures, or select **Copy** if you want to create duplicates.

5. In the new folder created in step 3, use the App bar to select **Paste**. The pictures appear, and the folder displays a thumbnail from one of the pictures in this new folder.

FIGURE 16.13

Use tools from the App bar to Cut, Copy, or even Select All when working with your pictures.

The methods you use to organize your folders will ultimately depend on which is easier for you. It takes time to keep pictures organized into folders, but it is well worth the effort. Otherwise, you will find that things spiral out of control, and trying to find a particular picture becomes a time-consuming effort when you can least afford it.

Renaming Your Pictures

One last detail that will help you keep things organized is to rename important pictures that you want to find later. You can use the powerful Search charm to quickly locate photos you have named. To try this, follow these steps:

1. In the Photos app, navigate to a folder in your Pictures library and select a picture. The App bar will automatically appear.

2. Select **Rename** from the App bar and type in a name for the picture, as shown in Figure 16.14. Select **Rename** or press **Enter** on your keyboard.

3. Open the Start screen and start typing the name of your picture. If you do not have a keyboard, bring up the Search charm and use the search field to type on your touchscreen. As shown in Figure 16.15, the results show local files at the top of the list.

Taking the time to rename all of your photos is probably unrealistic. Select pictures that you really like. It may be enough to name a couple of key pictures in a folder, because selecting the search item opens the Photos app and, from there, it's easy to look at other pictures in the same folder.

FIGURE 16.14

Give your pictures a unique name that will make it easier to identify them.

FIGURE 16.15

Use the Search charm to quickly find pictures that you have renamed.

THE ABSOLUTE MINIMUM

Keep these points in mind after you finish reading this chapter:

- The Photos app uses the App bar to provide you with many tools. Use a right-click or swipe in from the top or bottom to see which tools you can use when working with folders or pictures.

- SkyDrive is integrated into your Photos app, which makes it a very good choice for saving pictures. Weigh the benefits against the possibility of not having access to SkyDrive if traveling and not having an Internet connection.

- Take time to familiarize yourself with the tools available in edit mode. You may not use some tools as often, but knowing how to use Selective Focus or Vignette to enhance a picture can make you even prouder of your great pictures.

- Organize your pictures using folders, and keep them in the Pictures library. Consider how renaming pictures will make it easier for you to locate them later using the Search charm.

17

SHARING YOUR WINDOWS COMPUTER WITH OTHERS

The easiest way to share your Windows 8 computer with other users is to provide your username and password to whomever you want to share with. However, you probably would prefer a more secure solution for giving others access to your Windows 8 computer—yet another reminder that the easiest way is seldom the best way. The best way to share your Windows 8 computer is to create a separate account for anyone to whom you want to provide access. The process to create an account is easy, with just a few settings that require some thought. This chapter also shows you how to choose between and configure Windows 8's different password options, and how to remove an account and keep your computer secure.

Windows 8 Users and Account Basics

You can give as many persons access to your Windows 8 computer as needed. The portrait for every user account you've configured appears on the Sign-in screen for each new user, as shown in Figure 17.1.

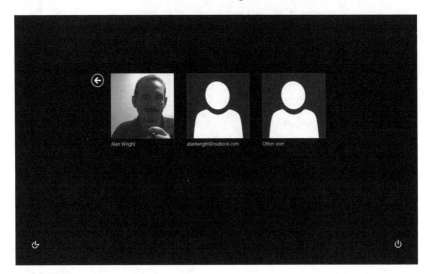

FIGURE 17.1

You may have a number of persons sharing your Windows 8 computer.

A new user in Windows 8 is automatically created as a *standard* user. A standard user contrasts with an *administrator* in that the person doesn't have access to some of the more sensitive settings, including those related to security. This means only an administrator can add new users to Windows 8. So, to try out and then put to use the instructions and walk-throughs in this chapter, you must be logged in as an administrator-type user. If you are not sure if your account is an administrator type, follow the steps in the section "Adding a New User with a Local Account." If, at step 3 of that section, you do not see the option to add a user, you are not an administrator. If you find your account is not an administrator type, try one of these fixes:

- If you were not the person who set up your computer, ask the person who did to change your account to an administrator type. (You can't promote yourself to an administrator.)

- If you did set up Windows 8, the account you created when you installed Windows is an administrator type. Sign in with that account.

Any person who wants to use Windows 8 must sign in with a valid account and a password. The account may be one of two types. A Local account is used only with the computer where it was created. A Microsoft account is stored with Microsoft on its servers across the Internet. This means you can use a Microsoft account on any Windows 8 device anywhere, including servers, desktops, laptops, phones, and tablets, if that account has been authorized to log in to the device beforehand by an administrator.

You have a choice as to which type of account to create and use. If you are the person who installs Windows, you can select which type of account to use to sign in to Windows 8 the first time. If someone creates an account for your use with Windows 8, be sure you understand which type of account is created for you. If you have a choice, it probably makes sense to use a Microsoft account. Here's why:

- All your Windows 8 preferences and settings, such as the color of the Start screen, a record of all the apps you downloaded, and approximately 10 more, are stored with your Windows 8 account. This means your preferences can be applied to any Windows 8 devices you sign in to. You don't need to spend time setting up any new computer you use. Refer to Chapter 4, "Making Windows Your Own," to learn how to specify which settings and preferences are saved with your account.

- Signing in to Windows 8 with a Microsoft account automatically signs you in to any app that you downloaded from the Windows Store that requires you to sign in.

- Signing in to Windows 8 with a Microsoft account automatically signs you in to any website that requires a Microsoft account. If you start Internet Explorer and browse to a site such as www.outlook.com, you do not need to sign in to those sites.

 NOTE For the purposes of this discussion, a Windows 8 account and a Microsoft account are essentially the same thing. Your Windows 8 account connects directly to your Microsoft account.

- If you forget your password, you can always reset it through Microsoft account services. If you forget the password to a local account, and you cannot recall it through one of the reminder features, you are probably out of luck and need to create a new local account.

You can create a Windows 8 account before you begin to install Windows 8. To do so, visit www.outlook.com or www.live.com (see Figure 17.2). If you already have a Hotmail, Live, or Outlook account, you are ready to sign in to Windows 8. Use the same credentials you use to sign in to those Microsoft online services to sign in to Windows 8. Your account must first be added to the Windows 8 device you intend to sign in to. This is covered next, in the "Adding a New User" section.

FIGURE 17.2

You can create a Windows 8 account before you add the account to your Windows 8 device.

NOTE If you installed Windows 8, you are granted administrator rights, which means that Windows 8 enables you to do anything with the software. Most relevant with administrator rights is that you can add new accounts, thereby giving other people access to Windows 8.

Adding a New User

Before you start the process of adding a new user to Windows 8, you should keep a few things in mind:

- You must be signed in with an administrator-type account. For information about administrator-type accounts, see the "Changing a User's Type" section later in this chapter.

- You must select whether the new user has a Microsoft account or a Local account. You can find information about account types earlier in the "Windows 8 Users and Account Basics" section.

Because there are differences in the process to create a Local account versus a Windows 8 account, there are separate walk-throughs for each in the next two sections.

Adding a New User with a Local Account

To add a user account that will be recognized only on a single Windows 8 device, create a Local account by following these steps:

1. Open the **Settings** charm and select **Change PC settings** at the bottom of the screen.

2. Select **Accounts** from the list of settings on the left side of the screen.

3. Select Other Accounts.

4. Select **Add a User**, which appears at the top of the Other Accounts pane.

5. Select the **Sign in Without a Microsoft Account** link at the bottom of the screen, as shown in Figure 17.3. You will be prompted one more time for the type of account you want to create; select **Local Account**. The screen shown in Figure 17.4 appears.

FIGURE 17.3

You must opt to log in without using a Microsoft account twice when creating a local account.

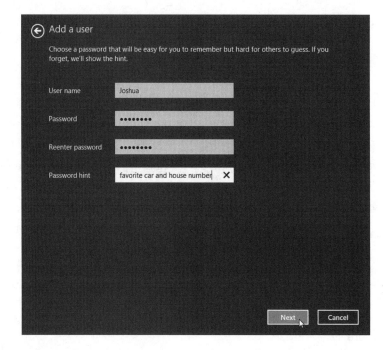

FIGURE 17.4

You need to supply a username, password, and a password hint to create a local account.

6. Enter a username (20 characters max; any combination of numbers and letters, including spaces; no ?|[]";|<>=+.?*%@), a password (any characters, including numbers, letters, spaces, and symbols), and a password hint into the fields provided. Click **Next**.

7. To track the user's online activity with Windows 8's Family Safety tools (Chapter 24, "Safe Web Browsing"), click the check box. Select **Finish**.

8. You return to the Sign-In options screen that appeared with step 2. Scroll to the bottom of the screen, and the listing should include your new user.

Adding a New User with a Microsoft Account

There are two scenarios in which you add a new user to your Windows 8 computer with a Microsoft account. You can add an account that already has been created, and you can add a user and create the user's Microsoft account at the same time. Both scenarios are covered in this walk-through.

To add an account that can be used with any Windows 8 device, follow these steps to create a Microsoft account:

1. Open the **Settings** charm and select **Change PC Settings** at the bottom of the screen.

2. Select **Accounts** from the list of settings on the left side of the screen. Your screen should look like the one shown in Figure 17.5.

FIGURE 17.5

The Accounts screen enables you to manage most aspects of the accounts authorized to use your Windows 8 device.

3. Select Other Accounts from the choices on the left and then select **Add a User**.

4. If the user you want to add does not have a Microsoft account, and you would like to create one, select **Sign Up for a New Email Address**. Then skip to step 6.

    If the user already has a Microsoft account, type the email address associated with that account into the Email address box. Then click **Next**. Windows attempts to verify the email address you entered.

5. If Windows does not recognize the email you entered, you are prompted to sign up for a new email address, as shown in Figure 17.6. If you want to create an account with this email address, skip to step 6. If you want to change or correct the email address you entered, click **Cancel**. You will be returned to the screen described in step 3.

FIGURE 17.6

If you enter the email address for an account that does not exist, you are prompted to create an account.

If the email address is verified, the screen shown in Figure 17.7 appears. If the person using this account is a child and you plan to use the Windows Family Safety tools to manage the child's online use, check the child's account option. Select **Finish**. Skip to step 8.

FIGURE 17.7

Your work is done if you enter an email address associated with a working Microsoft account.

6. The next three screens ask you to supply baseline contact information, such as your name and ZIP Code, phone number, alternative email, and security question. Be sure to note the email address and password you entered by either writing it down or by storing the information in a password storage application. You will find more information on passwords later in this chapter, in the section "Maintaining Security."

   When you've filled out all three pages of the form, click **Next** to continue.

7. The last prompt from Windows checks if you want to monitor the new user's web activity with the Windows Family Safety tools. Select the option if you like, and click **Finish**.

8. You are returned to the screen where you started at step 2. You should see the new account you created in the Other Accounts list at the bottom of the screen.

Creating a PIN or Picture Password

When you create your new account in Windows 8, you need to supply a password, but you can use one of two new sign-in options, replacing the use of the password after you initially supply it. These two options are PIN and Picture Password. Besides saving you the repetitive stress of entering your password often, these two new options are impressive, and you'll want to use them to impress your friends!

Adding a PIN to Your Account

A PIN is a 4-digit number you use to identify yourself when you sign in to Windows. Any 4-digit combination of numerals is acceptable, including repeats such as 9999. A PIN is particularly useful to tablet users who normally don't have a physical keyboard. On a tablet, a virtual keyboard appears on the screen as you sign in to Windows, enabling you to enter just your PIN to access Windows.

To add a PIN to your account, follow these steps:

1. Open the **Settings** charm and select **Change PC Settings**, which appears on the bottom right of the screen.

2. From the menu of settings, select **Accounts**.

3. Select Sign-in Options.

4. Select **Add under PIN**. The Create a PIN screen appears.

5. You first must verify your password. Enter your password and select **OK**. The screen in Figure 17.8 appears.

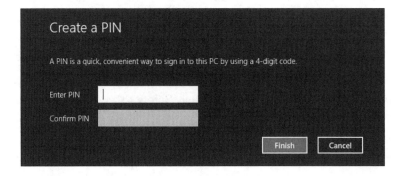

FIGURE 17.8

You can enter a PIN (and confirm it) to use as a substitute for your password.

6. Enter your PIN, and then enter it again in the **Confirm PIN** box.

7. Click **Finish**.

Adding a Picture Password to Your Account

If you are like me and enjoy drawing mustaches and other funny shapes on pictures of your friends, family, and your editor, this is the password option for you. A picture password is a combination of a picture and touch gestures. To set up a picture password, you choose a picture from your Pictures folder and then make three gestures, which can be your choice of tapping or drawing a line or circle. Windows records the position of the gestures, as well as the order in which you made them. This combination creates the picture password.

 TIP It's helpful if you have a picture in mind to use as your picture password. If you don't, you should locate or take a new photo and then load it onto your computer before you start this process. A good candidate photo has a number of recognizable items, as opposed to a broad, landscape photo. This way, it's easier to remember the objects on which you drew the required symbols.

To use a picture password with your Windows 8 account, follow these steps:

1. Open the **Settings** charm and select **Change PC Settings**, which appears on the bottom right of the screen.

2. Select **Accounts**.

3. Select Sign-in Options.

4. Under Picture Password select **Add**.

5. You first must verify your password. Enter your password and click **OK**. If you entered your password correctly, the screen shown in Figure 17.9 appears.

FIGURE 17.9

The first step in creating a picture password is to choose a picture.

6. Select **Choose Picture**.

7. Your screen displays the photos in your Picture folders. Look through the photos to find one to use as your picture password. Select the photo to use, and then select **Open**.

8. The picture you selected should be on the screen. The picture password screen uses only about three-quarters of the picture you chose. Click and drag or touch and drag the picture directly on the screen to a position you like. Tap or click **Use This Picture.**

9. The Set Up Your Gesture screen should be visible. This is the screen where you draw the three gestures. Windows asks you to draw them twice to be sure you can recall what they are and where they are drawn. Draw the three gestures. Figure 17.10 shows the example screen before any gestures have been drawn. The large number highlights itself with each gesture you draw.

   Select **Start Over** if you want to redraw all the gestures. If you want to save creating a picture password for another time, select **Cancel**.

FIGURE 17.10

You can see the gestures on the screen when you redraw each as part of the verification step.

10. After you confirm the three gestures for the picture password, you will see a Congratulations screen. Select **Finish**, and you are then returned to your account setting screen. You can sign out to try out your new picture password.

Making Changes to User Accounts

After you've created an account and a user has used the account to sign in to Windows 8, you can still make changes to it. You can change the account to an administrator from a standard type, or vice versa. You can also remove an account. Unlike the process for adding an account, which begins via the Start screen and Settings charm, you must make any modifications to existing accounts through the Desktop app.

Changing a User's Type

You may want to give certain users administrative access to Windows 8 so they can add more users, install software, or change security settings. Closely related, you may want to remove an individual's administrator rights and instead give them regular user capabilities. Making either change is easy.

To change a user's type, follow these steps:

1. Open the **Search** charm. Enter **change account**, which is enough to find the Change Account Type tool shown in Figure 10.11. Select **Change Account Type** from the list of results. The Manage Accounts window should be on your screen.

FIGURE 17.11

Use Search to quickly find the Desktop Manage accounts tool.

2. Select the account to change, which opens another window with a menu of actions, as shown in Figure 17.12.

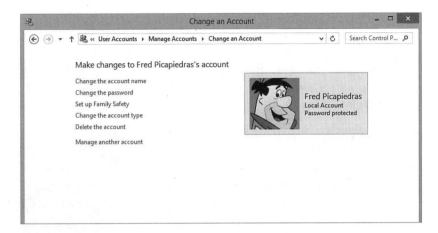

FIGURE 17.12

You can change several aspects of an account from the Change an Account screen.

3. Select **Change the Account Type** from the menu, and then select **Standard** or **Administrator** as the account type to change to.

4. Select **Change Account Type**. Windows returns you to the screen shown here.

Removing a User Account

You may need to remove an account from Windows 8. Perhaps the person who is associated with the account no longer should have access to this Windows 8 device, or perhaps the account was created in error. Regardless of the reason, it is easy to remove the account. You must be signed in with an administrator account to remove an account.

To remove a user account, follow these steps:

1. Open the **Search** charm. Enter **change account** and select **Change Account Type** from the list of search results. The Manage Accounts window should appear on your screen.

2. Select the account you want to delete. The Change an Account window appears (refer to Figure 17.12).

3. Select **Delete the Account**.

4. Depending on whether it's a local or Microsoft account, you will see one of the two windows shown in Figure 17.13. In either case, you can delete the account but keep the files used by the account, such as music files, photos, files stored on the desktop, all files in the Documents folder, and videos. To do so, select **Keep Files**. To delete the account and all the account files, select **Delete Files**.

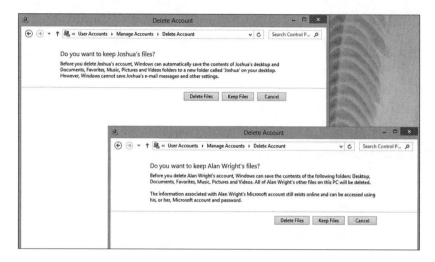

FIGURE 17.13

You have a few options related to user data when removing an account.

5. Windows asks you to confirm your choice. Select **Delete Account**. To keep the account, select **Cancel**.

6. You are returned to the Manage Accounts window. You can close the window if you choose, or you can return to the Start screen without closing it.

Maintaining Security

There are many aspects to security when using a computer. This section focuses on user account security. Perhaps you use a laptop or tablet away from home on occasion. If a curious workmate or acquaintance were to open or wake up your device, would it be secure or would it reveal unwanted details? If your device is lost, will it reveal sensitive information to others?

Windows 8 is the most secure operating system to date, encrypting your data by default. All the built-in security is useless, however, if you unwittingly leave your device open or reveal the password needed to unlock it. It is surprising how often data and identities are stolen because users themselves granted access to their information.

Consider a few practical suggestions to help you maintain security on your Windows 8 device. Obviously it is not a good practice to write a password down on a sticky note stuck to the side of your Windows 8 device. PIN numbers and even the picture passwords might not be practical in public places where social engineers can watch over your shoulder as you log in to your device. And never—ever—should you reply to an email, no matter who it appears to be from, requesting your system's login credentials.

Setting Password Policy

As you saw earlier in this chapter, passwords can be composed of traditional passwords, PINs, or pictures. Windows 8 has a couple of features that you should be aware of, depending on your device. One of these settings is the Password Policy. To check the setting your device currently has, follow these steps:

1. Open the **Settings** charm and select **Change PC Settings**, which appears on the bottom right of the screen.

2. Select **Accounts**.

3. Select **Sign-in Options**. You will see something like the screen in Figure 17.14. Notice that a password is required on this device if the display is off for 15 minutes.

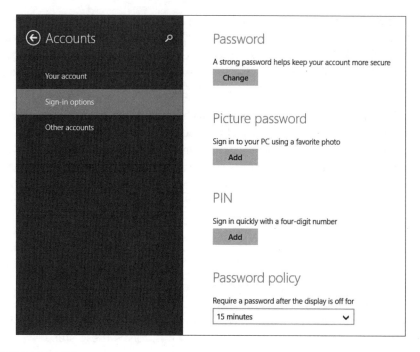

FIGURE 17.14

You may have an option to adjust how much time is permitted before a password is required to log back in to a device.

4. Review the current Password Policy. Use the drop down menu to change the current setting.

In the Sign-in Options you should see a setting listed regarding password policy, as shown in Figure 17.14. Using the drop down menu, you can select **Always Require a Password** or allow for a shorter or longer interval after the display goes dark before a password is required to log back in to your device. You may see only the option to require a password or not when waking this device. The setting you choose will likely depend on whether you use this Windows 8 device at home or in a work environment.

Using the Screensaver to Add Security

In the Desktop environment you can enable and adjust a setting to engage a screensaver and require a password to wake up a device after a time interval you establish. To use this setting follow these steps:

1. From the Start screen enter **screensaver**.

2. Select **Change Screen Saver** from the search results. The Screen Saver Settings dialog box will open on your desktop (see Figure 17.15). You can also navigate here using the Control Panel.

3. Select a screensaver from the drop-down menu and a wait time. Enable the check box On Resume, Display Logon Screen.

4. Select **OK**.

 NOTE Some devices may not have these settings. The Surface RT tablet, for example, does not have a screensaver.

FIGURE 17.15

Enable the screensaver settings to require a login with password to increase security.

THE ABSOLUTE MINIMUM

Keep these points in mind as you wrap up this chapter:

- To give others access to your Windows 8 device, you need to add an account to Windows 8. This is also known as "adding a user" in Windows 8. Unless you are told otherwise, create a Microsoft account when prompted as you add the new account.

- A Windows 8 account includes information about your settings and preferences. If you sign in to Windows 8 running on a computer other than your own, all your settings and preferences are applied to this new computer. This won't happen if you create a local account instead.

- A picture password replaces the standard password. To sign in with a picture password, swipe or tap three times on a picture you choose. Windows checks your gestures against what it recorded when you created the picture password.

- You can also use a PIN to substitute for a password.

- Check your Password Policy setting to ensure your device is protected from unwanted intrusions.

SHARING FILES AND PRINTERS

Say the word "network" to a novice Windows user and you're sure to notice a look of fear mixed with confusion. But for the person who simply wants to share some pictures or music, or perhaps all the family's important files, among the computers in their home, there shouldn't be too much panic. Windows makes this panic-free sharing possible with a function called homegroups. Homegroups provide exactly what you want from a small network to provide easy sharing without introducing any complexity. It strips away most of the tough network concepts and procedures and lets you focus on what sorts of files, folders, printers, and other stuff you want to share. This chapter helps you understand what you need to know about home networks, and it walks you through the easy process to set up sharing.

Setting up homegroup sharing is easy, although you need to leverage some information presented in other chapters. In particular, review the "Control Panel" section at the end of Chapter 10, "Performing Easy Windows Configuration." Also, be sure to review the "Navigating Through Your Folders" section in Chapter 19, "Managing Files and Folders."

Networking with Homegroup

This section eases you into the idea of creating a small network. Yes! You can boast to your pals that you know how to implement a computer network! The education begins with a brief review of the benefits of a small home network.

 NOTE Homegroup is appropriate for smaller networks, but how small is small? There is no reason why 10 or more computers can't be set up in a homegroup, or even 20 or more. But most homes have between 5 and 10 networked devices to share (everything from PCs and tablets to DVRs and game consoles), and a small home office probably has a similar number of computers and devices.

If you have more than one computer in your home or home office, it probably makes sense to connect the computers into a small network. Although the advantages and conveniences might not make sense right now, the Microsoft and Windows 8 view of computing is growing wide and deep. Here are a few benefits to setting up a small sharing network at home:

- Consolidate all the files of a certain type, such as music or pictures, on one computer. This way, it's easy to find a particular song or photo if they are all stored in one place.

- Set up one computer as a kind of home media player, storing all your movies and music, and also having all your audio equipment attached to it.

- Buy just one printer with lots of bells and whistles, connect it to one of your homegroup computers, and then share it with the rest of the homegroup.

There are usually a few settings to adjust, and possibly some hardware to acquire for a small group of computers to form a network. But the good news is that if all the Windows computers that you would like to join to a network can already connect to the Internet from your home (see Chapter 11, "Connecting to the Internet"), then very likely they are *already* joined to a network. It's as easy as that.

Using the Windows Homegroup

The homegroup is an incredibly helpful feature in Windows 8 that enables you to share files with other computers that belong to the homegroup. As a member of a homegroup, you can see all the files that other members of the homegroup make available for sharing, and vice versa, as if the files were on your computer. You usually can open and edit the shared files, make copies of them, and delete them as if they were your own. Figure 18.1 shows Windows Explorer displaying some shared photos on other homegroup computers.

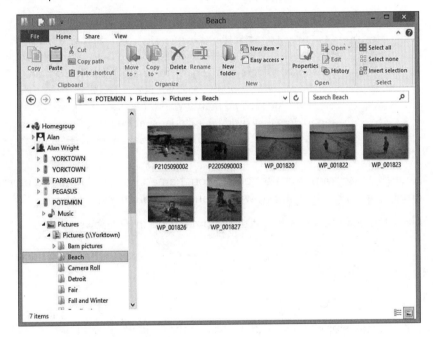

FIGURE 18.1

You can access shared files and folders as easily as files and folders on your computer's hard drive. In this picture, you can see pictures that Ellie has shared on her computer.

Here are a few things to know about homegroups and networks:

- Each computer whose files you want to share must join the homegroup; see the section "Joining a Homegroup."

- There may be only one homegroup on your network.

- If one computer on the network has created a homegroup, any computer on the network from which you want to share must join *that* homegroup.

- To create a new homegroup, all computers must leave the homegroup, including the computer that started it.

- One computer creates a homegroup, and all other computers then join it. This does not give ownership or responsibility for the homegroup to the computer that created it. All computers in a homegroup are on par with one another. None have any more responsibility or capabilities than any other.

- It might sound daunting to navigate through all your files and folders to find, discover, or identify what you might share. Windows 8 makes it easy to specify and organize the files you might share by using common folders you already use, such as Documents, Pictures, and Music. You specify which folders to share with your homegroup.

 NOTE To make things even easier, you can use a feature called a *library* to further organize your folders. Libraries, which are special folders that "point" to several other folders, are a convenient way to bring together all the files that share a particular use or function no matter where folders are located. The files and folders that reside in a folder specified by a library become members of that library. For a discussion of libraries, look ahead to Chapter 19.

Although these folders are set up for you, homegroups are not. You must create a homegroup as the first step toward sharing on your home network.

Follow these three steps to set up a homegroup in Windows:

1. Create a homegroup.

2. Join a homegroup.

3. Set up homegroup sharing.

Each of these steps is covered in detail in the following sections.

Creating a Homegroup

Creating a homegroup is a simple matter of clicking a few buttons and then making a password. Before you can start, however, you need to get to the homegroup screen. Here's how:

1. Open the Settings charm.

2. Select **Change PC Settings** at the bottom of the screen.

3. Select **Network** from the menu on the left side of the screen.

4. Select **HomeGroup** from the menu on the left side of the screen.

5. You should see a screen like the one in either Figure 18.2, Figure 18.3, or Figure 18.4.

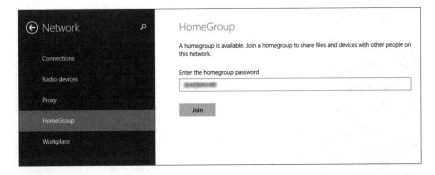

FIGURE 18.2

This screen indicates that a homegroup already is set up on your network but you haven't joined it yet.

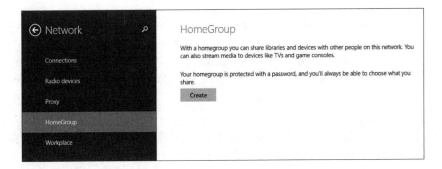

FIGURE 18.3

This screen indicates a homegroup has not been set up on your network.

 NOTE If your device is already connected to an existing homegroup, but you want to create a new one anyway, skip to the section "Leaving a Homegroup."

For now, we're interested only in Figure 18.3, which gives you the opportunity to create a homegroup. We'll get to the other two figures in a little bit. Follow these steps to create a homegroup:

1. Select **Create**. After a moment, the screen you see in Figure 18.4 appears.

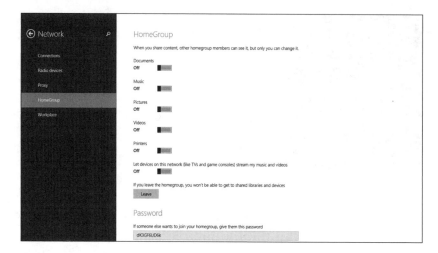

FIGURE 18.4

This screen indicates you belong to a homegroup but you have not shared anything yet.

2. The box under Password shows a string of 10 characters, indicating a homegroup has been created. The computer you've been using is a member of it.

3. Ignore the controls on this screen for now. Carefully write down the password shown in the box under Password. Note the case used for letters (7abc8 is not the same as 7ABC8). You need this password so that other computers can join in the homegroup.

At this point, your computer has created and joined the homegroup. The homegroup, though, is a quiet one with just this computer as a member. In the next section, you learn how other computers in the network can join the homegroup.

Joining a Homegroup

You can join a homegroup as long as one computer that belongs to the homegroup is signed on. Even if the computer that was used to create the homegroup is turned off, you do not need to wait for *that* computer to be signed in to join.

To join a homegroup, follow these steps:

1. Get the homegroup password. That password can be retrieved easily from another homegroup computer by bringing up the screen shown earlier (refer to Figure 18.4).

2. Open the Settings charm and select **Change PC Settings**.

3. Select **HomeGroup**. Your screen should appear like the one shown back in Figure 18.2.

4. Enter the password into the box, and select **Join**.

5. If the password is accepted, the sharing options become available (refer to Figure 18.4). You can set the sharing options immediately. For guidance, however, read the section, "Setting Up Sharing," later in this chapter.

Leaving a Homegroup

You read earlier that all computers must leave a homegroup before a new homegroup can be created. To leave a homegroup, follow these steps:

1. Open the Settings charm and select **Change PC Settings**.

2. Select **HomeGroup**, and then select **Leave**. (You can see this button in Figure 18.4.)

Troubleshooting Homegroup Connections

If you experience difficulty either joining a homegroup or leaving one, you can try one of these troubleshooting tips:

- You may experience difficulties joining a homegroup if you use a third-party (non-Microsoft) antivirus program. If you don't mind disabling your antivirus program for a short time, you can attempt to join or leave the homegroup again after temporarily disabling the software.

- You may experience difficulties joining a homegroup if you use an all-in-one Internet privacy or protection software suite. If so, disable the protection temporarily before trying to join the homegroup again. If you can connect, you may create an exception for Windows 8, enabling you to join a homegroup.

 CAUTION If you disable your antivirus or other Internet protection software, it's not a bad idea to disconnect from the Internet (but not your network) before you do.

- Windows networks are of a specific type: home, office, or public. The type defines the level of security for each. For example, a home network enables more computer-to-computer communication than a public network. A homegroup is allowed only on a home network.

WARNING **This fix is technical**. Get help restarting the Peer Networking Grouping and Homegroup Provider services. Another bit of advice from geek city is to be sure IPV6 is engaged. If this is Greek to you, it may be necessary to visit a computer expert.

Setting Up Sharing

Windows 8 organizes everything you might share into five categories. With your computer joined to a homegroup, turn sharing On or Off for each of these item types, as shown in Figure 18.5:

- Documents
- Music
- Pictures
- Videos
- Printers (and Devices)

To share any of these items, you simply need to move the toggle switch associated with it (from left to right).

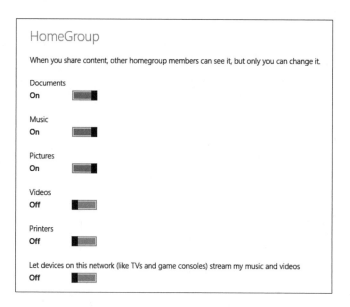

FIGURE 18.5

Documents, Music, and Pictures have been shared on this device.

You might recognize some of these options from elsewhere. They may appear when you browse for files using File Explorer as the names for some of the default folders listed when looking at content on This PC. An example of this is shown in Figure 18.6.

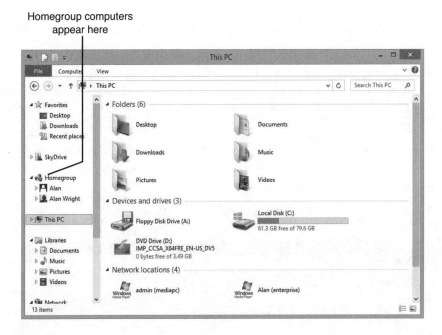

FIGURE 18.6

When viewing This PC, you will see Folders that point to your most commonly shared resources.

Before you share everything your device has to share, however, here are some things you need to know about sharing:

- By default, every file in a folder is shared with every computer in the homegroup (when you turn on sharing for that folder, of course).

- You can prevent one or more folders from being shared.

- You can prevent one or more files in a folder from being shared even if the folder is being shared.

- You can prevent one or more files in a folder or one or more entire folders from being shared with certain users in your homegroup.

The following sections show you how to deal with each of these cases.

Disabling Sharing for Specific Files or Folders

To prevent one or more files or folders in a library from being shared, follow these steps:

1. Start File Explorer.

2. Navigate to the folder where the file or folder you want to restrict from sharing is located. You can find assistance with navigating in Chapter 19.

3. Select the files or folders. You can use the multiselect approach (also described in Chapter 19) to select all the files or folders at once, or you can do them in small batches, or you can set sharing for each file or folder one at a time.

4. Under the Share tab in the **Share With** group, select **Stop Sharing** as shown in Figure 18.7. (The same options can also be found by right-clicking and selecting **Share With** from the context menu.)

5. You may have to repeat these steps a few times.

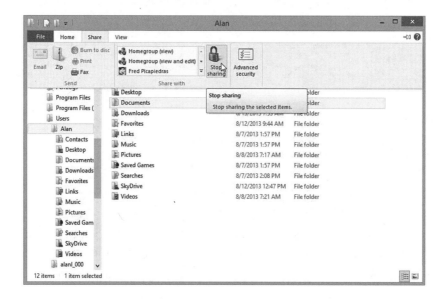

FIGURE 18.7

You can stop sharing selected folders or files with your homegroup.

Sharing Files and Folders Only with Specific Users

To share certain files or folders only with specific persons:

1. Start File Explorer.

2. Navigate to the folder where the file or folder you want to share with only certain people is located.

3. Select the files or folders. You can use the multiselect approach (refer to Chapter 19) to select all the files or folders at once, or you can do them in small batches, or you can set each file or folder one at a time.

4. Under the Share tab in the Share With group, expand the list of groups and individuals by selecting the More arrow button on the right side of the box (see Figure 18.8). You'll see a list of the persons with whom you can share.

5. Select **Specific People**. The dialog box shown in Figure 18.9 appears.

FIGURE 18.8

Select **Specific people** to display the list of users.

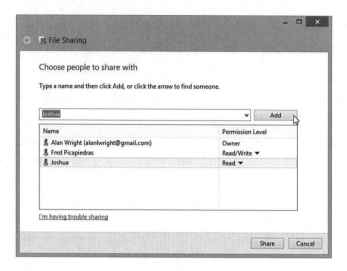

FIGURE 18.9

Select persons to filter sharing.

6. Enter the email address or the name of the person, and then select **Add**.

7. Repeat the last step if needed to select more persons with whom to share the files you selected.

8. To allow all the users you selected to edit the files and folders you share, select **Share**.

9. You may be asked to confirm the access you are granting if write permission is given. You will then have the option to email or copy a link to inform the users of the new shared file or folder. Select Done.

 NOTE When working with steps 6–8, refer to Figure 18.9. To allow some of or all the users you selected to *read* only the file you're sharing and *not change anything*, select **Read** from the Permission Level column for any user you won't allow to change the files you're sharing. Otherwise, leave the setting in the Permission Level column as Read/Write. To save your changes, select **Share**.

Sharing Your Printer

Sharing a printer in your homegroup is as easy as sharing files and folders, perhaps easier. When you turn on sharing for Printers (refer to Figure 18.5), each of your printers, scanners, and other devices potentially become available to all computers in the homegroup. Here is how to share specific printers:

1. Open Control Panel (use the Search charm if you need to), and then open Hardware and Sound. Finally, open Devices and Printers.

2. Locate the printer you want to share. Right-click or tap and hold the printer, and from the menu that appears, select **Printer Properties**.

3. Select the **Sharing** tab (see Figure 18.10).

4. Select **Share This Printer**. You'll notice a name for your printer is automatically filled in for you. This is the name everyone will see on the network. You can change it if you like.

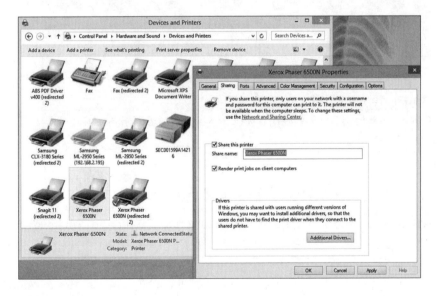

FIGURE 18.10

Use the Printer Properties dialog box to specifically share a printer.

5. Select **OK**.

6. Close the Devices and Printers window by selecting the **Close** button in the top-right corner of the window.

This printer will appear on other computers in your homegroup either automatically as a printer or you might be prompted to install drivers for a newly available device in the homegroup. Figure 18.11 shows a list of printers on a computer. Notice the selected printer is "on PEGASUS." That is the name of the computer shown in Figure 18.10 that shared the printer.

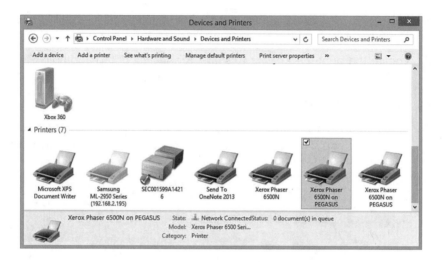

FIGURE 18.11

Printers that have been shared to your homegroup are identified with the computer that shared them.

Seeing Stuff Shared by Others

Although it's good to share, it's also really good to receive. Whatever your homegroup partners decide to share, you can access very easily via the Desktop. Follow these steps to access shared content.

1. From the Desktop, open File Explorer. If you are unclear how to open Windows Explorer, see Chapter 19.

2. Be sure the Navigation pane is displayed. To do so, from the View tab on the ribbon, select **Navigation Pane**. From the menu that appears, select **Navigation Pane** (yes, again) if there is no check beside the command. If the Navigation Pane command is checked, the pane is in view.

3. In the Navigation Pane, scroll down to about the third major group. It should show Homegroup at the top entry in the tree. Click the small arrow beside the word Homegroup to display homegroup computers, as shown in Figure 18.12.

4. Select the computer whose shared files you want to see. Then navigate through the folders in the Content pane as you would if browsing through files on your own computer.

Navigation pane

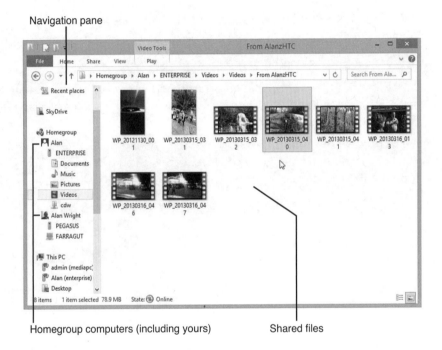

Homegroup computers (including yours)   Shared files

FIGURE 18.12

Browse through the folders shared on a homegroup computer as if the folders are on your own computer.

THE ABSOLUTE MINIMUM

- Homegroups is a feature in Windows 8 that makes it extremely easy to share files, such as pictures, music, and other files, with other nearby computers. Homegroups also enable you to share printers.

- Computers and tablets that connect to the Internet at your home or home office are already part of a network for which you can create a homegroup.

- There can be just one homegroup in a network.

- Use libraries to simplify what files get shared. When you turn on sharing, all the files in that library are shared. You must use the settings available through Windows Explorer to restrict sharing.

- The printers connected to your computer are automatically shared with all other computers in the homegroup as soon as you turn on sharing for printers on the Homegroup screen.

19

MANAGING FILES AND FOLDERS

The exciting new Windows 8 environment, with its broad palette of active tiles, some of them delivering news and other data to the Start screen, gives the perception that everything you do in Windows can be accomplished through the immersive, colorful screens you see on the Start screen, as well as on the Web in advertisements, videos, and reviews. The reality is that you'll certainly work with the Windows 8 apps and features often, but you'll also spend a lot of time just managing your files and folders as you might have done with the previous version of Windows. You can most efficiently work with files and folders on the Desktop using the File Explorer tool. This chapter helps you understand the basics about files and folders and how to keep them all under control using File Explorer.

Files and Folder Basics

Before diving into the methods and how-tos of managing your files and folders, it's a good idea to have a firm grasp of the basics. The following sections offer an overview of both, as well as a look at how you can use libraries to manage them all.

Understanding Files

At their absolute simplest, files store data. Different types of files serve different purposes. But for this discussion, it's best to categorize all files in two ways:

- System files
- User files

System files are the parts of the Windows 8 engine. Windows 8 uses these files to do its job, from connecting to the Internet to recognizing a mouse-click from a finger tap on the screen to figuring how much time you have before your battery runs out. These system files are important, and not only does Windows 8 expect that that they remain located on your computer, but also that they are in a specific location. You generally do not need to worry about accidentally erasing a system file and causing Windows to stop working. System files are stored in *System Folders*, and these folders are in a location generally difficult to access unless you are an administrator. Even so, it's best to avoid these folders and all their subfolders:

> \Windows
>
> \Program Files
>
> \Program Files (x86)

Many programs enable you to select the folders into which the system files for the program are installed. Unless you know better, it's best to use the default folder option the programs offer and remove them only via the Windows Uninstall a Program feature. The steps for uninstalling Desktop applications are covered in Chapter 9, "Working with Windows Desktop Programs."

These system files contrast with *user files*. User files are the files you use and create every day, such as your work files, music, photos, and many more. These user files and the folders that contain them are the main subject of this chapter. Software programs define the format of the user files that work with their program. You usually cannot use one of these files in a program other than the one that created it, although there are exceptions. For example, you can't open a file created by your tax preparation tool in your photo editing program, but you can open a Notepad text file in Microsoft Word.

User files are normally stored in a person's own folders. As you read next, all users in Windows 8 have their own set of folders that other users usually cannot access.

Understanding Folders

Whereas files store data, folders store files. It's as simple as that. A folder can store other folders, and those folders can store other folders, and so on. A folder in Windows is represented by, no surprise here, the Folder icon, as shown in Figure 19.1.

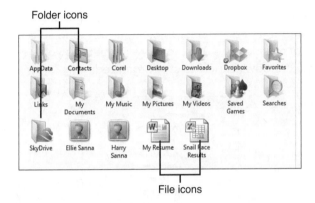

FIGURE 19.1

You can easily tell which of the items in Windows are files or folders.

When you add new users to Windows by creating an account for them, it also creates a set of unique user folders. Windows creates these folders in a parent folder. The folder is named after the user's first name if the account is a Microsoft account. If the account is a local account, the folder name is the same as the username you provided when you created the account. This folder is known as the user's *home folder,* and you can see an example of it in Figure 19.2. (To learn more about creating accounts and the difference between account types, see Chapter 17, "Sharing Your Windows Computer with Others.")

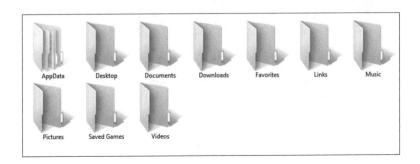

FIGURE 19.2

A set of folders is created for each Windows user.

You can store files anywhere you like in your own home folder and subfolders. You can create as many folders and subfolders as you like in your home folder. It makes sense to store certain special files, such as music files, in the folders specially designed for them. You cannot save or create files in any other folder in Windows, including the home folders of other users, unless you are a system administrator—and even then, it's generally not a great idea.

With some planning, you can create a hierarchy of folders to help organize all the files related to a task, subject, project, hobby, and so on. Figure 19.3 shows an example of a folder tree used to store recipes. As you'll soon see, you do not need to be a Windows expert to stay organized.

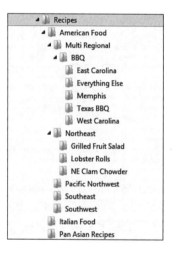

FIGURE 19.3

You can design a folder system for specific needs.

 CAUTION Software programs you purchase also leverage folders to organize their files. When you install programs, they often create their own folders. You should never move or delete program folders, even if you know you will never use the program again. Sometimes these folders contain files that are used by other programs. When you delete a folder that contains files, all the files are deleted along with the containing folder.

Exploring with File Explorer

You use File Explorer to manage your files and folders. Although Microsoft keeps changing the name, File Explorer has been around for many years, and the version that comes with Windows 8 probably is the easiest to use.

You can launch File Explorer from the Desktop, and its icon appears on the taskbar by default.

 TIP   You can also add a File Explorer tile to the Start screen by using the Search charm to locate an app named "explorer." When File Explorer appears in the list of results, right-click the icon and select **Pin to Start from the menu that appears**.

After opening File Explorer, you'll see a new window like the one in Figure 19.4.

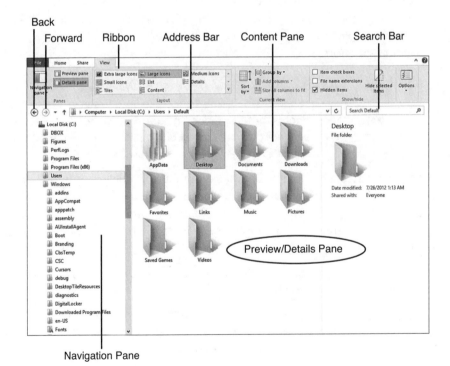

FIGURE 19.4

File Explorer includes a number of controls to enable you to navigate through your file system.

The Navigation pane, as shown here, drives almost all the activity in File Explorer. Whatever you select in the Navigation pane determines what appears in the Content pane.

Working with Libraries

The *library*, first introduced in Windows 7, is an extremely useful tool to organize your files. Windows 8.1 continues to use libraries even if you do not notice their presence right away. A library usually appears as a themed folder—Pictures, Documents, Music, etc.—in File Explorer that contains folders that can actually be located anywhere on your device, attached media, or even on separate computers. A library, then, is really just a collection of folders (and their files) that fit a specific category.

When you select a library, all the folders designated by the library appear as if they were in the same place. A library does not store a file the way a folder does, it does not actually move your files and folders. As an example of how you might use a library, you can add folders that have pictures that are saved on your Desktop, external storage device, and another computer that is always connected to the same network. When you open your Pictures library you will see all these folders in one place. This provides you with a very powerful way to organize with a minimum of effort.

 NOTE Libraries are already used by Windows 8.1 even if they have not been made visible in File Explorer. When you open the Video, Photos, or Music apps from the Start screen they will display the content of your corresponding library and not merely the folder of that same name in your user profile.

Windows creates a number of libraries automatically, including one for pictures, one for documents, one for videos, and another for music files. You can create additional libraries yourself. You might create a library to organize all the files related to your career, or you might consolidate all the folders for all the projects you're working on.

To work with libraries you first need to make sure they are visible in File Explorer. To do this, follow these steps:

1. Open File Explorer using the icon on the Desktop task bar. You will see a This PC window open. In the navigation pane to the left you will see Favorites, This PC, Network, and likely Homegroup and SkyDrive.

2. Select the View tab and then select the Navigation pane button as shown in Figure 19.5. Select **Show Libraries** from the list of options that appears.

3. You will see that a group of default libraries is now visible in the navigation pane of File Explorer. Select one of your Library folders to view its contents as shown in Figure 19.6.

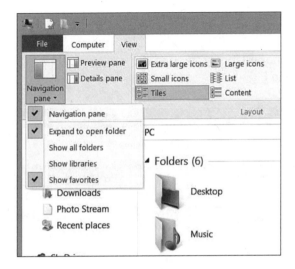

FIGURE 19.5

File Explorer does not show libraries by default.

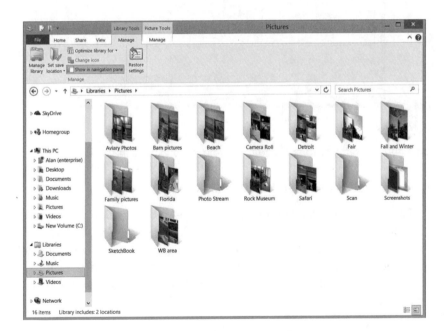

FIGURE 19.6

Once you have enabled Show libraries, you will see them in your navigation pane as a cluster of folders.

4. When you have a library selected, File Explorer shows a Library Tools tab on the ribbon at the top. Select this tab.

5. Select **Manage Library** to open the library locations dialog box for that library as shown in Figure 19.7.

FIGURE 19.7

Edit a library's settings to add additional folders to include in the library.

There are a few basic ways that you can manage a library:

- To add a folder to a library, use the steps in this section to open the library locations dialog box shown in Figure 19.7. Select **Add**. A small File Explorer type window appears. Navigate to the folder to include and then select **Include Folder**. In this example, the third folder is actually located on a different computer in the Homegroup. You can read how to navigate in File Explorer later in this chapter.

- To remove a folder from the library, select the folder and then select **Remove**.

- To define where files are stored when you save to a library, close the library locations dialog box. With the library still selected in the Navigation pane, under Library Tools, on the Manage tab, select **Set Save Location**. Then, select the library folder to which files are to be saved.

- When navigating in File Explorer you can right-click a folder and select **Include in Library**, and then select the library from the context menu. This is the easiest way to add folders to your libraries.

- To create a new library, right-click/press-and-hold on Libraries in the Navigation pane and select **New,** then select **Library**. An empty library appears in the list of libraries. Enter a name for the new library and select **Enter**. Next, add folders to the library.

Navigating the Folder Tree

The center of attention of the Navigation pane is the folder tree. The folder tree shows all your computer's drives, folders, libraries, and other content, in a format that makes it easy to see how everything is related. Think of your computer as the main trunk of the tree, and think of those leftmost-positioned items as the primary branches growing from the trunk. In many cases, those branches have other branches growing from it.

Each of the five primary branches in the Navigation pane folder tree contains related kinds of items.

- **Favorites**—Just as you can specify websites as Favorites, making it easy to reach these sites by choosing from the Favorites menu, you can do the same with folders. Folders that have been made Favorites appear off the Favorites branch.

- **Libraries**—As you read earlier in this chapter, a library organizes related folders, making it easy for you to see and work with all the related files and folders. The Libraries branch contains all your libraries. Once enabled, you will see this branch below the library name showing all of a library's folders.

- **Homegroup**—This node shows all the content shared with the workgroup that your Windows 8 belongs to. The tree is organized by the user that joined the computer to the workgroup. Under each user are the computers the user has access to. You will not see anything in this branch until you join or start a homegroup.

- **This PC**—This PC is the branch that contains all the computer's physical objects, such as hard drives, folders, removable drives, network drives, and so on. This branch excludes the virtual items, such as libraries and Favorites.

- **Network**—The Network branch shows all the computers on the network that the computer connects to.

You can tell a branch that has other branches growing from it by the appearance of the small triangle symbol beside its name. That triangle icon is black or white, as shown in Figure 19.8. If it is black, the branches growing from it are visible. When the triangle is white, the branch's sub-branches are hidden.

To display more branches in the tree, select the white, triangle-shaped icon. To hide the branches growing from a main branch, select the black, triangle-shaped icon.

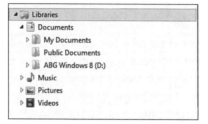

FIGURE 19.8

Show and hide branches in the folder tree by clicking the triangle-shaped icon.

Following are a few options to help you organize the Navigation pane. Each of the following, with the exception of the Navigation pane width, can be set by accessing the Navigation pane options menu. Under the View tab in the ribbon's Panes group (refer to Figure 19.4), select the Navigation pane down arrow.

- **Show/hide the Navigation pane**—After you navigate to the folder you want to work with, you can close the Navigation pane to maximize your screen real estate.

  To show or hide the Navigation pane, on the View tab in the Panes group, select the Navigation pane down arrow. Then select the Navigation pane to toggle the appearance of the pane on and off.

- **Change the width of the Navigation pane**—If your folder names are particularly long, or if you have several levels of folders in your file system, you can increase the width of the Navigation pane. You can also decrease the width of the Navigation pane to see more of the Explorer pane.

  To change the width of the Navigation pane, point to or tap-and-hold on the right edge of the slider bar that separates the Navigation pane from the Content pane. When the pointer becomes a double-headed arrow, drag the bar to change the width of the Navigation pane.

- **Showing/hiding Favorites**—If you tend to work with some folders more than others, even temporarily as you work on a project, you can add a folder to the list of Favorites. Keeping a folder on the Favorites list makes it easier to access the folder than having to navigate through your file system each time you want to work with it. You can hide or show your Favorites List in the Navigation pane.

  To show or hide the Favorites in the Navigation tree, on the View tab in the Panes group, select the Navigation pane down arrow. Then select **Show Favorites** to toggle the appearance of the Favorites on and off.

- **Showing/hiding all folders**—A few objects in the Navigation pane are a bit different from files, folders, drives, or libraries. The Control Panel, Recycle Bin, and Desktop are actually special folders. Control Panel contains small programs used to configure Windows 8. Recycle Bin stores files and folders you have deleted. Desktop is a special folder that holds anything you see on the main Desktop screen. You can hide these folders if you like, although this author sees no good reason to do so.

  To show or hide these special folders in the Navigation tree, on the View tab in the Panes group, select the Navigation pane down arrow. Then select **Show All Folders** to toggle on and off the appearance of the Control Panel, Desktop, and Recycle Bin.

- **Automatically expand to current folder**—If you open a folder without using the Navigation pane, you can configure the folder tree in the Navigation pane to expand automatically to that folder. You can also turn this feature off.

  To update the folder tree in the Navigation pane when the address is entered, under the View tab in the Panes group, select the Navigation pane down arrow. Then select **Expand to Open Folder** to toggle this feature on or off.

Customizing the Content Pane

The Content pane is the main attraction of File Explorer. The Content pane shows you the contents of the folder, drive, branch, or computer selected in the Navigation pane (see Figure 19.9). Think of the Content pane as your workbench. It's the place where you maintain and organize your computer's folder and files, such as copying, renaming, moving, deleting, burning, and so on.

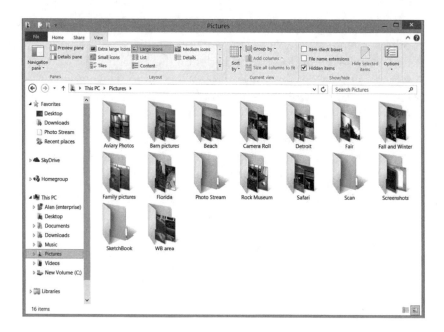

FIGURE 19.9

The Content pane shows the contents of the folder selected in the Navigation pane.

Selecting items in the Content pane is important because the commands you execute, such as Copy, Share, Delete, and all the others, affect the items selected in the Content pane. Refer to "Selecting Files and Folders" later in this chapter to review how to select.

You can change the appearance of the icons listed on the Contents pane by choosing the size or layout you want from the ribbon under the View tab in the Layout group. The Current view group contains commands to change the order in which objects appear.

- The choice of icon size: small, medium, large, and extra large is a matter of personal choice and the size of your display. If you have a large display (perhaps greater than 24") and a high resolution (greater than 1024×768), you can fit more of the large icons on the screen.

- The List view is helpful when you must select items, especially when you need to make a noncontiguous selection, as shown in Figure 19.10.

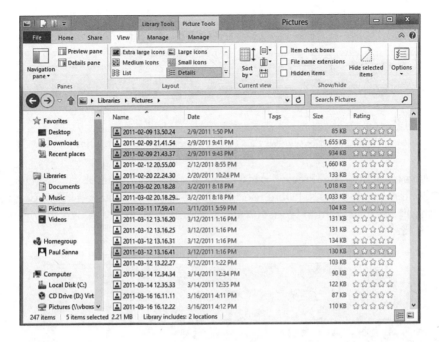

FIGURE 19.10

The List view is extremely helpful when you need to select items that do not appear next to one another.

- The Content and Details views are useful if you need to see (and sort by) the size, type, and the date the items were last modified. Click the name of the column to sort by that field. Click it again to change the sort order. Select **Add Columns** in the Current view group on the View tab to add more information in columns to the view.

- Experiment with the various options on the View tab. As the name of the tab indicates, the commands change only the appearance of the icons on the screen. It is impossible to mistakenly delete anything by making a selection from the View tab.

Exploring the Preview and Details Pane

The rightmost area of File Explorer displays one of two panes: the Preview pane and the Details pane. Only one of these panes is visible at a time. Select the view you want from the ribbon's View tab, as shown in Figure 19.11.

FIGURE 19.11

You can select one of two views to show in the Preview/Details pane.

Where possible, the Preview pane shows a snapshot of the object selected in the Content pane. If the software used to create the file is installed in Windows 8, or if the file is of a common type, you see a snapshot, such as the one shown in Figure 19.12.

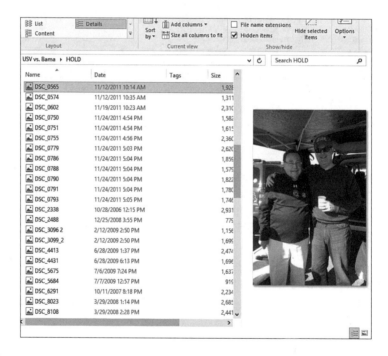

FIGURE 19.12

The Preview pane gives you a look at the file selected in the Contents pane.

The Details pane shows information about the file. The information in the fields you see may have been entered by persons who worked with the file, whereas other fields may have been filled by the software when the file was created. The two images shown in Figure 19.13 illustrate how the Details pane can show different information for different file types.

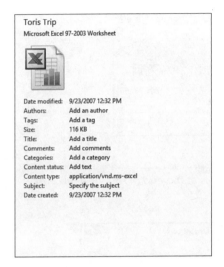

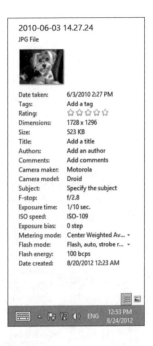

FIGURE 19.13

The Details pane displays information about the item selected in the Contents pane. The left example is of a Microsoft Excel file, and the right example comes from a photograph file.

 NOTE If you want to see a preview of how the Preview pane will appear using any of the icon views shown in the Layout section under the View tab, just pass the mouse cursor over each choice without clicking. The Preview pane changes to the view you hover over.

Folder Options

A number of options affect how folders work and appear. To change one or more of these settings, follow these steps:

1. On the ribbon under the View tab, you should see a panel labeled Options on the far right of the ribbon. Select **Options** and then **Change Folder and Search Options** (see Figure 19.14). The Folder Options dialog box appears, as shown in Figure 19.15.

2. Select the **View** tab.

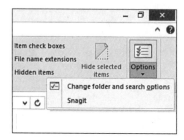

FIGURE 19.14

The command to show folder options is at the end of the View tab.

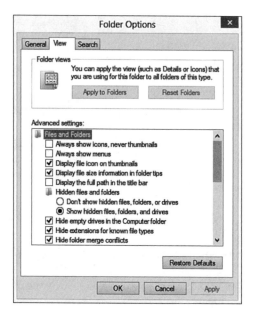

FIGURE 19.15

Nearly 20 options help you control exactly how folders work in File Explorer.

3. Adjust the options you're interested in.

4. Click **OK**.

You can review the most useful of these options in Table 19.1.

TABLE 19.1 Folder Options

Option	Description
Always Show Icons, Never Thumbnails	Displaying thumbnails requires extra computing power. You can help Windows run faster by clearing this option.
Always Show Menus	The ribbon provides much of the same functionality as provided by the menus and the commands on them in File Explorer. This option ensures the menus are always available, because certain processes in Windows hide the File Explorer menus.
Display the Full Path in in the Title Bar	This option displays the full path to the content displayed in the Explorer pane.
Hidden Files and Folders	Show Hidden Files, Folders, and Drives. Some files and folders are hidden automatically in Windows. This option displays these hidden files and folders.
Hide Empty Drives in the Computer Folder	In addition to the main hard drive installed into your computer, you might have additional drives plugged into your computer, such as small, removable USB drives (known as thumb drives). This option hides these drives if no device is plugged in.
Hide Extensions for Known File Types	As you learned earlier in this chapter, some file extensions are associated with a software program. For example, files with an XLS extension are almost always associated with Microsoft Excel. This option saves a little space by hiding the extension for a file when the filename displays and when the file's extension has an association with a program.
Restore Previous Folder Windows at Logon	When you sign on to Windows and start File Explorer, this option automatically opens folders just as you left them when you signed off. This is a useful option if you routinely work with the same set of folders or you are working on a special project that requires you to work with several folders.
Show Status Bar	This option displays the status bar at the bottom of the Windows Explorer window.
Use Check Boxes to Select Items	If awards were given out for Windows features, this option would win year after year. This option creates a small check box with each file's icon, making it simple to select the file. Read the section "Selecting Files and Folders" to learn more about this option.
Use Sharing Wizard	Sharing files and folders with members of your family at home can be tricky. There are a few settings that must be just right for the information you've intended to share to be accessible by the other party. Using the wizard assures that you will see each setting necessary for sharing to work. There is no reason why a beginning user would have this option cleared.

Option	Description
When Typing into List View	This option is driven by personal preference. If you routinely work with long lists of files or folders, a quick method to moving to a file you want to work with is to type its name. If this option is set to Select the Typed Item, the cursor moves to that file. If you prefer to search for the files whose name you entered, select the Automatically Type into the Search Box option.

Navigating Through Your Folders

Although Windows makes it easy to do most of your work from the shiny Windows 8 interface described in Chapter 2, "Interacting with Windows," occasionally you must get your hands dirty and work directly with your folders and files. That's why you're reading this chapter, right?

There are many potential reasons for you to work hands-on with your folders and files. You may need to move to a folder to copy a file to another folder. There might be an occasion when you must locate a file on your system, although you are not sure of its exact name or location. You might need to move a folder from a removable hard drive to your machine's hard drive, or vice versa. And as described earlier, you might need to organize some of the folders in your collection to store information for a new project. For these reasons and numerous others, you must know how to move through your file system.

 TIP In several places in this chapter, you can read instructions to reach certain locations in Windows 8, particularly files and folders. What might not always be clear is where you are starting from or what folder you happen to be in. The File Explorer title bar always shows the current folder.

This section of the chapter doesn't show every possible way to navigate through your files and folders because there are several, but you do see the simplest ways to get around.

Following are some direct tips for navigating in some special cases:

- To navigate to a folder by typing its name, tap or click once in any empty spot in the address bar. This highlights the contents of the address bar. Enter the name of the folder and press **Enter**.

- To navigate to a folder you recently opened, on the right end of the address bar, tap or click the down arrow, and then select the folder from the list (see Figure 19.16).

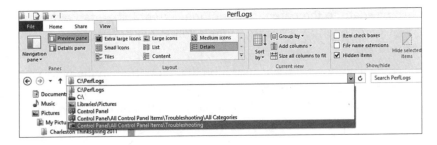

FIGURE 19.16

You can quickly navigate to a folder you visited by selecting the folder from a list of recently visited folders.

- To navigate to the folder you most recently opened, click the back-arrow button or click the Recent Locations button next to the Back and Forward buttons and select the first item in the list (see Figure 19.17).

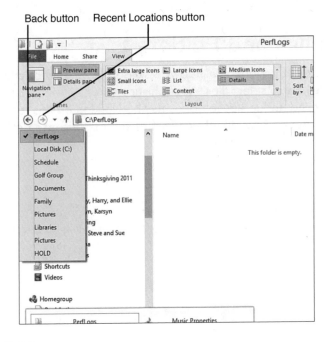

FIGURE 19.17

Choose the Recent Locations button or the Back button to move to the previous location you visited.

- To navigate to the parent folder of the current folder, tap or click the Navigate Up arrow adjacent to the address bar or press Alt+up arrow on the keyboard.

- To navigate down a branch through the folder tree, in the Navigation pane, click any folder that you believe is higher in the hierarchy than the folder you're looking for. In the Content pane, double-click/tap a folder to reveals its content, and so on.

Here are a few other useful tips:

- Double-clicking a folder in the Navigation pane expands the folders and reveals what's in the folder.

- Selecting a folder name in the address bar displays its children folders in the Content pane.

- Selecting a small arrow in the address bar pops open a list of children folders of the folder to the left of the arrow.

Selecting Files and Folders

One of the most important Windows 8 skills to learn, particularly for use with File Explorer, is how to select files. As sophisticated as Windows 8 is, it cannot yet read your mind (though developers may be working on this feature), so you need to let Windows 8 know directly which files you may want to delete, copy, move to a thumb drive, burn to a CD, and so on. It's easy to select just one file and only slightly complicated to select multiple files, but there's no doubt you can learn to select files like an expert.

 NOTE Although the author refers specifically to files in these instructions, you can use the same techniques to select folders as well, including if you must select files together with folders.

Selecting a Single File at a Time

To select one file, first navigate to the folder where the file is located. Then do one of the following based on the device you use:

👆 Tap once on the file.

⌨ Press the arrow keys to move the cursor to the file. If the cursor doesn't seem to be moving, press the **Tab** key repeatedly until the cursor appears in the Content pane.

🖱 Click once on the file.

Selecting Multiple Contiguous Files

To select multiple contiguous (next to one another) files, first navigate to the folder where the files are located. Then do one of the following based on the device you use:

👆 Swipe over the list of files. Be careful not to strike the screen when you start to pan or Windows will interpret the start of the pan as a tap.

⌨ Press the arrow keys to move the cursor to the first file in the list of those to select. If the cursor doesn't seem to be moving, press **Tab** repeatedly until the cursor appears in the Explorer pane. With the cursor over the first file, press and hold down the **Shift** key while you use the arrow keys to highlight the files.

🖱 Click and drag the mouse pointer over all the files and folders to select. To do so, point to a spot slightly above and to the left of the group of files, and then drag until all are highlighted, as shown in Figure 19.18. This process is easier if you use the Medium Icons view.

 TIP   It is easier to select multiple files when the contents of the Preview pane display in List or Details view. Read the earlier section "Exploring the Preview and Details Pane" to learn about changing the view.

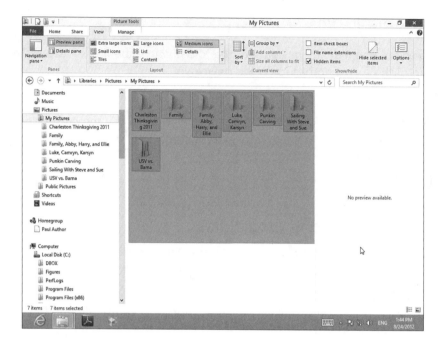

FIGURE 19.18

Select the files with your mouse by dragging over the entire group.

Selecting Multiple Noncontiguous Files

To select multiple noncontiguous (not next to one another) files, first navigate to the folder where the files are located. Then do one of the following based on the device you use:

- Select the **Use** check box to select the option described earlier in Table 19.1, Folder Options. Tap the check box for each file to select, as shown in Figure 19.19.

- Press the arrow keys to move the cursor to each file in the list. If the cursor doesn't seem to be moving, press **Tab** repeatedly until the cursor appears in the Explorer pane. With the cursor over the first file in the list, press and hold the **Ctrl** key while using the arrow keys to move the cursor to other files you want to select. When you reach a file to select, press the **spacebar**. Repeat this process for each file, remembering to hold the **Ctrl** key down.

- Click once on the first file. Next, press and hold **Ctrl** while you click each of the remaining files. Do not release Ctrl until you have clicked each of the files you intend to select.

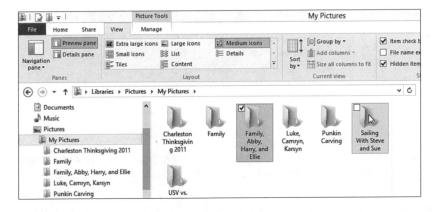

FIGURE 19.19

The Use Check Boxes option makes it easy to select files.

 TIP   Selecting multiple files not adjacent to one another can be tricky. If you accidentally release the Ctrl key before you have selected all the files you are interested in, you must start over. An alternative to using the Ctrl+click technique is to use the Use Check Boxes to Select Items option in Table 19.1.

Typical Files and Folders Tasks

If you have been reading straight through this chapter, you've read about navigating and selecting. At this point, you can put together the skills you read about to finish some basic tasks in Windows.

Each of these tasks are completed with File Explorer, which was covered earlier in the section "Navigating the Folder Tree."

If you are copying or moving several files, or if the files you are copying or moving are large, a message might appear onscreen showing the progress (see Figure 19.20). The message displays a chart illustrating the task. You can see more information about the task by selecting the **More Details** button.

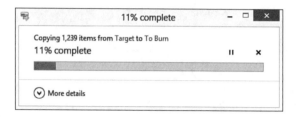

FIGURE 19.20

A dialog box appears when you copy or move files, helping you monitor progress, as well as giving you the opportunity to pause or cancel the process.

If you start another copy or move a task while an earlier one is running, the new task is added to the status screen.

 TIP   In each of the following instructions you can also use simple keyboard combinations to cut (Ctrl+X), copy (Ctrl+C), or paste (Ctrl+V).

To Copy One or More Files or Folders

1. Navigate to the folder where the files and/or folders to be copied are located.

2. Select the files and/or folders to be copied.

3. From the ribbon, on the Home tab and in the Clipboard group, select **Copy**.

4. Navigate to the folder to which the file and/or folder will be copied. Be sure not to select a folder or file in the Explorer pane.

5. From the ribbon, on the Home tab and in the Clipboard group, select **Paste**.

To Move One or More Files or Folders

1. Navigate to the folder where the files and/or folders to be copied are located.

2. Select the files and/or folders to be copied.

3. Right-click with your mouse, or with your finger or stylus, press and hold on top of one of the items being moved. Select **Cut** from the menu that appears.

4. Navigate to the folder to which the file and/or folder will be moved. Be sure not to select a folder or file in the Explorer pane.

5. Right-click with your mouse, or with your finger or stylus, press and hold any blank spot on the Explorer pane. Select **Paste** from the menu that appears.

To Rename a File or Folder

1. Navigate to the folder where the file or folder to be renamed is located.

2. From the ribbon, on the Home tab and in the Organize group, select **Rename**. A small border around the existing name of the file or folder appears, enabling you to edit the text.

3. Type the new name and press **Enter**.

To Create a Folder

1. Navigate to the folder where the new folder is to be created.

2. Right-click with your mouse, or press and hold with your finger, on an empty spot in the Explorer pane.

3. Select **New** and then **Folder** from the menu that appears. A new folder appears with its label highlighted.

4. Type the name for the new folder and press **Enter**.

To Delete a File or Folder

1. Navigate to the folder where the file or folder to be deleted is located.

2. Select the file(s) and/or folder(s).

3. From the ribbon, on the Home tab in the Organize group, click the arrow below the Delete icon.

4. Select **Recycle** to delete the file(s) and/or folder(s) with the chance to recover them if you find you made a mistake. To delete the file(s) and/or folder(s) with no chance to recover them, select **Permanently Delete**.

THE ABSOLUTE MINIMUM

Here are the key points to remember from this chapter:

- The raw materials of your Windows 8 system are files and the folders that store and organize them. Files are categorized as either system files, which are used by Windows 8 and the programs that run in Windows 8, or user files, which are the files you work with every day. You normally do not directly interact with system files.

- File Explorer, which runs in the Desktop app, is the tool used to manage your user files. You can start File Explorer from a tile on the Start screen. You should locate the tile and then pin it to the Start screen if you anticipate using File Explorer often.

- If you work with photos or music files or with work files on a regular basis, you'll work with File Explorer.

- The organization of the folders in Windows, plus the location of your files in your system, is known as your file system. You use specific techniques with your mouse, stylus, finger, or keyboard to navigate through your file system.

- You must select those files that you need to interact with, such as to copy or move. You use specific techniques to select files (and folders).

IN THIS CHAPTER

- Learning About Microsoft SkyDrive
- Using SkyDrive to Store Files
- Configuring SkyDrive to Keep Your Pictures
- Using SkyDrive to Sync Your Preferences

WORKING WITH SKYDRIVE

Cloud storage is by no means unique to Windows 8. You can choose from many cloud storage services and many websites—and even apps in the Windows Store to manage their use from Windows. Microsoft created SkyDrive to provide a valuable alternative to traditional storage methods. It has become an integral part of Windows 8, which makes it incomparable for ease of use and availability. If you have never used SkyDrive before, you will certainly have questions about what it is, how to use it, and why it will become increasingly important to you. If you have used SkyDrive in the past, you may be surprised how integrated it is in Windows 8. This chapter helps you understand how to manage SkyDrive.

roducing SkyDrive

It's amazing how much content, files, and data users have access to today. You may have several gigabytes (if not terabytes!) of pictures, video, and music that you have accumulated. Documents may be small, but they add up. Many people find that they work with several devices between home, work, and when traveling. It isn't practical to carry all your important data with you. That's where the cloud comes in. SkyDrive is an Internet-based (cloud) storage area in which you can put files such as pictures and documents and have access to them from virtually any Internet-enabled device.

If you are skeptical about "free stuff," be assured that SkyDrive is the real thing. You automatically get 7GB of free cloud-based storage with your Microsoft account, and you can pay a fee to add storage to your SkyDrive. If you have an Office 365 subscription, SkyDrive Pro is included which means you have 25GB of SkyDrive space by default. As you read through this chapter's contents, it's important to keep in mind that I'm assuming that you are logged in to a device with a Microsoft account and that you have an Internet connection. Both are needed to access SkyDrive.

 NOTE During the writing of this book, Microsoft announced that the term SkyDrive had to be replaced due to a lawsuit over the use of the word 'sky' in the brand name. At the time of this writing there was no word from Microsoft as to what the new name would be. So, as you read this chapter and see references to SkyDrive throughout this book, just be aware that whatever its new name, the Microsoft cloud storage service formerly known as SkyDrive, is what I'm referring to.

A SkyDrive tile on the Start screen provides quick access to the contents of your SkyDrive. To open SkyDrive, select the SkyDrive tile, shown in Figure 20.1.

The SkyDrive tile

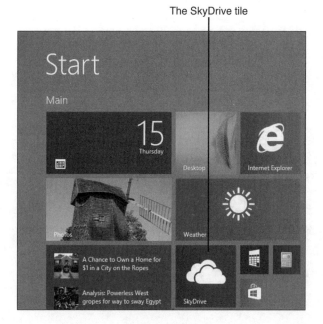

FIGURE 20.1

The SkyDrive app is available from the Start screen.

As you can tell from Figure 20.2, SkyDrive is organized by three default folders: Documents, Pictures, and Public. The picture also shows the App bar, which gives you access to a few tools for working with your SkyDrive. You also can explore more information about SkyDrive by selecting the Learn More Online link. Otherwise, select **Close** to remove the small splash screen to the left.

FIGURE 20.2

The default view in SkyDrive shows your primary folders.

There are many practical reasons to use this new form of storage. Consider some of these common uses:

- If you work with the same document on a number of computers, such as your work computer and your home computer, or if you also work on a tablet, use the SkyDrive account to store the documents. This saves you from emailing the document to yourself. You can even access your SkyDrive from most smartphones.

- If you have a tablet, you may be faced with the reality of having limited storage space on the device itself. SkyDrive provides a flexible storage solution to hardware limitations on your device.

- SkyDrive enables you to easily share with other folks. You can specify by email address those people who have access to one or more of your SkyDrive folders.

- If you work with a small team, all the documents can be stored in the Public folder of a SkyDrive account. Instead of emailing files around the group, the SkyDrive folders can be the source for all team or project documents.

NOTE   Sharing files from your SkyDrive can be done using the Share charm which sends the selected file(s) as an attachment via your email. If you want to share files using a link or control the permissions that others will have when accessing the file, you need to log in to your account using a web browser and share from the web browser interface, which offers greater control over sharing. This chapter focuses on SkyDrive features that are built in to the Windows 8 operating system.

Adding Files to Your SkyDrive

The process to load your files to SkyDrive is easy when using the mouse or touch interface. To load files and folders to SkyDrive, follow these steps:

1. Open the SkyDrive app.

2. To upload to a folder on your SkyDrive, open that folder. To open the folder, click or tap the folder.

3. Open the App bar and select **Add Files** (refer to Figure 20.2).

4. Navigate through your file system to select files to upload. Select each file you want to add to your SkyDrive, as shown in Figure 20.3.

5. When you have selected all the files to upload, select **Copy to SkyDrive**.

6. You will now see your files appear in the SkyDrive folder you added them to, as shown in Figure 20.4.

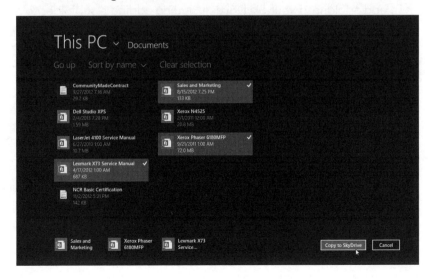

FIGURE 20.3

You can select files to copy to your SkyDrive folder from local storage locations.

Click to check upload progress

Uploading 1 item...

⊕ SkyDrive ⌄ Documents

Lexmark X73 Service Manual
4/17/2012   687 KB
Available offline

Sales and Marketing
8/15/2012   133 KB
Available offline

Xerox Phaser 6180MFP
9/21/2011   72.0 MB
Uploading...

FIGURE 20.4

Files you have selected appear in your SkyDrive folder as they are uploaded.

 NOTE It may take some time to upload especially large files. Status messages appear in the upper right, as shown in Figure 20.4. You can also click these status messages to view details from the Progress pane.

Managing Files on Your SkyDrive

You have as many options for managing your SkyDrive as you do for your local drives. You can create folders and subfolders, select multiple files, delete files, and see thumbnails of a file's contents. Here are a few of the options:

- To add a folder to your SkyDrive, including adding a subfolder to a folder on SkyDrive, start by opening the SkyDrive app. Open the folder on SkyDrive where the folder will be created. Open the App bar and select **New Folder**. The pop-up shown in Figure 20.5 appears. Enter the name of the folder and select **Create**.

FIGURE 20.5

You can create additional folders to keep your files organized.

- If you are moving or copying all the files in a SkyDrive folder, you can easily select all files. Open the folder where the files are located. Next, open the App bar and select **Select All**. You will see a view like the one in Figure 20.6.

- To delete one or more files on your SkyDrive, open the folder where the files are located. Select the files to be deleted. To do so, right-click on the file or, if you are using a touch interface, tap and swipe up on the file. Tap additional files to add to your selection, if needed. Next, from the App bar select **Delete**.

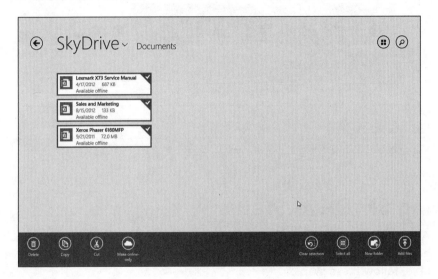

FIGURE 20.6

You can perform many basic tasks with selected files on your SkyDrive.

- To work with a SkyDrive-based file, select the file to open with your default application for that file type. To specify which application should open it, select the file(s) and then select **Open With** from the App bar. You will be able to select from applications you have on your device and even assign default applications from here.

- To change how files appear in your SkyDrive, use the View button in the upper-right corner of your app to switch from detailed view to thumbnail view. Compare Figures 20.6 and 20.7 to see the difference. This changes the view in all folders in SkyDrive.

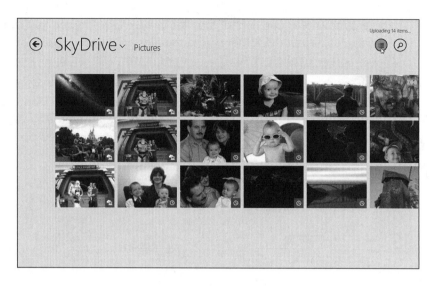

FIGURE 20.7

Viewing files as thumbnails in SkyDrive.

Viewing SkyDrive Status

As you start to add files to your SkyDrive storage, you might begin wondering just how much storage space you have left. To see how much space you have available, follow these steps:

1. From the Start screen select the Settings charm, then select **Change PC Settings**.

2. Select **SkyDrive** from the menu to the left.

3. You should see File Storage on the left and your current SkyDrive storage space on the right, as shown in Figure 20.8.

4. If you need more space, there is a convenient Buy More Storage button. Select this to see current options, as shown in Figure 20.9.

FIGURE 20.8

Check your storage space status using the Change PC settings, SkyDrive menu.

FIGURE 20.9

You can buy additional SkyDrive space for an annual subscription price.

You might hesitate to purchase additional space. Consider a few factors that perhaps will put things into perspective:

- **Ease of use**—You do not need to carry a flash drive around, and it will be there any time you log in to a computer with your Microsoft account—even if you choose to log in to your Microsoft account from a web browser on someone else's computer.

- **Security**—What happens if you lose a flash drive or, worse yet, your laptop? Will you get your data back if your hard drive fails? SkyDrive space is encrypted and is backed up on Microsoft servers, so you do not have to worry if a hard drive fails.

- **Convenience**—By sharing files with other people you can simplify collaboration and avoid issues with email attachments.

Before buying additional space, make sure you are wisely using the space you already have. Just because you can save all your music and videos to your SkyDrive does not mean it is practical or even a good idea. Things that you share or that need to be highly available should get priority. In the following sections you may also want to look at how SkyDrive space is used by default by your device to see if you want to be more or less conservative in configuring these options.

Configuring SkyDrive File Storage

There are a few settings that allow you to customize how your device uses SkyDrive storage. You learn about some of these settings in this and the following sections.

Saving to SkyDrive as Default

Windows allows you to save your files to the Documents folder on your SkyDrive automatically. This will already be enabled by default on your device if you chose the option to use SkyDrive when first logging into the device with your Microsoft account. To check this setting, follow these steps:

1. From the Start screen select the Settings charm, then select **Change PC Settings**.

2. Select **SkyDrive** from the menu to the left.

3. You should see File Storage on the left and your current SkyDrive storage space on the right, as shown previously in Figure 20.8. Notice that the setting to save documents to SkyDrive is set to On.

4. If you want to turn this off, slide the selector to the Off position. You can still select files from your Documents folder to copy to your SkyDrive Documents folder manually following the steps from earlier in this chapter.

An example of what happens is shown in Figure 20.10, where I've saved a Word file to my Documents folder and it was saved to SkyDrive\Documents. Notice the highlighted path that appears to be on the C drive. The only location where this document is saved is on the SkyDrive; no local copy is saved. If you don't want this to happen, you should turn off the Save Documents to SkyDrive by Default option specified in step 3.

FIGURE 20.10

Files you save to the Documents may be saved to your SkyDrive Documents by default.

This is a matter of preference and is meant to save you a few steps if you intend to keep a copy of the file on your SkyDrive. It is important to understand the behavior of this setting so that you will know where your files are later.

Managing Photo Storage Considerations

Another important setting to consider is how your device handles photos and storage. Associated with this are videos that you might record using the camera on your Windows 8 device. Figure 20.11 shows the default settings for the Camera Roll. Camera Roll is simply a way of referring to images created by this device. Photos are often kept at full resolution on the device and a lower resolution is uploaded to your SkyDrive.

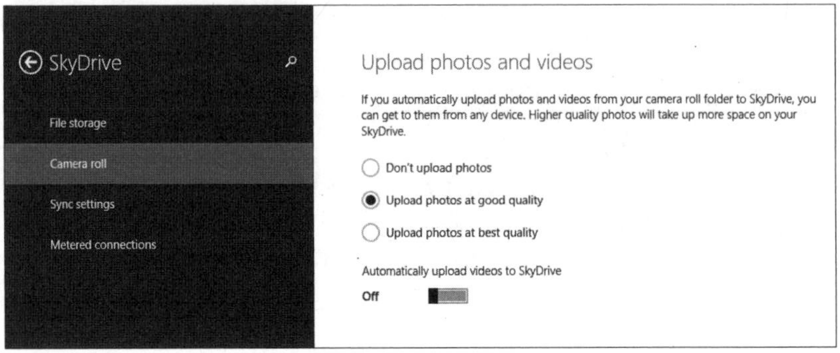

FIGURE 20.11

Make changes to how your device saves pictures and video to SkyDrive through the Settings charm.

To check the setting on your device, follow these steps:

1. From the Start screen select the Settings charm, then select **Change PC Settings**.

2. Select **SkyDrive** from the menu to the left.

3. Select **Camera Roll** from the menu on the left to see your current SkyDrive storage options for the device on the right. Select **Don't Upload Photos** to prevent this feature altogether. Good quality is fine for sharing photos on other devices.

4. Automatically Upload Videos to SkyDrive is off by default. Video files are large and can quickly consume your SkyDrive space if you enable this and you tend to take lots of video.

I have used a Windows Phone and a Surface tablet for some time, and the good image quality displays nicely on other devices, including my wife's iPad. Use the best quality setting if you need to have much higher resolution copies saved to the SkyDrive. Just be aware that as devices get higher resolution cameras, this also uses up your drive space faster. A good compromise is to leave the setting at good and manually upload any photos that you want to keep at a higher resolution.

Synchronizing SkyDrive

Another nice feature that is built in to Windows 8 is to synchronize your settings with any other Windows 8 systems or devices associated with your Microsoft account using SkyDrive. This includes theme and wallpaper choices, Start screen layout, language, and Windows settings. Figure 20.12 shows Sync settings for a Windows 8 device.

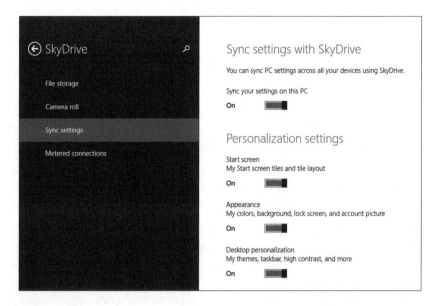

FIGURE 20.12

You can customize how settings from one Windows 8 device affect other devices you use.

To check your settings follow these steps:

1. From the Start screen select the Settings charm, then select **Change PC Settings**.

2. Select **SkyDrive** from the menu on the left.

3. Select **Sync Settings** from the menu on the left. Your current SkyDrive sync settings are displayed to the right. By default, everything is likely enabled.

4. Scroll down through the list on the right and disable settings that you do not want synced by sliding the switch to the Off position.

If you have a tablet device and a Windows 8 desktop PC, for example, you might prefer some settings to remain unique to each device. You will find that changes you make on one device are automatically made on another device when sync is enabled. It is a very nice feature that enables you to quickly navigate your devices without having to manually save favorites or change personalization settings for each device you use. If you want to turn Sync off, turn the first slider switch shown in Figure 20.12 to the Off position.

Manage Metered Connections Considerations

Occasionally I am out on the road and I will share the Internet from my smartphone. This allows me to use a process called tethering to connect to the Internet with my laptop and tablet using the same cellular Internet connection my smartphone uses. This is handy, but depending on your plan it could quickly suck up your monthly data allotment. I exceeded my quota for the month the first time I used it because my older Windows XP-based laptop downloaded a bunch of updates and I didn't notice what was happening in the background until it was too late. This illustrates why it's important that you protect your more costly connections to the Internet from unnecessary data consumption.

Another factor could be bandwidth. Hotels can be terribly slow and stingy with "free Wi-Fi," and I have friends who still live with dial-up connections. If you have a slow connection, you may need to consider what type of data gets priority when you connect to the Internet.

Microsoft uses the term metered Internet connection to refer to a connection that has restrictions on data, especially related to quotas or limits. Fortunately, Windows enables you to categorize a connection as metered, which allows you to control what type of data is downloaded over that connection. Figure 20.13 shows the settings related to SkyDrive when using a metered connection.

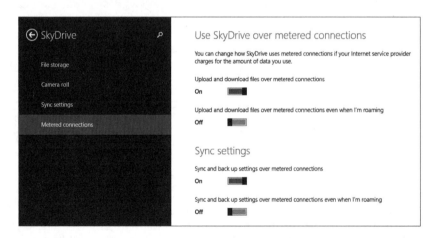

FIGURE 20.13

Change how your device uses SkyDrive while on metered connections to conserve data consumption.

To check your settings follow these steps:

1. From the Start screen select the Settings charm, then select **Change PC Settings**.

2. Select **SkyDrive** from the menu on the left.

3. Select **Metered Connections** from the menu on the left. Your current Use SkyDrive Over Metered Connections settings are displayed on the right.

4. Based on your data concerns, you may choose to disable everything, or you might leave just Upload and Download Files Over Metered Connections enabled.

If you disable everything, it will affect your access to pictures and other files that are saved to your SkyDrive. The Sync settings you see here relate to personalization settings that I showed you in the previous section.

To let Windows know a connection should be considered metered, navigate to your current network settings by opening the Settings charm. Select the network you are connected to and look for the slider to Set as a Metered Connection, as shown in Figure 20.14.

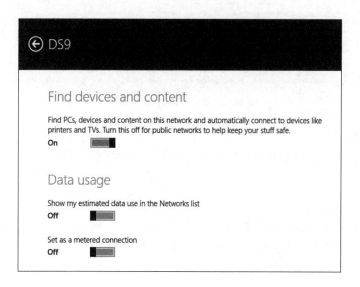

FIGURE 20.14

Make sure you identify a network as metered if you are concerned about data consumption.

Set this slider to On, and now the options you have selected for using SkyDrive over a metered connection will kick in. By default, Windows also will prevent system and app updates from using a metered connection. To learn more about options related to your network connections see Chapter 11, "Connecting to the Internet."

Using SkyDrive from the Desktop

SkyDrive has become so integrated into Windows 8.1 that you may forget you are connected to cloud-based storage. Everything you've read about so far about creating folders and copying in files can also be done while working directly with the File Explorer tool (see Figure 20.15).

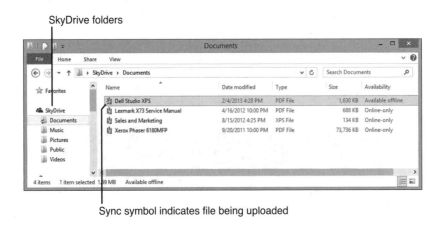

FIGURE 20.15

You can manage SkyDrive folders straight from the File Explorer.

If you look at the Navigation pane you'll see a node for SkyDrive along with the five folders it contains. Files can be copied to this folder just like any other folder on your system. The only difference is that when you copy or move files to a SkyDrive folder, you'll see a small sync symbol on the file while it is being uploaded to your SkyDrive.

Offline Availability

Offline availability is another great feature that makes SkyDrive versatile. Notice in Figure 20.15 the column labeled Availability. This indicates whether the file will be accessible when you are not connected to the Internet. If you are traveling or are without Internet for some reason, you will still have a cached copy of a file that shows Available Offline. Files that are marked as Online-only require Internet connectivity to open them; they usually appear grayed out when you are without an Internet connection, although you will still have information regarding the file's last known date, size, and thumbnails. If you try to open one of these files, you will see something like the warning in Figure 20.16.

FIGURE 20.16

You will be unable to open files from your SkyDrive that are Online-only if you do not have an Internet connection.

To make changes to this setting from File Explorer, follow these steps when connected to the Internet:

1. From the Desktop, open Windows Explorer and navigate to a folder in the SkyDrive node.

2. Right-click or tap and hold a file to bring up the context menu.

3. Select **Make Available Offline** or **Make Available Online** only as needed. The status in the Availability column will change to match your selection.

THE ABSOLUTE MINIMUM

Keep the following points in mind after you read this chapter:

- SkyDrive is an integral part of Windows 8. Take some time to open your SkyDrive and add files and folders.

- You can check your available drive space and even purchase additional SkyDrive space by opening the Settings charm and selecting **Change PC Settings**, **SkyDrive**.

- The SkyDrive app lets you add files, create and manage folders, and delete files.

- Use the View button to switch between thumbnails and tiles with detailed information for your files.

- Check your settings to see if documents are being saved to your SkyDrive or locally by default. Adjust settings as needed for syncing your settings from one device to others you use.

- Check your settings for metered connections and tag connections as metered if data consumption is a concern.

- Make sure files are available offline if you will need them when you're away from an Internet connection.

21

HAVING FUN WITH MOVIES AND VIDEOS

If you watch movies and other videos on your computer, you should begin a friendship with the Video app that uses Microsoft's Xbox Video service. The app is easy to use, yet it has enough features and capabilities to meet just about all your needs, especially after major upgrades have been made to the app. Certainly some folks with a bit more experience in integrating digital media with personal computers might bellyache at the lack of interesting features in the app, but you cannot argue with the price (free) or the ease of adding in your content to the library. This chapter covers all the basics, from navigating through all the movies and TV shows offered in the marketplace to renting or purchasing a selection that interests you.

Getting Started with the Xbox Video App

The Xbox Video app is an easy-to-use program that enables you to watch videos from both your private collection and from the enormous Xbox LIVE marketplace. If you are bored with your own collection, you can purchase almost any video offered in the marketplace. If you don't want to make a purchase commitment, you can rent one or more of the videos offered. If you don't have the time to watch a full movie, you can always occupy a few minutes by watching the 10-minute previews available for each movie. You can also amuse yourself reading the artist profiles.

To start the Xbox Video app, select the tile, as shown in Figure 21.1. If you cannot locate the tile, open the Charms bar and then select **Search**. When the Search pane opens, enter **videos** and then select **Apps**. Select the Video tile from the list of results on the left side of the screen.

FIGURE 21.1

Launch the Xbox Video app from the tile on the Start screen.

Setting Up Your Xbox LIVE Account

A few seconds after the app starts, Windows 8 tries to sign in to Xbox LIVE with the same Microsoft account you use to sign-in to Windows. Xbox LIVE is Microsoft's online digital media service. In addition to a host of features and benefits associated with the Xbox game console, it provides videos, music, and games to Windows 8. Connecting to Xbox LIVE makes it easy to buy and rent video content, as well as to take advantage of the other services that Microsoft offers.

If you aren't using a Microsoft account to log in to Windows or if you haven't connected your Microsoft account to an Xbox LIVE ID, the app's main screen displays a message in the upper-right corner prompting you to click to sign in (see Figure 21.2).

This account isn't signed in to Xbox Live

FIGURE 21.2

You will be directed to sign in if you do not have an account with Xbox LIVE.

At this point you may be wondering how many accounts one person needs to get along in Windows. In this case it's because LIVE services, originally created for the Xbox game consoles, existed long before Microsoft accounts came along. Fortunately, linking the two is a simple process that you need to do only once (if you haven't done so already). If you see the Click Here to Sign In link, go ahead and give it a click.

 NOTE   If you have an Xbox LIVE ID already, but it's not connected to your Xbox account, you can find more details about joining the two at www.xboxlive.com.

Follow the prompts Windows throws your way until you're asked to create an Xbox profile (see Figure 21.3).

To continue, create an Xbox profile

Your login: alanlwright@outlook.com
Adding an online Xbox membership to your Microsoft account lets you participate in great Xbox gaming and entertainment.
Already have an Xbox LIVE account?

Date of Birth

Country/Region

United States (English)

☑ I'd like to receive information and offers about music, videos, and games from Xbox and related entertainment providers in email.

☐ Share my contact information with partners of Xbox and related entertainment products so they can send me information and offers.

Clicking 'I Accept' means you have read and agree to the Xbox LIVE Terms of Use and Privacy Statement.

| I Accept | Cancel |

FIGURE 21.3

Your account is initially created after you supply just a few pieces of information.

Before you click the I Accept button you might want to check the settings regarding additional marketing options. After you have indicated your preferences, select **I Accept**.

After accepting the provisions of your account, you're next presented with some information about your account, most notably your gamertag (see Figure 21.4).

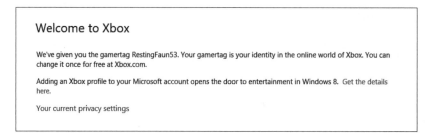

Welcome to Xbox

We've given you the gamertag RestingFaun53. Your gamertag is your identity in the online world of Xbox. You can change it once for free at Xbox.com.

Adding an Xbox profile to your Microsoft account opens the door to entertainment in Windows 8. Get the details here.

Your current privacy settings

FIGURE 21.4

Your gamertag is your unique identifier in the Xbox LIVE universe.

The gamertag is the ID you use to identify yourself in the Xbox LIVE universe. Select **OK**. At this point, Windows 8 finishes creating your account, and you are returned to the app. You can browse through the videos in the app and see rates to rent a title that interests you. To set up your account for purchases and to perform any kind of account maintenance, open the Settings charm again and select **Account**. A menu of account choices appears, from which you can supply credit card information to pay for videos you rent or purchase, upgrade your Xbox LIVE account, and more. If you have any questions about the Xbox LIVE service, visit www.xbox.com. Microsoft often makes changes to the services, and promotions are usually available. Visit the site to read the most up-to-date rules and news.

Adding Your Videos to the Videos Library

If you have acquired digital movies and TV shows in the past, or if you have downloaded and saved lots of the fun and informative videos from the Internet (legally only, please), you'll want to add those movies to this library. You can also load videos you've recorded into Windows 8. By loading all your video content into Windows 8, you can access all your onscreen digital content from one place. Until you add your own content to the Xbox Video app, the screen shown in Figure 21.5 appears.

FIGURE 21.5

This message almost begs you to load your videos into the library!

If you have no digital videos—that is, you have never purchased videos online and you have never imported videos into your computer—you can skip this section. If you do own movies, TV shows, home movies, and other videos, you can link their location to the Videos folder in Windows 8. The Xbox Video app uses that folder, which is actually a special folder referred to sometimes as a library, as its source for your videos. You can learn about libraries in Chapter 19, "Managing Files and Folders."

Keep in mind, though, that you must maintain the link to your video collection's location, such as across your home network or to a removable hard drive, for your videos to be available. If your Windows 8 computer is a laptop, it's likely you'll move that computer to a location away from the network or drive where those videos are located. If your computer stays in one place, of course, you won't have this problem.

 TIP To find your personal videos easily, you should name them. A name like "WIN_20130818_190138" is much harder to remember than "Joshua's first bike ride." Later in this chapter, you see how to use search in the Video app. The easiest way to rename files is to use File Explorer, which we covered back in Chapter 19.

Follow these steps to link your collection of videos to Windows 8 and the Xbox Video app:

1. Select the link shown in Figure 21.5, **Choose Where We Look for Videos on This PC**. (If you already have some videos but would like to add more, you will need to select the Settings charm, **Preferences**, and then select **Choose Where We Look for Videos on This PC**.)

2. A pop-up screen, shown in Figure 21.6, appears that invites you to build your collection. It points to the Videos folder by default, but if there's someplace else you want Windows to look, select the button with a large plus sign (+). This opens the file picker, which allows you to choose locations on your hard drive, SkyDrive, or elsewhere on your device. If you have videos scattered in different locations, either consolidate all the content to one place or repeat these steps for each location where videos are stored.

3. Open the Xbox Video app. Check **My Videos** to verify that your videos are present.

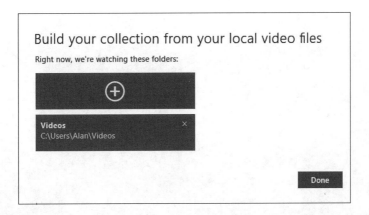

FIGURE 21.6

Add the location of your videos to the Windows 8 Video library.

Moving Through the Xbox Video App

The **Xbox Video app** is organized into four main sections. These sections are organized laterally across the screen and are broken up, so at first it may appear to show more than four groups. You'll also notice that each section is also a link that, when clicked, allows you to explore a category in more detail. Here are the main sections, in order from left to right:

- **My videos**—The first section on the left gives you access to videos in your Video library (see Figure 21.7). It's divided between Personal Videos, My TV, and My Movies, the latter two of which appear only if you have purchased content in those categories.

- **Home/recommendations**—This section is the first section showing Xbox LIVE marketplace selections (see Figure 21.8), and it is the first thing you see when you open the Video app. It shows the current hot videos or those Microsoft and its partners want to make noise about.

FIGURE 21.7

Personal Videos displays content from your Video library and purchases you have made from TV and Movie selections.

FIGURE 21.8

Review the selection of hot current movies and videos.

- **Movies store**—This section appears with new movies and featured movies (see Figure 21.9). Some movie tiles offer bonus content or sometimes a 10-minute preview; watch for these to appear as badges on the movie tile itself.

FIGURE 21.9

The movies store offers a huge selection of films with a focus on the latest and greatest.

- **Television store**—Very similar to the way movies are organized, this section enables you to shop for and then watch shows that appear and have appeared on TV. You can pay for and then watch selections from the main networks and from the specialty and pay networks. There are free shows offered, as well.

To access the content organized in these sections, scroll through the sections of the app. With your mouse, point to the scrollbars at the bottom of the screen. With your finger or stylus, swipe left or right to move around. Use the Tab or arrow keys on the keyboard to move across the screen.

When you select a TV or movie, you see a screen with detailed information providing purchase and rental prices, and possibly a trailer that you can watch. Reviews are offered for movies, and a list of cast members appears. As with many things on the detailed screen in Xbox Video, these names are links that you can select to find more information about the director, actor, or writer. There's also a section with a list of related movie titles. When looking at television shows, you will see a Metacritic rating, and you can indicate your own rating of the TV program. A list of episodes allows you to purchase individual episodes rather than an entire season.

Inside a marketplace, select the category to reveal additional lists by which you can filter the content you see, such as featured movies or top-rated TV shows (see Figure 21.10).

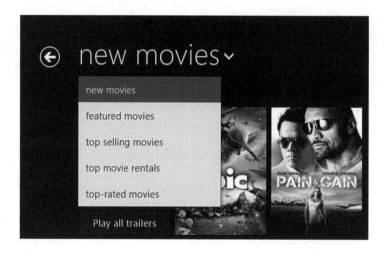

FIGURE 21.10

You can quickly jump from one list of movies to a different list.

While you are looking at a list of movies or television programs, you can filter them even further using the subcategories that appear beneath the section title (see Figure 21.11). To back up at any time, select the Back button that appears at the top left of most screens. If you open a small screen, for example, to view details about a movie, you can click anywhere outside of the screen to close it.

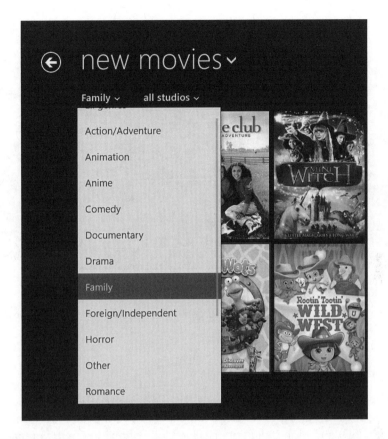

FIGURE 21.11

When viewing a list, you can filter the list in a couple of ways.

You might be wondering how to find something that is not in a featured or top list. From anywhere in the Video app, you can select the search icon in the upper right to initiate a search for any movies, TV shows, and personal videos. If you search for *Casablanca*, for example, and select it from the search results, you'll see the movie's information page (see Figure 21.12).

FIGURE 21.12

Search makes it possible to easily find gems that may not be in the current top-viewed lists.

Shopping for Videos

You can browse through the movies and TV shows presented in each section with an eye toward buying or renting. You usually have a choice between standard edition (SD) and high definition (HD) versions of a video, and you can generally choose to download or stream either selection.

If you are unfamiliar with the idea of renting or purchasing a digital movie or TV show, especially with Xbox LIVE, this section explains how that works. Just keep in mind that the screens and options used to process your purchase or rental certainly can change, so what you see here may have some variation compared to your own experience.

Making a Purchase

Select the movie or TV show you want to take in. You may also purchase a season pass for certain TV shows, in which you pay upfront to watch new episodes as they air during the season. When you decide to make a purchase, select **Buy** or **Rent** on that video's page in the Xbox Video app. You may then be asked to confirm your credentials by reentering your Microsoft account password. You will be presented with a summary of your purchase options, as shown in Figure 21.13.

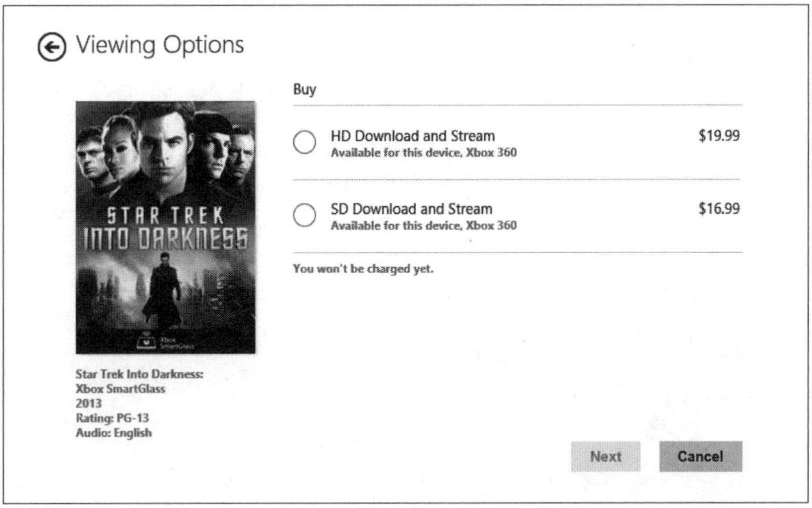

Viewing Options

Buy

HD Download and Stream $19.99
Available for this device, Xbox 360

SD Download and Stream $16.99
Available for this device, Xbox 360

You won't be charged yet.

Star Trek Into Darkness:
Xbox SmartGlass
2013
Rating: PG-13
Audio: English

Next   Cancel

FIGURE 21.13

After you choose to buy or rent a selection, you may have to select from available options.

After making your selection to Buy or Rent, a confirmation of your order appears on the screen. The confirmation shows the amount your purchase costs and the details for the purchase. Read the details carefully as some movie purchases may have an expiration. After you select **Confirm**, you are charged. If you have questions about your account or purchases, look at the support information on Microsoft's Xbox LIVE website at www.xboxlive.com.

After you confirm your order, the video appears in the Personal videos section of the app. To see the physical movie in file form, open File Explorer and navigate to the Videos library. You see a folder for the movie you purchased and the movie file in the folder designated as the Save folder for the library. Refer to Chapter 19 for information about libraries.

Renting a Selection

If you prefer not to make your purchase permanent, you can rent most titles. Terms tend to change on an unannounced basis, so you should certainly check for the most current details about Microsoft's rental policies on www.xboxlive.com. Figure 21.14 shows the rental terms for an HD download of a movie. Even though it is to be downloaded, the video will be available for only 14 days in this example. Following are other details regarding rentals that you should consider:

- After you start playback of a rental, you must complete watching it in 24 hours before the rental becomes nonfunctional.

- During the 24-hour rental period, you can watch the movie as many times as you like.

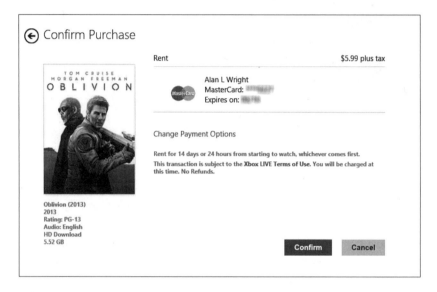

FIGURE 21.14

Read the terms carefully when renting or purchasing video content before selecting Confirm.

THE ABSOLUTE MINIMUM

Keep the following points in mind after you've completed reading this chapter:

- If you plan to purchase or rent a video in the Windows 8 Xbox Video app, be sure to create your Xbox account before you start. It can save some work by doing it upfront.

- If you have different IDs for your Microsoft account and an existing Xbox LIVE account, look into merging these two accounts. You can find information about merging accounts on www.xboxlive.com.

- Move your videos to your Windows 8 computer so that they can be integrated into the library with other selections you might acquire. Doing so also enables you to watch your videos whenever you choose.

- You can also consider linking to the existing location of your videos by adding the physical folder location of your videos to the Video library accessed through File Explorer. This is an easier option than moving your videos, but you can't access this content if you move your computer to a place where it can no longer connect with your video library's location.

22

ENJOYING MUSIC

The Music app in Windows 8 is fun to use, attractive to look at, and generally does everything you'd expect it to do. You can play music you've purchased in the past, and you can buy new music. The Music app isn't full-featured, though. You may want to play music that resides on a CD, or someone else in your home may want to play tunes on your computer. These and a few other features are not available in the Music app; however, other tools in Windows can substitute for the Music app for these tasks. In this chapter, you learn the basics—playing music, setting up your library, looking through your library, shopping for music online—and learn when you must use another tool.

Getting Started with the Music App

You can use the Music app to play and manage your music in Windows 8. You can bring into the Music app the music you've already purchased online or imported from CDs, and you can purchase new music.

As a Windows 8 app, you can play music full screen and enjoy the animated collages that play in the background. Or you can dock the Music app while you do other work in Windows 8. You can play a single song, a playlist of your own design, an entire album, or perhaps all the music you can find from one artist. From using other programs like iTunes from Apple, you might be wondering how you create a music CD or import music from a CD. These capabilities are available from the Windows Media Player program, but not the Music app. You can find a brief overview of these tasks at the end of this chapter.

To start the Music app, select the tile, as shown in Figure 22.1. If you cannot locate the tile, open the **Charms** bar and then select **Search**. When the Search pane opens, enter **music** into the search box. Select the Music tile from the list of results.

FIGURE 22.1

Select the Music app from the Start screen.

Learning What's Where in the Music App

The Music app is loosely organized into three sections: Collection, Radio, and Explore. These appear off to the left on the sidebar:

- Collection shows music from your library, as shown in Figure 22.2.

- Radio is a new feature allowing you to listen to streamed music generated by a music artist that you indicate (see Figure 22.3). You can listen to content from that artist and others that match that genre. Like other radio services, you can purchase a subscription to eliminate advertising and monthly time limits.

- Explore allows you to look for new music from a huge library of Xbox Music selections.

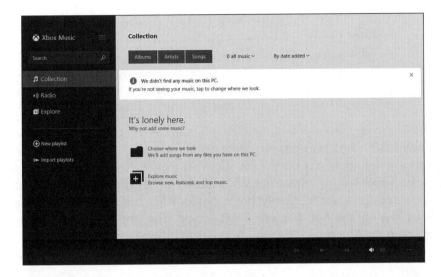

FIGURE 22.2

The Collection area will show music from your library and other devices.

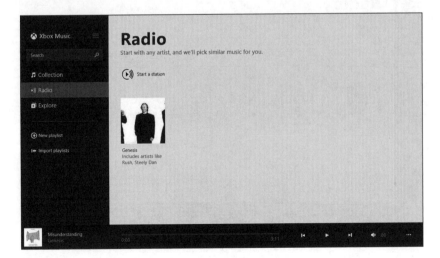

FIGURE 22.3

Radio enables you to select the type of streaming music you want to listen to.

TIP To reduce the space that is taken up on the screen by the vertical control bar on the left side of your Music app, you can select the icon composed of three horizontal lines to the right of the Xbox Music title. It reduces this bar to simple icons, as you can see in Figure 22.4. Select the icon again to restore the bar to its original appearance.

The Music app displays a music player bar across the bottom of the screen that is always visible and presents the exact commands you need, no matter what you're doing in the app. For example, as shown in Figure 22.4, when you play music, the music player bar presents commands to play the next song, repeat the current song, and more. Although this bar might look like the App bar present in most apps, it is not the App bar for the Music app. The App bar now has very limited usage in the Music app. Use the App bar to browse for a file when you want to manually play a song in the Music app that may not be in your Music library at the moment.

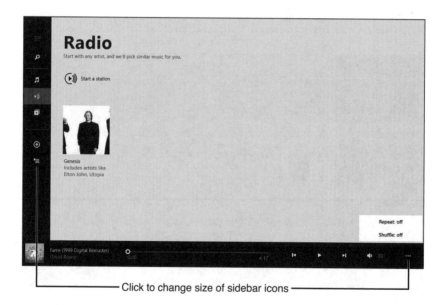

Click to change size of sidebar icons

FIGURE 22.4

The music player bar gives you access to commands you would see on an MP3 player as you play music in the Music app.

Setting Up Your Xbox LIVE Account

A few seconds after the app starts, Windows 8 tries to sign-in to Xbox LIVE with the account you used to sign in to Windows. If you have not established an Xbox membership yet, in the upper-right corner of the Music app you will see a notification inviting you to sign in, as shown in Figure 22.5. The steps to set up your Xbox LIVE account are shown in detail in Chapter 21, "Having Fun with Movies and Videos."

FIGURE 22.5

You may need to supply information to create your Xbox membership.

Once your Xbox LIVE account is created, a menu of account choices appears, as shown in Figure 22.6, from which you can supply credit card information to pay for music you want to download and own or simply want to listen to with an Xbox Music Pass account. You can also manage other aspects of your account from the same screen. If you have any questions about the Xbox LIVE service, visit www. xbox.com. Microsoft often makes changes to the service, and promotions are often available. Visit the site to read the most up-to-date rules and news.

FIGURE 22.6

After your account is created, you are linked to the Xbox LIVE service.

TIP   When you're working in other apps or even the desktop, you can still interact with the Music app, even if it is out of sight. If your Windows 8 device includes its own play or volume controls, go ahead and use them. When you do, a compact music player temporarily appears. This is a nice hidden feature that avoids your needing to dock the player to the screen while working in other apps.

Loading Your Music into Windows 8

Along with buying new music, the whole point of the Music app is to listen to your music, right? Before doing so, you need to bring your music into the Music app. If you have no digital music—that is, you have never purchased music online and you have never imported CD music onto your computer, you can skip this section. However, you should be prepared for your library to grow quickly (and your expenses to rise as quickly) because the Music app makes it incredibly tempting and easy to buy new music.

The Music app does a lot with a little. The app presents an attractive, well-laid-out, informative, and well-organized library of music. As you learn shortly, you can get the same benefits if you specify where your music collection is located rather than moving your music. The point is that a number of benefits included in the Windows 8 design don't commit you to a specific system of storing your music file.

You have two options to bring your music into the Music app:

- You can link to your existing collection of music, even if it's on another computer or on a removable drive.
- You can either copy or move your entire collection from a different system to the computer running Windows 8.

The following two sections explain how to connect your music to Windows 8 using these approaches.

How to Link Your Music

Linking to your music takes advantage of the libraries function in File Explorer. A *library* is a special folder type that consolidates folders from different locations on your computer to make all the folders appear to be in the same location. The Music folder is actually a built-in library in Windows 8. The Music app uses the music library to populate the My Music section. You can find detailed information in Chapter 19, "Managing Files and Folders," for instruction on working with libraries.

When you first open the Music app, your collection may appear rather empty. If it does, you can select the alert notification, if visible, or select the Choose Where We Look with the folder icon to bring up the Music app interface to the Music library. You will see the current folder included in the library, and you can select a large button with a + (plus sign) to add more folders using the file picker. Figure 22.7 shows the results after I added a folder containing some music. The locations you can add include networked folders, folders from devices in your homegroup, and removable drives. If you wish to add a location later, select the Settings charm and then select **Preferences**. You will then see a link to Choose Where We Look for Music on This PC, select this to add more folder locations to your Music library.

 CAUTION   Keep in mind that if you cannot reach the network or you cannot travel with your removable drive, you will not have access to your entire collection of music. Also network locations that Windows 8 cannot index for one reason or another are not added to your Music library.

FIGURE 22.7

The Music library points to all the music on your computer. The Music app leverages the Music library to present your music in the app.

Another unique way to link music with Windows 8 is from the cloud, as indicated by an alert in the Collection view shown in Figure 22.8. You can listen to music you already have on other devices you log in to from the cloud. Select the alert to use a feature called Match Music to compare music you currently own to music in the cloud-based Xbox music library. These songs are then matched and made available from the cloud; you do not need to copy or repurchase on another device.

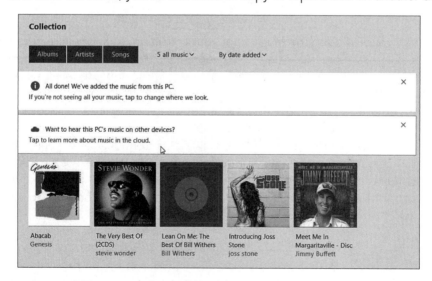

FIGURE 22.8

You can add songs you currently have to the cloud thus making your songs available from the cloud to other devices you use.

Depending on your device, you may also see the option to listen to music that is on another device without having to take any action at all. Figure 22.9 shows the Collection view on a Surface RT that has no music on the device itself; however, music is on the cloud. The music shown is on a Windows Phone 8, which also uses Xbox music.

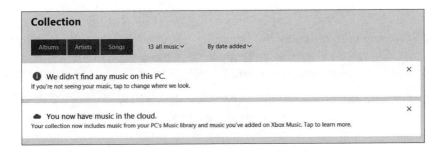

FIGURE 22.9

Your Windows 8 device may allow you to stream songs automatically from other devices that use the Xbox music service.

You may notice that some songs have an icon next to the song title. Icons will indicate one of the following when they appear next to a song or album:

((•))   This icon indicates that a song is available for streaming only while connected to the Internet. It cannot be played while offline.

    This icon indicates that a song is available on this device and from the cloud when you log in to other devices. You can play this song while offline.

 NOTE The absence of any icon indicates that a song is available only on this device. You need to take action to make it available to other devices you log in to.

 TIP You may see a couple of alerts that appear in your Collection view. The first is related to your Music library. The second is related to cloud-based options that you may have. After you have made use of these alerts to configure your collection, these alerts can be closed by selecting the **X** on each one.

How to Move Your Music

If Music libraries and cloud options are not for you, follow these steps to move your music to the computer running Windows 8:

1. The first step is to prepare your music. It will be easier, but not required, to move your music if all your music is in a single folder or grouped in subfolders within a single folder.

2. Check that your Windows 8 computer has enough free disk space to accommodate your music. Ensure that you have more than 10% of the total drive capacity available after copying your library.

   For example, suppose your music takes up 10GB, you have a 250GB hard drive, and 50GB is free. When you add your music to your hard drive, you have just 40GB free space remaining, but 40GB is greater than 10%, so in this example, you are clear.

3. Move or copy your music folder to the My Music folder on the Windows 8 computer. You may need to use a removable drive to move the folder, or you can use a homegroup network to complete it.

4. Open the Music app. Inspect your Collection to verify that your music is present.

Browsing Through Your Music

You can easily review your music library in the Music app. You might need to review your library to verify that you set up your music library correctly. More likely, you'll browse through your library looking for something interesting to play.

You can view your music by album, artist, or song title. To look through all your music, select Collection from the vertical bar on the left, and select Songs to display your entire collection of songs. The screen shown in Figure 22.10 appears. From Collection, you can

- Group and sort your library.
- See all the music for an artist or on an album.
- Create a playlist.

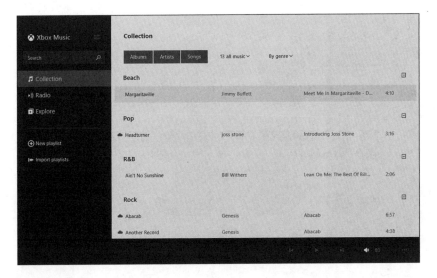

FIGURE 22.10

Collection gives you the opportunity to review your entire library.

When viewing your collection, you can sort the view further by selecting from the two drop-down options that by default display All Music and By Date Added. All Music enables you to filter by location, on this PC or in the cloud. Changing By Date Added allows you to sort the list using other common criteria, such as genre or alphabetically, as shown in Figure 22.11.

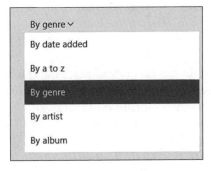

FIGURE 22.11

Choose from the sort options to rearrange the current displayed sort order.

When you have one or more album covers on the screen, you can click or tap to see the details about an album (see Figure 22.12). Any songs that you have in your collection from that album, either on your device or available to you via the cloud, appear here.

FIGURE 22.12

Select any album cover to play one or more songs from the album or add the album to a playlist.

An album cover also can link you to details about an artist, where you can inspect all the music loaded for that artist. Selecting the **"i"** sends you to the Artist Details page, where you can view all the artist's work and buy music, filling in your collection. This is a convenient way to shop for music for an artist. You will find that this informational icon also appears if you right-click on an album cover in your collection at the bottom of the screen with the text Explore Artist.

Playing Music

You can play a song from a number of places in the app. Just look for the Play button, which appears on an artist's album page, as well as in the album song list when you have a song selected (refer to Figure 22.12). To add a song to the queue of music to play, select **+** and then select **Now Playing**. To play a selection immediately, select the **Play** button. As the song plays, the music player bar on the bottom of the screen shows your song.

To see the full screen Now Playing window, tap or click the music player bar and you will see something like Figure 22.13.

FIGURE 22.13

Click or tap the music player bar to bring up a full screen Now Playing window with a variety of images for the current artist.

Creating Playlists

A big part of playing music is the *playlist*. If you've used a previous version of iTunes or Windows Media Player, you probably know about creating playlists. Playlists are custom song selections that you pick to play together. Maybe it's a "best of" Tom Petty mix or a selection of your favorite classical music. The Music app has made it much easier to create and manage playlists. To create a playlist from your collection or add a song to an existing one, select the **+** sign when a song is selected, and choose an existing playlist or select **New Playlist** (see Figure 22.14).

You can see that a few tools have been added to the left vertical bar in the Music app to manage playlists. From here, you can create a new playlist or select an existing one. If you have a playlist from a different application, such as iTunes, in your Music folder, you can select **Import Playlists** to bring up the screen shown in Figure 22.15.

FIGURE 22.14

Add songs to an existing playlist or create new ones on-the-fly.

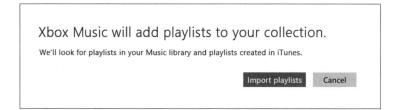

FIGURE 22.15

Import existing playlists that are located in your Music library.

Purchasing Music

You can purchase music wherever you see the option to buy, which may appear as a shopping cart button or a link. Occasionally, this option may appear while you are looking around in your Collection, but the place you will most likely encounter purchase options is in the Explore portion of the Music app. Select albums or songs to see information about them and use the … button to purchase individual songs or complete albums (see Figure 22.16). Here's more of what you need to know about purchasing music:

FIGURE 22.16

The Buy Album button can be found on portraits for songs and albums you don't own.

- Music purchased in the Music app is accomplished using the payment methods you have set up in your Account profile.

- Songs you purchase appear in your Collection. To see the actual files, open File Explorer and look at the Music library. You can read about libraries in Chapter 19.

- If you have not already created an account or set up payment methods when you attempt to purchase music, you will be prompted for billing information (see Figure 22.17).

- To find music in the Xbox LIVE music marketplace, select the Search tool at the top of the vertical Music app bar on the left side of the app. Enter the artist's name or song. Select the appropriate result. Select a song or album to see purchase options.

- To listen to Xbox LIVE music without having to purchase every song you want to hear, purchase an Xbox music pass. This allows you to play any music you like.

FIGURE 22.17

If you have not set up payment methods, you will need to do this first in your account profile.

Importing Music and Creating Music CDs

So far in this chapter, you've read about managing music stored on your computers and hard drives, as well as music in the Xbox marketplace. With all the great music in your library, it's a sure bet you'll want to create a music CD of your own design. And it's also a good bet that you'll purchase new CDs or come across CDs in your home or office whose music you want to add to your library. These two likely scenarios are the focus of this section.

As mentioned in the beginning of this chapter, the Music app isn't up to the task of addressing all your music enjoyment needs. To import a new CD into your library or to create a new CD, use the desktop app called Windows Media Player. Users of past Windows versions probably know the Windows Media Player, which is a handy tool that manages all your digital media, such as photos, movies, videos, and music.

 NOTE If you use your Windows 8 computer as part of a home theater setup, where you control it from the comfort of a couch, you should look into using Windows Media Center, a purchasable add-on for Windows 8.1.

Importing Music from a CD

Windows Media Player is the Desktop music player that is included with Windows 8. Besides listening to music, you can also import songs from music CDs using Windows Media Player. The music you import becomes part of your music library. In almost all cases, and as long as you have an active Internet connection, Windows can identify the CD. The name of the artist, the name of the album, and the name of each selection is automatically loaded into the library. If not, you need to enter that information manually.

 TIP   If you find that you need to use Windows Media Player often, it's not a bad idea to pin it to your Start screen. Just search for Windows Media Player using the Search charm, right-click (or tap and hold) it in the search results, and select **Pin to Start**.

Follow these steps to import music from a CD:

1. Open the Windows Media Player. The program opens on the Desktop, as shown in Figure 22.18.

FIGURE 22.18

Windows Media Player runs on the Desktop.

2. Load your CD and wait for Windows to recognize it. Do not press any buttons for a few moments.

3. The CD's tracks plus a snapshot of the cover artwork associated with the CD appears, as shown in Figure 22.19.

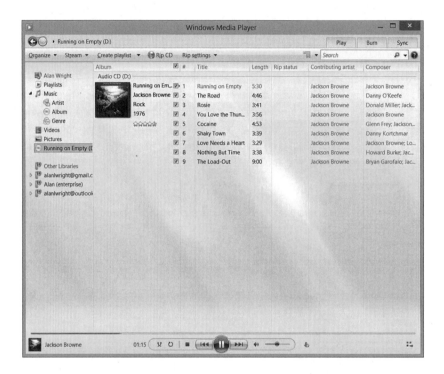

FIGURE 22.19

The CD's contents appear, enabling you to deselect songs you do not want to import.

4. Select **Rip Settings** from the menu bar if you want to adjust any quality settings, otherwise select **Rip CD** to begin.

5. Wait for each track's Rip Status to become Ripped to Library. You may eject the CD when complete.

Creating a Music CD

Burning a CD using Windows Media Player is just an extension of creating a playlist, although any playlists you create in the Music app don't appear in Windows Media Player. So, to burn a CD, you first need to create a playlist. Follow these steps to create a music CD based on a playlist you've created:

1. Open Windows Media Player. Note the tree structure of your media on your computer on the left side of the screen (refer to Figure 22.19). This is known as the Navigation Tree.

2. If you have a playlist you want to burn to a CD, skip to step 7.

3. Select **Create Playlist** from the menu bar. Select **Create Playlist** again.

4. Type the name of the playlist and press **Enter**.

5. Under Music in the Navigation Tree, click **Artist**, **Album**, or **Genre** to choose music to burn to the CD.

6. Drag the song to the playlist you created in the Navigation Tree. Repeat steps 5 and 6 until the playlist contains all the music you want to burn to the CD.

7. Insert a blank, writable CD into a drive on your computer capable of burning CDs. Select the playlist to burn.

8. Select the **Burn** tab on the right side of the screen. Then select **Start Burn**.

9. Remove the CD when Windows Media Player reports that the CD is complete.

 NOTE Even though Windows Media Player can't access playlists you created in the Music app, playlists you create in Windows Media Player can be imported into the Music app. Go figure.

THE ABSOLUTE MINIMUM

Keep the following points in mind when you're finished reading this chapter:

- You can play existing music in the Music app either by moving the music directly into the Music folder on your Windows 8 device or by using the library feature in File Explorer to indicate where the music is located.

- You may also connect to a music source over a home network, but this solution will fail when you move your computer out of range of the network, such as if one of the computers is a laptop you typically travel with.

- Either create an account in the Xbox LIVE marketplace or have a credit card at hand if you plan to purchase music.

- A large number of hidden features are available throughout the Music app. Try these out now so that you can remember them later. For example, the music player bar can expand to the full screen Playing Now screen when you listen to music, and it can appear as a small, temporary pop-up when you're working in other apps.

- You need to use Windows Media Player if you want to import music into your library from a CD or if you want to create a new CD.

23

HAVING FUN AND PLAYING GAMES

Microsoft's Xbox LIVE service and the Xbox 360 console together play an important role in Windows 8, and the role is a fun one. Windows 8 leverages the console and its Xbox LIVE online service to bring music, movies, videos, and games to Windows. This digital content is presented and managed in Windows 8 through the new Music, Video, and Games apps. Read Chapter 21, "Having Fun with Music and Videos," for information about movies and videos as well as signing up for Xbox LIVE, and see Chapter 22, "Enjoying Music," for information about playing and purchasing music in Windows 8. With the Xbox SmartGlass app, you can control your Xbox from your Windows 8 device, deliver Xbox content right to your tablet, server, laptop, or desktop, and use it in conjunction with some Xbox games. In this short chapter, you'll learn how to connect your Windows 8 device to Xbox 360. You'll also get an overview of the Games app.

Of course, the prerequisite for this chapter is that you own an Xbox 360 or the new Xbox One platform. While the Xbox One is still unreleased at the time of publishing this book, the features and capabilities described in this chapter will be available for Xbox One owners. Without one of these consoles, your reading of this chapter should be very short.

Using Xbox LIVE with Windows 8

Xbox LIVE is Microsoft's online gaming and digital media service. It has evolved since it was introduced around 2002, and it is certain to continue to grow and evolve, especially as the services it provides have become a part of Windows 8. Here are the features that Xbox LIVE offers today to the Xbox 360 console community:

- Enables players to compete online in Xbox games. Members can also try out demos of new games, as well as purchase games.

- Enables members to enjoy music, movies, and TV shows from an enormous library of selections. Content can be rented, played, or purchased; although not every selection can be rented.

- Enables members to share content, chat, issue voice commands, consume content from other providers (such as HBO), find opponents, find people who share the same interests, and much more.

A BRIEF HISTORY OF THE XBOX

Before diving into the Xbox LIVE service, it makes sense to go back in time and review the origins of all this cool digital content: the Xbox 360 console. Released in late 2001, the Xbox was Microsoft's first game console. Less than five years later, Microsoft launched the Xbox 360, which went on to become the most successful game console of its generation. Xbox One hopes to build on the success of the Xbox 360 both by adding more power to the console for games and tying it even more closely to your living room experience for music and video as a true all-in-one entertainment console.

Few other aspects of a game console contribute more to its success (or demise) than the quality of the games that run it. The Xbox-only game *Halo*, with four major installments (and a couple spinoffs), is among the most popular console games of all time. The Xbox 360 is also noted for its comfortable, innovative controller design, its sharp high-definition (HD) graphics, plus the online environment it creates for players. It's easy to find friends to compete against online, and to download game demos and experience movies, videos, and music online.

Some of these benefits don't translate exactly to Windows 8. Here's how Windows 8 works with Xbox LIVE's services:

- From the Music app, you can shop the Xbox LIVE music service, also known as Xbox music, for both current and past songs and albums. You can audition music you might like, and then purchase and download music you want to keep. You can snap the Music app next to another app you're working with, giving you some entertainment as you toil away. (Refer to Chapter 22.)

- From the Video app, you can review the Xbox LIVE library of movies and TV shows, also known as Xbox videos, both current and past. You can rent some titles and purchase and download others. You can watch the video content on your device, including projecting it on a wall or screen to get the movie theater experience. (Refer to Chapter 21.)

- From the Xbox LIVE Games app, you can play games against other Xbox LIVE gamers. You can also shop for Xbox games, as well as download game demos and full games. If you were impressed by the *Solitaire* game loaded into many versions of Windows over the years, you will be astounded by the great Xbox games you can run on your computer or tablet.

- With the Windows 8 SmartGlass app, you can control Xbox 360 from your Windows 8 device and review Xbox content on that device. Your Windows 8 device becomes a remote control for Xbox, as well as another display for Xbox.

Access to all this great content on Xbox LIVE does not come automatically. You need to connect your Windows account to Xbox LIVE to enable all the cool functionality described previously. If you have already set up the Music app or the Video app with an Xbox account, your job in this chapter is easy. You use the same Xbox LIVE account throughout Windows 8. If not, read the next section to understand how to join your Windows account to Xbox.

Setting Up Your Xbox LIVE Account

Each time you start the Xbox Games or Xbox SmartGlass apps, shown in Figure 23.1, Windows 8 tries to sign in to Xbox LIVE. You are sure to notice the Signing In message on the top-right corner of the screen. If you have not created your account yet, you will see a message in the upper-right corner of the app inviting you to sign in (see Figure 23.2). In this case, skip back to Chapter 21 for more information about setting up a LIVE account and then return here.

FIGURE 23.1

The Xbox Games and Xbox SmartGlass app tiles.

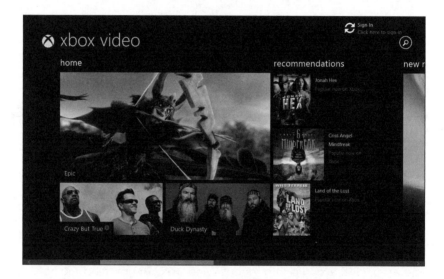

FIGURE 23.2

If you do not currently have an Xbox LIVE ID, you will be asked to sign in to create one.

 NOTE If you signed in to Windows 8 with a local account and you want to enjoy the Xbox Games, you have two choices. You can convert your local account to a Windows account or create a Windows LIVE account if you don't have one. You won't be forced to sign in to Windows 8 with this new account. Rather, you use it only to access Xbox LIVE. You are prompted for this account when you access the Xbox apps. It's clearly much more convenient to sign in to Windows 8 with a Windows account.

Controlling Xbox from Windows 8

Xbox SmartGlass is a Windows 8 app that is a companion app to the Xbox and it enables the computer or other Windows 8 device to control an Xbox console. At first thought, perhaps you don't consider this to be all that useful. Why would anyone want to use a computer to control Xbox when the console's own controls are easy to use? Also, why would you want to be tethered to a computer to manage your console? These are reasonable questions. Here are, hopefully, some reasonable answers:

- Its midday and you are already thinking of the evening's activity. There is a movie that you missed at the theater that is now available to download and watch online. Use Xbox SmartGlass to either buy or rent the movie so that the movie is ready to go when you get home.

- A game you have been looking forward to playing on Xbox Live Arcade finally is released. You can't wait to play it, but you have an evening of work in front of you. With Windows 8, you can snap your work to one side of the screen, and snap Xbox SmartGlass to the other side. This way, you can do some work and do some gaming at about the same time!

- You have a new Windows 8 tablet. Use the Xbox SmartGlass installed on that tablet to control everything you see on the screen right from your couch or favorite chair.

- You can play your Xbox 360 anywhere you like, as long as your Windows 8 device can reach your console over your home network.

SMARTGLASS AND XBOX ONE

This chapter focuses on the Xbox 360 and the SmartGlass app designed for Xbox 360. In principle the same capabilities will be available for owners of the Xbox One. The Xbox One console uses a different SmartGlass app that is designed specifically for the Xbox One console. Expect the name of the Xbox SmartGlass to be updated to reflect that it is for the 360 console as well.

Connection speed and performance between SmartGlass and Xbox One are said to be much faster, about three and a half times faster than between it and the 360! More devices can be connected to an Xbox One console at a time which opens up interesting possibilities for gaming developers.

Installing Xbox SmartGlass with an Xbox 360

The Xbox SmartGlass app is available in the Windows Store and it may already be installed on your Windows 8.1 device. In addition to installing the application from the store, you need access to your Xbox console to set everything up. Be sure your Xbox is configured to connect to the Internet and has any available software updates. Also you will need to use the same Microsoft account on both devices to use SmartGlass.

 NOTE Your Xbox console checks for updates automatically when it's connected to the Internet. When it notifies you that an update is available, all you need to do is give it permission to download and install it.

Follow these steps to install the app from the store:

1. Open the Windows Store. The Store tile is on the Start screen.

2. Open the Search charm.

3. Enter **Xbox** into the search box, and then select **Xbox SmartGlass** from the results on the left.

4. Select **Install**. You will see a notification that SmartGlass is being installed as shown in Figure 23.3.

FIGURE 23.3

Install SmartGlass from the Microsoft Store.

5. After the installation process finishes, open the app. You may be asked to log in with your Microsoft account password.

6. Do not select Connect to your Xbox in the upper right corner of the SmartGlass app as shown in Figure 23.4. Instead, turn your attention to the Xbox 360 console.

FIGURE 23.4

When SmartGlass is unable to connect to your Xbox you will see a notification to Connect to your Xbox.

7. Turn on your Xbox 360 console and make sure you are signing in with the same Microsoft account that is used for your Windows 8 device.

8. On the console, select **Settings,** and then select **Console Settings**.

9. Locate the Xbox SmartGlass setting.

10. Turn Xbox SmartGlass to **Available**.

11. Go back to Windows 8 and select **Connect** if it has not already connected automatically.

12. If everything is connected properly you will see the heading now playing and the current game or screen on the Xbox console is indicated as shown in Figure 23.5.

FIGURE 23.5

When SmartGlass is connected you will see the heading now playing *indicating the current game or screen being viewed on the game console.*

Using Xbox SmartGlass

The Xbox SmartGlass is an app that enables you to manage some aspects of your Xbox 360 console and can be used to provide you with second screen content on your Windows 8 device from the gaming console. You can direct the console to download or purchase content from one of the Xbox LIVE marketplaces, as shown in Figure 23.6, and, depending on the game, you can even control the game while you play it from your Windows 8 device.

Before commanding Xbox 360 to download great new music or to blow up the bridge separating you from the bad guys in a fun, interactive game, you need to start the app. To start the Xbox SmartGlass app, locate the tile on the Start screen (refer to Figure 23.1) and then select it. SmartGlass is a new Windows 8 type app, so be sure to review Chapter 1, "Your First Hour with Windows 8," if you need help navigating through the screens and options.

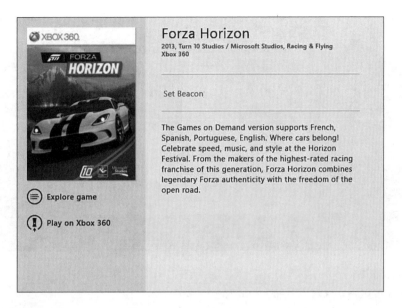

FIGURE 23.6

The SmartGlass app provides access to the Xbox LIVE services as if you were working at the console.

With the SmartGlass app open, you can navigate through menus and screens on your device as if you are operating a controller and viewing the monitor to which Xbox is connected. You can use your mouse, finger, or keyboard to navigate through the app. Most of the content you can access is already available through the Music, Video, or Games apps. Figure 23.7 shows a movie that offers SmartGlass content, a movie guide in this case that enhances the movie viewing. Other examples of SmartGlass features include maps for games and tips that can be consulted as a game is being played. When you see content you are interested in, select it to see more detail. Depending on what you selected, you see options like the following:

- Explore
- Play a game on Xbox 360
- Play a movie trailer
- Review information about an artist

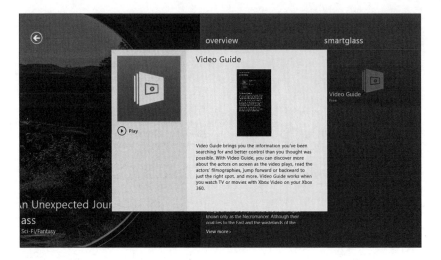

FIGURE 23.7

Start the SmartGlass app from the Start screen.

You will typically be transferred to the appropriate app when you need to see detail or to review the content without Xbox 360. When you do need to use the Xbox controller interface, such as to play a game, open the App bar and select **Remote**, as shown in Figure 23.8.

Figure 23.9 shows how to send commands that simulate your use of the Xbox controller by clicking or touching locations on your computer monitor or tablet screen.

FIGURE 23.8

You engage the Xbox controls from a command on the App bar.

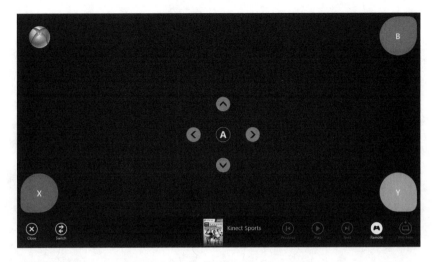

FIGURE 23.9

You tap or click your computer or tablet screen matching the buttons you would press on your Xbox controller.

Learning the Xbox Games App

Perhaps the most fun-filled app in Windows 8 is the Xbox Games app, though it is often referred to simply as Games. To start the app, select it from the Start screen. The Games app is organized in a few sections. As you scroll across the screen, you can review the following:

- Current games Microsoft and its partners are promoting in the Spotlight section

- Windows 8 games you can acquire from the Windows Store

- Xbox games you can download and then play from your Windows 8 device with the SmartGlass app

- See Xbox games that are installed across various devices and activity and achievements (see Figure 23.10)

- Review your gamer profile

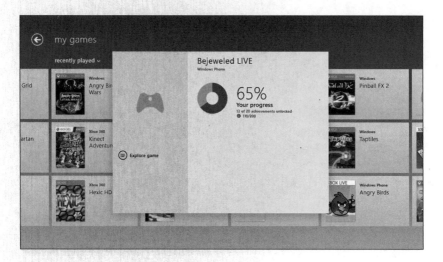

FIGURE 23.10

You can see Xbox game activity from the Games app for Windows 8 phones, computers, and Xbox 360 game consoles.

Fortunately, as is expected, this app is simple to use. Here are some tips for use with the app:

- If you purchase an Xbox 360 game, it can be used only on the console to which it was first downloaded.

- If you issue the command to play a game, you are automatically switched to the SmartGlass app.

- When you install a Windows 8 game from the Windows Store, you can also launch it from the Games app.

That's it for the overview. It would be troublesome if a games application required long instruction. My best advice to you is to click where intuition tells you to. The game should do most of the work for you, at least until the competition starts.

THE ABSOLUTE MINIMUM

Keep these points in mind after you've completed reading this chapter:

- The Xbox movies, videos, and games apps make content available to you (the user) from the Xbox LIVE service.

- You must supply a Windows account to access the Xbox LIVE content that plays through the Xbox-powered apps in Windows 8. You may still sign in to Windows with a local account, but you need to supply your Windows account credentials every time you access one of the apps.

- Xbox LIVE prompts you for information to connect your Windows account to Xbox LIVE when you open one of the Xbox apps. After you answer the prompts, you won't hear from Xbox LIVE again.

- Games you acquire from the Windows Store can be played from the Games app.

SAFE WEB BROWSING

For something so exciting, enormously helpful, always entertaining, and extremely valuable, the Internet can be a dangerous place. There's risk at every corner of having your personal information stolen, of viruses spreading to your computer, of fake versions of your favorite websites appearing, designed to fool you into entering private information, and of software secretly loading itself on your computer to track your every Internet move. It's certainly sad that individuals try to take what's yours, but after you accept the reality of the situation, you must address the threat and prepare your defenses. This chapter reviews all the important tools available to a beginning Windows 8 user to ensure safe and private Internet computing.

WINDOWS 8 APPS VERSUS DESKTOP APPS

You learned in Chapter 12, "Surfing the Web," that two versions of Internet Explorer are installed with Windows 8: a Windows 8 app version and a Desktop version. The Windows 8 version generally offers fewer opportunities for malicious software to find its way onto your computer through the browser, but there is more you can do with the Desktop browser. The instructions in this chapter refer to the Desktop version of Internet Explorer unless noted otherwise. This means, for example, if you are instructed to select **Tools** and then **Safety** from the menu, you should do so with the Desktop browser. Any settings you change in the Desktop browser automatically apply to the Windows 8 version, too, where appropriate. This means you don't need to switch between both browsers to adjust the same setting.

Understanding Internet Threats and Risks

You might be surprised at the large number and variety of risks and threats in the Internet world. Despite the increasing proliferation of all these threats and risks, there's just two parts to the strategy needed to protect you: Learn the threats, and raise the defense. The first part of the strategy is the goal of this section. You learn about the myriad ways you can find trouble browsing the Web, emailing friends and family, and just plain staying connected to the Web.

Web Browsing Risks

The web browser is your doorway to information, news, fun stuff, art, science, and everything in between. The browser can also be a doorway to your personal information, as well as to a launchpad for viruses and other malware. The following is a list of risks that exist while you simply and innocently browse the Web:

- Most websites use small files known as *cookies* to help keep track of your preferences as you move from page to page, as well as to remind the site who you are when you return to the site. These cookies are created and then stored on your computer. Cookies can contain whatever information a website needs to provide a pleasant browsing experience, including personal information. You have probably figured out by now that cookies would be attractive to people interested in you and your personal details. Although cookies are not a risk on their own, a risk is created when access to them is not controlled.

NOTE There is some wisdom to never allowing cookies onto your computer. You can direct Internet Explorer to reject all cookies. Doing so, however, prevents some sites from working with your browser. Instead, you can use a feature of Internet Explorer called InPrivate Browsing, which enables cookies to be temporarily stored only in a secured area of your computer and then they are removed when you leave the site. You can read about InPrivate Browsing later in the chapter in the section "Browsing Quietly and Invisibly with InPrivate Browsing".

- Web pages cannot on their own run programs on your computer, except to show pages in your browser. Websites with bad intentions have been known to display a pop-up message in which the buttons, if selected by the user, trigger a program that *can* run on your computer. These programs can do anything, including installing a virus, spreading the virus through your contacts, accessing the network you're attached to, and so on. Not only are pop-up messages annoying, but they represent a potential high safety risk. Never activate a pop-up message if you don't know what it is.

- If you download software from the Web, either to try out or for purchase, you are introducing risk to your system. Most of these software downloads are safe, particularly if they come from a known publisher or developer. The installation program does nothing more than load the software onto your computer. Some of these installation programs, especially for smaller try-before-you buy programs, secretly install spyware when they install the program you selected. Spyware is software that secretly tracks your clicks and web browsing, creating a profile of your interests. Worse though, spyware can capture your keystrokes, making it easy to determine your passwords, as well as credit card and banking information.

There are other less-significant risks associated with browsing the Web, but the preceding list represents the most significant threats. To summarize, viruses can land on your computer from pop-ups and other malicious sites (see phishing threats later), cookies can expose personal information, and downloads from the Web potentially can contain dangerous, hidden spyware.

Understanding threats exposed by browsing the Web is just half of the story. Up next is a review of threats exposed through email.

Learning About Risky Attachments and Other Email-Related Threats

If you have ever opened an attachment in an email sent by someone you didn't know or barely knew, or if you opened an attachment—even from someone you do know—when you were not quite sure of the contents, you may have dropped yourself in the middle of a minefield.

Attachments represent more risk than just about any other email or computer practice. A party looking to ruin your day can package anything they like in an otherwise friendly looking attachment, including viruses. What might appear to be a file filled with jokes or containing a cute movie (maybe the file is called "funny_kitty_video") can contain a program that not only infects your computer, but also sends a virus in an attachment to every address in your contact list. I don't imagine that's something your family and friends would appreciate.

Be suspicious of an email with an attachment. If your suspicions outweigh your confidence, see if you can figure out the email address of the sender. Maybe you already have it. Ask if the person sent the email before you open the attachment. If so, you should be in good shape. If the sender doesn't recall sending it, delete it immediately because it's likely a piece of malware automatically sent through email from your associate's email account.

Consider the following questions. If you answer no to even one of the questions, you should not open the attachment.

- Do you know the sender?

- Have you received email from the sender before? Have you received an email with an attachment before?

- Were you expecting an email with attachments? Can you guess what's in the attachment?

There is one more feature to worry about when it comes to preventing Internet monkey business while reading email. Your email program might have a feature in which email is automatically displayed in a small window as soon as you scroll over the message in a list, as shown in Figure 24.1. This feature is known as the Preview pane in Microsoft Outlook. Without specifically intending to, you are opening an email when it appears in your Preview pane, and some malware is programmed to run or spread the moment the email containing it is displayed.

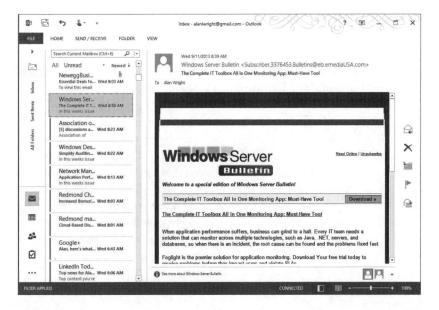

FIGURE 24.1

Scrolling an email through the Preview pane of your email application can sometimes trigger the loading of a virus.

Learning Phishing Threats

You may have come across the term *phishing* as something you should be concerned about. This term has nothing to do with pulling creatures out of the sea, nor does it refer to the popular improvisation band formed at the University of Vermont. Rather, phishing refers to the practice of trying to gain access to personal information by posing in email (or Twitter, or instant messaging, and so on) as a reputable or official organization, like your bank, credit card company, or another online company that you respect.

Phishing scams usually come in the form of an email informing you of some situation that requires confidential information from you. The email appears official, possibly incorporating the organization's colors or logo. You may be told that your account has been upgraded, although your account number or some other form of ID is needed to complete the process. Phishing scams also involve a request for your help in claiming millions of dollars for a cousin or friend (which would require use of your personal account to hold the funds) or even yourself (see Figure 24.2).

A typical phishing practice is to use a website address that resembles that of a real organization. For example, the website address of one of the largest banks in North America is www.bankofamerica.com. You might find yourself directed to a website with the address www.bankamericacom.net that has absolutely no relation to the actual Bank of America website whatsoever.

 NOTE The techniques described in this section are sometimes referred to as *Social Engineering*, the use of pressure, surprise, or misdirection to trick you into clicking something, opening a website, or providing information that opens you or your system up to persons that are trying to exploit you. This is always evolving, and currently Facebook and Twitter are popular methods used to get you to click or open things that may expose your computer to malicious individuals. The greatest security risk a computer will face is likely to be caused inadvertently by the user himself.

```
RUGBY2011 LOC AWARD TEAM
Johannesburg
South Africa
0001


Dear Sir/Madam

We wish to notify you that your email address was automatically selected during the RUGBY 2011 world
cup finals kick off in New-Zealand and has won you Cash (Cheque) of £3000.000.00 GBP (Three Million
Great Britain Pounds) Payable through our Paying Bank.

Kindly note that you're Ref: RUGBY2011/00453/NL/11 falls within our Afro booklet Regional
Headquarters representative office in Johannesburg, South Africa as indicated in the play coupon.
All participants were selected automatically World Wide through a computer draw system and emails
were generated from over 1 0, 000.00 internet email service providers. For security reasons, you are
advised to keep your winning information confidential until your claim is processed.

You are hereby advised to Contact Mr. Harry A. Dominic the appointed agent for the immediate release
of your winnings fund:

Your winning prize has been insured and Deposited in our Paying bank an Escrow Account Pending your
Claim with this Payment Reference File Number of Deposit"PPC/ZA5622/2011
```

FIGURE 24.2

Scams can arrive at your desktop in many forms, including news about rugby winnings.

The best and only advice is to ignore and delete these emails if you have even the smallest bit of suspicion. Here are some other thoughts about phishing emails:

- Ignore the urgency of the request. Just because the request claims action must be taken in some period of time or something terrible will occur, that doesn't mean you should trust the claim.

- A bank would never request your account information or Social Security number through an email—wouldn't your bank have this information already?

- Ask the question, "Why me?" Why would you be singled out to help a needy individual get the fortune of money due to them?

- Do not click a link. A link could launch a program or collect information you didn't plan to provide.

- Resist the urge to reply with some sort of message saying they didn't fool you. That just tells them your email address is current and active and should be targeted in the future.

CAUTION Be careful about using your email for everything. Many people will keep a "junk" email account with Gmail, Yahoo, or some other free email service just for filling out those website forms for free contests, newsletters, coupons, and other situations where a website may ask for your email. Their intention is often to share your email with other advertisers and bombard you with their own emails in the future.

One more useful strategy to defend against phishing attempts is to use a SPAM blocker. *SPAM* is the term used for unwanted email or advertisements or junk email. In fact, most large email providers such as Gmail, Yahoo, and Outlook.com, already include filtering for this type of email by default. A SPAM blocker monitors your inbound email and traps SPAM as it travels to your inbox. With most SPAM blockers, you can configure whether SPAM is immediately deleted, filed to a Junk email folder, or left for you to deal with. A SPAM blocker can sometimes capture phishing scam emails. Your Internet service provider (ISP) also probably provides a SPAM blocker. If you do not have any option for filtering SPAM on your email account, you should search the Web for a highly-rated option, free or otherwise.

Avoiding Virus Threats

If you have heard anything about Internet risks, it's probably about viruses. A *computer virus* is a piece of software introduced to a computer that can reproduce itself. Usually, a virus doesn't simply reproduce itself and then go dormant. Viruses can make unwanted changes to your computer's setup, sometimes significantly damaging your system. And because a virus replicates itself, a virus usually is concerned with finding its way to other computers, such as by leveraging a contact list or by attempting to infiltrate other computers if you connect to a network.

A virus can get onto to your computer in a number of ways:

- On a CD/DVD you acquire

- Attached to an email

- Through downloaded software or files

- On a removable drive you attach to your computer
- From a network you connect to

A good antivirus program defends against a virus accessing your system in each of these methods. The good news is that with Windows 8 you have built-in protection for these threats by means of Windows Defender which you'll learn more about later in this chapter. In addition, all the safe computing guidance presented throughout this chapter also can help protect you. Follow the advice later in the "Absolute Minimum" section.

 CAUTION It's worth overstating that your antivirus program can do its job only if it's kept up to date. You should regularly confirm that your antivirus program is updated with the latest virus definitions.

Defending Yourself

You need to maintain a number of defenses to ensure your data, equipment, reputation, privacy, personal information, and finances are protected. Each of the following sections describes a component of your Internet defense strategy. The last section of the chapter describes how to bring the various pieces together to create a whole strategy.

Reviewing All-in-One Internet Defense Suites

Many beginners ask the same question about protecting themselves and their computers from Internet threats: Should they buy one of those all-in-one Internet defense suites? With Windows 8 you have a solid antivirus and malware protection already included. Even so, you may feel more comfortable with one of the top Internet security suites for a few reasons:

- Internet threats are constantly evolving and growing. It makes sense to rely on a larger organization that can keep pace with new threats.

- Many purchased Internet security suites offer additional features such as email virus scanning, enhanced parental controls, or more robust firewall features.

- Protecting yourself requires a wide strategy of defense. Although you are capable to raise this defense using the tools available in Windows, a commercial suite has a more vested interest in ensuring that there are no holes in your defense.

- Many of the solutions also provide coverage for more than one computer.

You should expect to pay approximately $100 and then a nominal annual fee to stay up to date from year to year. There are plenty of unbiased reviews available on the Internet to help you select a suite.

WINDOWS DEFENDER AND THIRD-PARTY INTERNET SUITES

With the Windows 8.1 update, Windows Defender has been enhanced to assume all responsibilities for viruses and malware. If you install a third-party Internet security suite, Defender is deactivated but not uninstalled. If you uninstall the third-party application, Defender resumes operation.

Defending with Windows Defender

Windows 8 has a built-in antivirus/spyware application known as Windows Defender. Although free software sometimes is viewed skeptically, Windows Defender is quite good. There is no reason not to use it.

Some of the most important Windows Defender features and options you should know about include the following:

- **Updated Definitions**—Windows automatically and regularly updates both virus and spyware definitions. You can also force an update if you like. As soon as the Microsoft security engineers detect the introduction of a new virus into the Internet, a definition of the virus is created and downloaded to all Windows Defender users by means of updates.

- **Choose How to Deal with Potential Problems**—Windows Defender enables you to review past situations in which the software identified content that had the potential to be a problem. You can see the list of everything suspected as being malicious, the list of those that you identified as known and okay, and you can see the list of programs that indeed were found to be malicious and have been quarantined.

- **Real-Time Protection**—This option determines whether Windows Defender continually scans your system activity, assessing programs and files your computer comes in contact with. The alternative is to set up Windows Defender to review for malicious files during a regularly scheduled scan. Real-Time Protection should be enabled at all times.

- **Exclude File Types, Names, Locations**—You can specify that certain files be excluded from scanning. You can identify these files by their name, location, or their type. Many people exclude their photos library and their music library if they know for sure that they were the provider of the songs and pictures.

- **Scan Removable Drives**—This option determines whether external drives connected to your computer also should be scanned for viruses, and so on.

Configuring Windows Defender

Windows Defender protects your system from the moment you install Windows 8, but you can change how it operates. Follow these steps to configure Windows Defender:

1. Open the Charms bar and select **Search**.

2. Enter **defender** into the Search box and then select Windows Defender when it appears at the top of the results list. A screen like the one shown in Figure 19.3 should appear on your Desktop.

FIGURE 24.3

Windows Defender is built in to Windows 8.

3. Select the **Settings** tab.

4. Select **Real-Time Protection** from the list of settings, and be sure Turn on Real-Time Protection is checked. This way, dangerous or malicious programs are identified instantly as soon as they approach your computer.

5. Select **Excluded Files and Locations** from the list of settings. Unless you have been told to exclude certain files, folders, or drives from protection by Windows Defender, the lower of the two lists on the screen should be empty. To remove an entry from the list, select it and then select **Remove**. You would not want a key folder, such as Documents, or a key drive, such as C, excluded.

6. Select **Excluded File Types** from the list of settings. Unless you have been told to exclude certain types of files from protection by Windows Defender, the lower of the two lists on the screen should be empty. If there is an entry in the bottom of the two lists that you do not recognize, such as EXE files, select the entry and then select **Remove**.

7. Select **Advanced** from the list of settings. You should accept the default choice under **Remove Quarantined File After 3 Months**. Otherwise, leave all settings as you found them. The only exception is if you find yourself exchanging removable drives often, perhaps as a way to share photos; then select **Scan Removable Drives**.

8. If you made any changes in steps 4–7, click **Save Changes**. Otherwise, click **Cancel**.

With the steps completed, Windows Defender is set up to provide solid protection against viruses and spyware.

Using Windows Defender

There is little for you to do when Windows Defender runs, especially if you have set up the program to automatically receive updated definitions. The only occasion in which you need to take action is when Windows Defender detects a threat, and even then, the only action to take is to look at the offending file. Figure 24.4 shows the message you see when Windows Defender detects malware.

For this example, I used a stream of text characters that resemble a virus saved to a file on the Desktop. Figure 24.5 shows the file in quarantine. At this point, Defender has already removed the file from the Desktop. This is exactly how the program would react to a real virus introduced to your computer.

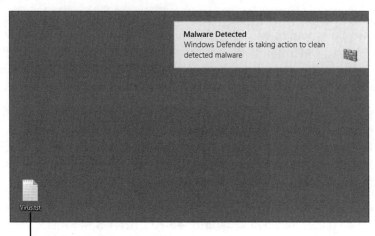

Test "infected" file placed on the desktop

FIGURE 24.4

Windows Defender displays a simple, small message when it believes it has detected a virus.

FIGURE 24.5

You can view files quarantined in Windows Defender.

Checking Your Security Status at the Action Center

Windows 8 provides a screen that shows the status of all the settings and controls for protecting your privacy and important personal information. To access the Action Center, search for a setting named Action Center. When the Action Center appears, open the Security section by selecting the down arrow to the right of the label, as shown in Figure 24.6.

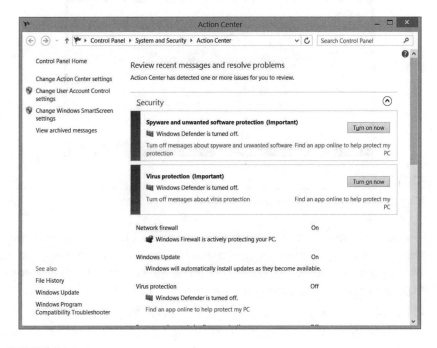

FIGURE 24.6

The Action Center shows you a status of your security options and settings.

Using SmartScreen to Avoid Dangerous Websites

All this discussion about bad people and dangerous sites is made worse by how difficult it can be to tell the good from the bad sites. The SmartScreen feature in Internet Explorer is designed to stop you before visiting bad sites, and it assists you in a few other areas related to malicious websites.

SmartScreen is a feature in Internet Explorer that monitors the sites you browse to and the files you download for both suspicious files and sites, as well as for sites that are confirmed dangerous and malicious. SmartScreen is passive and unobtrusive, which means you can usually do your thing and not be bothered unless it notices you are doing something that it considers dangerous. There is no reason to turn off SmartScreen filtering except if advised to by a knowledgeable, reputable technical support professional.

Figure 24.7 shows a typical warning when you try to browse to an unsafe site.

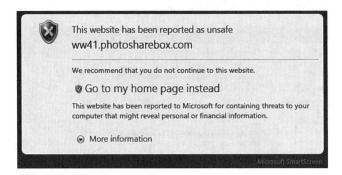

FIGURE 24.7

This is how SmartScreen reports an unsafe website.

If you come across a site that you believe is suspicious, you can easily report it. Even the most innocent-seeming sites, with puppies on the home page, can be phishing sites. If you do not want to report a site but would rather check it against Microsoft's list of dangerous sites, you can do so with just a few clicks:

- To report a site you think is dangerous, select **Tools**, **Safety**, and then **Report Unsafe Website** (see Figure 24.8). A page displays, asking a few questions about the site you are concerned with.

- To check a website, select **Tools**, **Safety**, and then **Check This Website**. You are prompted to continue checking the website. Click **OK**. If the site checks out to be safe, the message in Figure 24.9 appears.

FIGURE 24.8

Although Benji looks lovable, you can report the site where his picture appears as unsafe with just a few menu commands.

FIGURE 24.9

This is the message you receive when SmartScreen detects no threats with the site you reported.

Covering Your Internet Tracks

Internet Explorer keeps a record of the sites you have visited recently. It keeps this record to help speed up your browsing experience the next time you visit those sites, as well as to make it easy to select a site from a list of those you know the next time you want to visit. This browsing record presents a clear picture of the sites you visit and the pages you browse to. If your computer has multiple users, you should consider deleting your browsing history when you are done with Internet Explorer.

- To delete your browsing history, select **Tools**, **Safety**, and then **Delete Browsing History.** You can select certain pieces of information not to be deleted, but you won't break anything if you delete everything. The worst result from deleting all history is having to reenter passwords that were stored earlier in the browser (which is never a good idea) or reenter certain form data, such as your address and phone number. Select **Delete**.

- To always delete your browsing history when you close the Internet Explorer, select **Tools** and then **Internet Options**. From the Internet Options dialog box that appears, under the General tab, select **Delete Browsing History on Exit**. Click **OK**.

 TIP If you use the Windows 8 browser, deleting browsing history clears the sites listed in the Frequent Sites section, not sites collected in the Tabbed sites.

Browsing Quietly and Invisibly with InPrivate Browsing

Internet Explorer provides a mode of browsing that leaves no trail, evidence, or history of your browsing. It is virtually impossible for anyone using your computer to determine the sites you visited using InPrivate browsing. Windows uses a number of features and tools to make your browsing experience a good one, including recording information about your activity at a website and using different technologies to show different content (such as movies or animation) on websites. With InPrivate browsing, Windows engages these tools only as needed and quickly erases any evidence that they were used. Although InPrivate browsing might seem similar to the Delete Browsing History explained earlier, InPrivate browsing actively maintains anonymity while you browse instead of just after the fact.

To switch to InPrivate browsing, select **Tools**, **Safety**, and then **InPrivate Browsing**. Using the Windows 8 browser, right-click with your mouse or tap and hold with your finger or stylus. Select the Tab tools button, which appears as three dots, and then select **New InPrivate Tab**. You'll be able to tell when you are using the InPrivate mode by the icon that appears adjacent to the address bar, as shown in Figure 24.11.

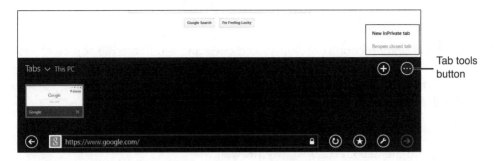

FIGURE 24.10

The Tabs Tools button gives you access to the InPrivate browsing option in the modern Windows 8 app version of Internet Explorer.

FIGURE 24.11

The InPrivate logo appears adjacent to the address bar when the InPrivate mode is in use.

Using Windows Firewall

A software firewall is a barrier between the computer and the network outside of the computer; the Internet is the network firewalls are most concerned with. Like a physical firewall, a software firewall blocks traffic at the most critical point. A firewall running on a computer like yours usually works with a policy. The policy mandates what information can come through and reach the computer and what can't. The Windows Firewall is aware of most of the mainstream and popular software programs, services, and sites, and it permits traffic out and back between these known sources and your computer.

When the firewall detects communication from an unknown source, it prompts you for action. You can decide whether to permit or deny access. When you acquire new software, there is a chance that the firewall might not recognize it, and you will be asked to·create a policy that determines how the firewall should handle communication with the program in the future.

There are dozens of rules that control the firewall's behavior, and each rule has at least one dozen settings. It makes sense to keep the firewall running. When the firewall detects a new application/service/site and alerts you to it, you can determine whether to allow it. If you recognize the application/service/site, allow it. If you don't recognize it, you should deny and then note the source of the warning. You can look into the source, perhaps by searching the Internet, and you can later change the rule of the firewall to either deny always or allow connections for this application/service/site.

To check your Firewall settings follow these steps:

1. From the Search charm, enter **firewall**.

2. Select **Windows Firewall** from the search results, and the Windows Firewall dialog box opens on your Desktop.

3. You can see the current status and policy on incoming connections as shown in Figure 24.12. The Notification state lets you see if you are to be notified or not for specific events.

4. To make changes to policies or settings, select from the choices to the left. This is not recommended unless you have instructions directing you to make specific changes to your firewall. If you or another user made changes here that you want to revoke, choose the Restore defaults link in the Navigation pane.

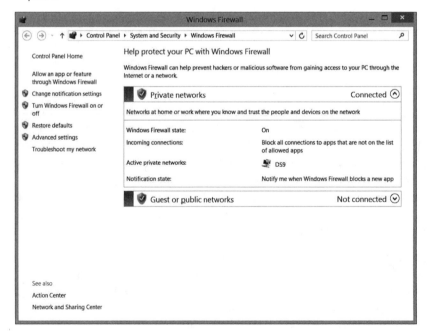

FIGURE 24.12

You can make changes to your firewall using the Windows Firewall dialog box.

Managing All Your IDs and Passwords

If you've used the Internet for any length of time, you know that most sites these days allow (and want) you to register with them, providing at least your email address and asking you to create a password. It can be frustrating, but unless you want to be a web hermit and visit only sites that enable you to use all their features anonymously, you must comply—and that's how the trouble starts. How do you maintain all those user IDs and passwords?

You are certain to have read advice that says not to use the same user ID and password at every site that requires credentials. The thinking is that if somehow your user ID and password is disclosed from one site (which does happen, unfortunately, on a regular basis), then you have put at risk your information at all the other sites where you must sign in. But if you follow that advice, how do you possibly remember all those IDs and passwords? Here's some advice you can put to good use:

- Group the sites you visit as follows: 1) Sites that hold important financial or personal information, such as credit card, bank, and health-related sites; 2) Sites that have your credit or bank information to make purchases or renew a service; 3) Sites that ask you to register simply to save your preferences; and 4) Sites that do not ask you for credentials. Use just one user ID/password combination for Group 3. Create unique user ID/password combinations for each site in Group 1 and Group 2.

- There are a number of password generators on the Web. Generate a password for each site in Group 1 and 2.

- Avoid any of the following in any part of your password:

  - Your name, first or last, or the name of a family member

  - Your pet's name

  - A favorite anything, such as food, car, color, actor, and musical act

  - Any number relevant to you, such as a street address, part of your birthdate, age, number of children, and so on

  - Anything descriptive about you, such as CheerDad, JuneTeen, or JustTurned30

You can use one of the online password managers, but they are a hassle to download and keep updated, and not every website works well with them. Also, people tend to create passwords that are easy to use if they have to remember them. If you commit your passwords to paper, there's no reason not to go with a complex format. There is little chance of losing the book if you do not take it out of the house.

If you need a password outside of the house, write down the password and place it in your wallet. When was the last time you lost your wallet? Besides, if someone found the small piece of paper in your wallet, what would they do with this information: *t^^Gr11m(xA)*?

THE ABSOLUTE MINIMUM

The following are the absolute minimum steps you should take, as well as how often, to protect yourself from Internet threats:

- Consider investing in an all-in-one Internet security suite. This way, you gain access to all the tools you need in one package. Or configure Windows Defender as recommended in this chapter.

- Set Internet Explorer to delete your browsing history when you leave the browser.

- Exercise extreme caution when you receive an email with attachments. Unless you know the sender and you expect the email with attachments, do not open the attachment.

- Ignore any emails from anyone that asks you for any kind of personal information. Show extreme caution when these emails appear regardless of how official they appear. Just think, would your bank or other financial institution ask you for your account number? Wouldn't they have it already?

25

TROUBLESHOOTING AND SOLVING COMMON PROBLEMS

Microsoft has invested tens of thousands of hours of testing to ensure Windows runs properly, but with a system as complex as Windows, you can bet a few issues snuck out the door. These issues aren't limited to a feature not working, which is known as a bug in the software business. Sometimes a feature or capability is difficult to use, making it easy for a user to make a mistake or to configure Windows the wrong way. You don't have to be a Microsoft engineer to solve some of the problems you will encounter in Windows. The troubleshooting tools in Windows 8 can help solve some of those problems. In addition, the Task Manager can help shut down a program that gets stuck. And when all else fails and you want to start over, the Refresh and Reset functions enable you to do that. These problem solving tools are covered in this chapter. First up, though, is some advice for handling problems that might arise when you start Windows.

Handling Special Windows Startup Situations

Starting up Windows is usually a predictable and boring event. The computer lurches into action when you press the power button, a stream of messages appear on the screen, and after you enter your credentials, the Windows Desktop or Start screen (your choice) appears. Every once in a while, though, the unexpected happens. A message appears from Windows that you've never seen before, or perhaps Windows refuses to start. When the unexpected happens, it's worth the time it takes to identify the cause. A bit more important than considering what happened is to proceed past the interruption.

Restarting Windows After a Problem

The Microsoft engineers built Windows to handle many problems, but there is always a chance that something can go wrong. Some software programs might interfere with others; hardware you add to your computer might interfere with Windows; and programs you download from the Internet can cause issues. As a result, Windows can freeze, become sluggish, or shut down unexpectedly, and sometimes you may need to force your computer to power down. If Windows shuts down while experiencing problems, you might see the screen shown in Figure 25.1 when your computer restarts.

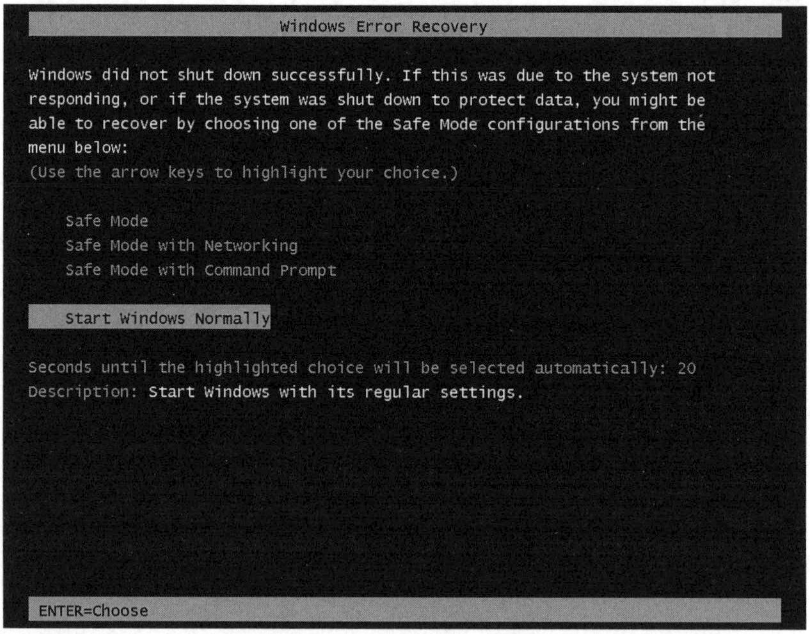

FIGURE 25.1

Windows guides you when it restarts if it crashes or shuts down unexpectedly.

If you have experience running Windows in one of the diagnostic modes listed, such as Safe Mode or Safe Mode with Networking, you can use one of those options. If you are like most users, select Start Windows Normally and press Enter. Because Windows has gotten very good at self-correcting common issues, everything should run just like normal at this point.

Messages You Might Receive While Signing In

You might see a message when you sign in letting you know that your password will expire soon. Unless you have extremely tight controls over computer use at home, you will see this message only at work. If you see this message at work, it means your company has established a policy requiring you to change your password on a regular, scheduled basis.

If you see the message shown in Figure 25.2, your password has expired and you need to create a new one before you can use Windows 8.

FIGURE 25.2

This message appears if your password has expired.

If you see the message shown in Figure 25.3 when trying to change your password, it is indicating your new password may be too easy to figure out, based on password complexity requirements. Perhaps your password is too short or does not have a required uppercase character, or perhaps it does not contain a symbol. Also, you need to follow the complexity rules when you create your password for the first time.

FIGURE 25.3

The password entered did not meet the minimum complexity requirements.

Here are the complexity requirements:

- The password cannot contain the user's account name or any more than two consecutive characters from the user's full name.

- The password must contain at least six characters.

- The password must match three of these characteristics:

  - Contain at least one English uppercase character (A through Z)

  - Contain at least one English lowercase character (a through z)

  - Contain at least one digit (0–9)

  - Contain at least one nonalphabetic character (for example, !, $, #, %)

Using the Troubleshooting Wizards

Windows 8 has almost 30 different tools for dealing with difficulties and trouble you encounter in the software. Each of these troubleshooting wizards focuses on a particular aspect of the software, such as sound problems or connecting to the Internet.

To use a troubleshooting wizard, follow these steps:

1. Open the Search charm and enter **troubleshooting** into the Search box.

2. Select **Troubleshooting** from the list of results. A screen like the one shown in Figure 25.4 appears.

3. Select **View All**. The entire list of troubleshooting wizards appears, as shown in Figure 25.5. Select the wizard that matches your issue.

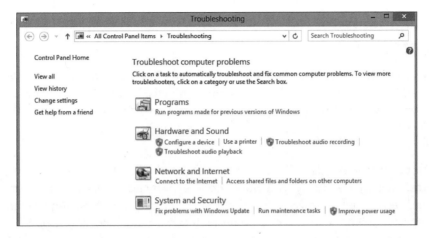

FIGURE 25.4

Windows shows troubleshooting wizards for the areas of the system you've been using lately.

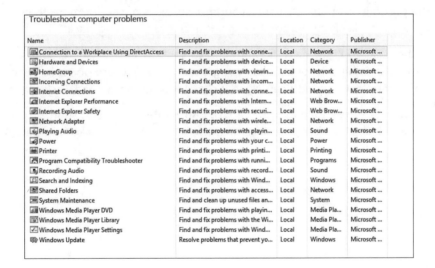

FIGURE 25.5

You can leverage a number of troubleshooting wizards to solve problems you encounter.

Using Task Manager to Close Unresponsive Programs

The Task Manager is a utility that lets you see the programs running in Windows 8 and the impact they have on system resources. You can see how much memory a program is gobbling up, whether one program is dominating use of the CPU or other system resources, how much data is transmitted by certain programs, and lots more.

Not everyone needs a deep appreciation for all the information presented in Task Manager. Actually, you would need expert knowledge in computer science and technology to truly understand the significance and meaning of many of the reports shown. However, one item of interest a beginning Windows 8 user might appreciate and learn to leverage is how to shut down a stuck program.

Once in a while a program stops functioning for no apparent reason. You know when this occurs because the program seems to dim on the screen, and the title of the program has the phrase Not Responding tagged on to the end of it. When the program is unresponsive to your mouse clicks or tap for more than a couple minutes, it's likely the program has left and is not coming back.

In the past, you may have been forced to shut down your entire computer to bypass an issue with one locked program. Those days are gone. In Windows 8, if a program locks up, you can close it down with help from the Task Manager.

To open the Task Manager, press **Ctrl+Alt+Delete**. A menu should appear with just a few choices; Task Manager is one of them. Select **Task Manager**. After doing so, the Task Manager should appear, as shown in Figure 25.6.

FIGURE 25.6

The Task Manager enables you to review performance and resource use in Windows.

Select **More Details** to view every application or program running in your system. Find the entry for the program that seems to be frozen. Right-click or tap and hold on the problematic program. Select **End Task**, and then verify your action by clicking **OK** if you are prompted. The program will halt almost immediately.

Understanding Refresh and Restore

Once in a while, no matter how much advice you've received or troubleshooting you have tried, you may need to take a step back and restart your experience with Windows. This doesn't refer to forgetting what you've learned. Rather, it may be wise to reinstall Windows or to go back to a point before you started customizing Windows 8. Short of backing up everything, deleting everything on your computer, and reinstalling Windows and all your other programs, you have two options to start over. The options are named, simply enough, Refresh and Reset.

Getting a Do-Over with Refresh

Refresh is designed to undo everything that might have been done that has made the computer perform less sharply than before. The refresh does not delete your personal files or any of the settings that affect the appearance of Windows. Rather, the settings that control how Windows 8 operates are set back to their original value. Any software that was not installed through the Microsoft Store is removed, apps acquired from the Windows Store are *not* affected. Refresh is a great way to restore Windows to a state where it was running properly without investing the time to reload all your files and programs.

To refresh your system, follow these steps:

1. If you installed from a DVD, insert the DVD into your computer but cancel the setup program when it starts, or close the AutoPlay dialog box if it appears.

2. Open the Charms bar and select **Settings**. Select **Change PC Settings** and then select **Update and recovery** from the menu.

3. Select **Recovery** on the next page that appears, and then select **Get Started** under the Refresh Your PC heading as shown in Figure 25.7.

4. Read through the instructions. If you want to continue, click **Next**.

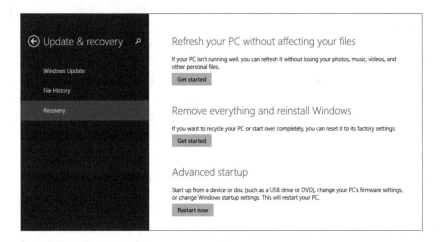

FIGURE 25.7

Refresh your Windows 8 device to get a fresh start without losing your files and settings while returning Windows to its just-installed state.

5. At this point, you may be prompted for the Windows 8 DVD if it was not inserted in Step 1. Insert it if required.

6. If you are sure you want to proceed, select **Refresh**.

7. The Refresh program runs, and eventually your computer restarts. This process takes approximately 15 minutes.

Restarting from Scratch with the Reset Option

Reset is designed to restore the computer to its state before you ever touched it. The reset returns the computer to its factory-shipped settings, removing any trace of your applications or your files from the system. Use the Reset option in these situations:

- You want to rebuild your Windows 8 environment from scratch, installing everything again and setting every option again. Use the Reset option in this scenario only if you have backed up your personal information to an external drive (not to the drive on which Windows 8 is installed).

- You want to give away or sell the computer but you would like Windows 8 running on it when you do.

Before Windows 8 is reinstalled, the Reset program can clean the hard drive of your files. You also have the option to completely erase the drive beforehand. You might have heard that some clever individuals can still access files that have been deleted or were stored on a file that has been formatted. This option specially formats the drive so that it would be extremely unlikely for someone to recover your files from the drive.

To reset your system, follow these steps:

1. If you installed from a DVD, insert the DVD into your computer but cancel the setup program when it starts, or close the AutoPlay dialog box if it appears. Have the original product key handy for when the Reset program reinstalls Windows 8.

2. Open the Charms bar and select **Settings**. Select **Change PC Settings** and then select **Update and recovery** from the menu.

3. Select **Recovery** on the next page that appears, and then select **Get Started** under the Remove Everything and Reinstall Windows heading. The screen shown in Figure 25.8 appears.

FIGURE 25.8

The Reset program enables you to start from scratch with Windows.

4. Select **Next**. A screen like the one shown in Figure 25.9 appears.

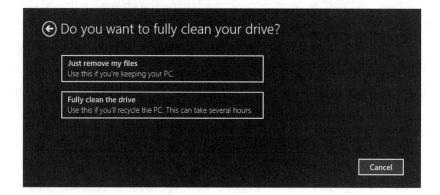

FIGURE 25.9

You can choose whether your entire drive is erased when Windows is reinstalled.

5. To remove your files during the reset, select **Just Remove My Files**. To remove your files and to prepare the entire drive so it is hard to recover them (for example, if you want to sell or donate your PC), select **Fully Clean the Drive**.

6. You will be prompted one more time. Select **Reset** to continue or click **Cancel** to return to the Start screen.

7. The reset process runs for approximately 20 minutes if you choose to just remove your files. It can take at least twice as long if you choose to also prepare the drive. When it finishes, you will be prompted for your Windows 8 product key. Enter it and click **Next**.

8. Proceed through a few more guided steps to finish the reset program. When complete, Windows 8 will have been reinstalled to an otherwise empty drive.

THE ABSOLUTE MINIMUM

Keep the following points in mind after you've completed reading this chapter:

- Use the Task Manager to close an unresponsive program rather than restarting Windows 8.

- Use the Refresh program to retain your files while resetting Windows 8 to the default settings.

- Use the Reset program to prepare your computer to be sold or donated or to create a fresh copy of Windows 8 loaded on your computer.

Index

D

G

H

I

N

O

P

U

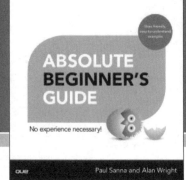

Your purchase of **Windows® 8.1 Absolute Beginner's Guide** includes access to a free online edition for 45 days through the **Safari Books Online** subscription service. Nearly every Que book is available online through **Safari Books Online**, along with thousands of books and videos from publishers such as Addison-Wesley Professional, Cisco Press, Exam Cram, IBM Press, O'Reilly Media, Prentice Hall, Sams, and VMware Press.

Safari Books Online is a digital library providing searchable, on-demand access to thousands of technology, digital media, and professional development books and videos from leading publishers. With one monthly or yearly subscription price, you get unlimited access to learning tools and information on topics including mobile app and software development, tips and tricks on using your favorite gadgets, networking, project management, graphic design, and much more.

Activate your FREE Online Edition at
informit.com/safarifree

STEP 1: Enter the coupon code: KGAMNVH.

STEP 2: New Safari users, complete the brief registration form.
Safari subscribers, just log in.

If you have difficulty registering on Safari or accessing the online edition,
please e-mail customer-service@safaribooksonline.com